THE FAMILY QUIZ BOOK

THE FAMILY QUIZ BOOK

BARDFIELD
PRESS

First published by Bardfield Press in 2004

Bardfield Press is an imprint of
Miles Kelly Publishing Ltd
Bardfield Centre, Great Bardfield, Essex, CM7 4SL

2 4 6 8 10 9 7 5 3 1

Editorial Director: Belinda Gallagher
Assistant Editor: Rosalind McGuire
Design set-up: Jo Brewer
Designer: Louisa Leitao
Picture Researchers: Rosalind McGuire/Liberty Newton
Production Manager: Estela Boulton

British Library Cataloguing-in-Publication Data
A catalogue record of this book is available from the British Library

ISBN 1-84236-383-2

Printed in China

www.mileskelly.net
info@mileskelly.net

Introduction

See Quiz 192

The Family Quiz Book has something for everyone. The questions cover ten different subject areas and are presented in five levels, each one becoming progressively more difficult. Level 1 is just right for children and the images provide simple clues to guide them to the correct answer. Level 5 is the trickiest – designed for the supremely confident!

See Quiz 53

You can play in pairs, in teams, or individually. Work your way through the book quiz by quiz, or choose a subject you feel confident about – it's up to you how you play. The answers are at the bottom of each quiz for quick reference – they'll also solve any disputes! However you decide to play, have fun. Remember – this isn't just a quiz book, it's also a brilliant source of information.

Level 1

QUIZZES 1–57

Global Matters

15, 47

Great and Famous

13

Lights, Camera, Action!

22, 37, 39, 44, 55

Making History

4, 8, 21, 28, 31

Music Mania

25

Natural Selection

2, 6, 16, 20, 29, 34, 38, 40, 49, 52

Scientifically Speaking

7, 10, 14, 18, 41, 45, 53, 56

Sporting Chance

3, 5, 19, 26, 32, 42, 50

Total Trivia

1, 9, 17, 23, 27, 30, 33, 35, 46

Written Word

11, 43, 51, 54, 57

Level 2

QUIZZES 58–119

Global Matters

65, 92, 113, 117

Great and Famous

97, 100

Lights, Camera, Action!

67, 71, 76, 78, 90, 95

Making History

59, 69, 74, 80, 91, 99, 102, 106

Music Mania

62, 93

Natural Selection

79, 83, 88, 98, 111, 119

Scientifically Speaking

63, 82, 104, 107, 112, 115

Sporting Chance

61, 68, 73, 77, 81, 86, 103, 116, 118

Total Trivia

58, 64, 66, 70, 75, 85, 87, 94, 101, 105, 110, 114

Written Word

89, 109

Level 3

QUIZZES 120–178

Global Matters

150, 164

Scientifically Speaking

122, 128, 135, 140.
153, 159

Lights, Camera, Action!

127, 133, 141, 155,
165, 172, 174, 178

Sporting Chance

136, 143, 151, 158,
163. 167, 177

Making History

125, 130, 147, 154,
161, 166

Total Trivia

121, 129, 134, 138,
142, 148, 160, 170,
173, 175

Music Mania

124, 131, 137, 176

Written Word

146, 152, 162, 169.
171

Natural Selection

123, 126, 139, 145,
149, 157

Level 4

QUIZZES 179–242

Global Matters

184, 202, 212, 217, 237

Natural Selection

185, 190, 205, 209, 229, 233

Great and Famous

181, 195, 218, 225

Scientifically Speaking

182, 186, 193, 200, 221, 224, 227

Lights, Camera, Action!

189, 198, 206, 208, 231, 234, 242

Sporting Chance

183, 187, 214, 223, 236, 238, 241

Making History

194, 199, 207, 211, 222, 230

Total Trivia

179, 188, 191, 197, 203, 213, 215, 219, 226, 232, 235

Music Mania

196, 201, 210, 220

Written Word

239

Level 5

QUIZZES 243–249

Picture Quizzes

How to use this book

Your book is split into five levels, each containing more than 50 quizzes. Level 1 is the easiest, with each level becoming progressively more difficult. The quizzes cover ten subject areas ranging from Music to Sport. The answers can be found at the end of each quiz.

Different Subjects
Each of the ten subject areas has its own tinted strip. Look for the red strips if you want to play the Total Trivia quizzes.

Levels 1 to 5
Each right-hand page tells you which level you are playing in.

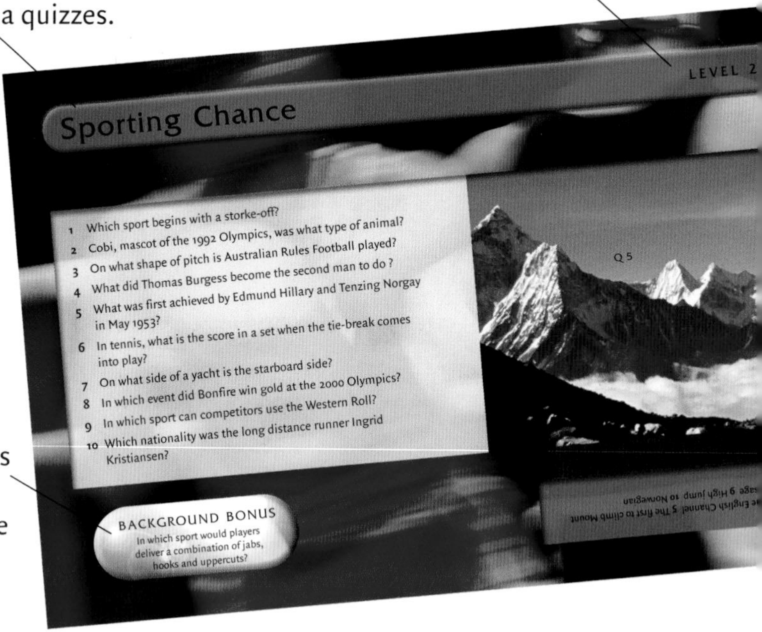

LEVEL 2
Sporting Chance
1 Which sport begins with a storke-off?
2 Cobi, mascot of the 1992 Olympics, was what type of animal?
3 On what shape of pitch is Australian Rules Football played?
4 What did Thomas Burgess become the second man to do ?
5 What was first achieved by Edmund Hillary and Tenzing Norgay in May 1953?
6 In tennis, what is the score in a set when the tie-break comes into play?
7 On what side of a yacht is the starboard side?
8 In which event did Bonfire win gold at the 2000 Olympics?
9 In which sport can competitors use the Western Roll?
10 Which nationality was the long distance runner Ingrid Kristiansen?
Q5
BACKGROUND BONUS
In which sport would players deliver a combination of jabs, hooks and uppercuts?

Background Bonus
Look out for the Background Bonus panels. The large background image acts as a clue to the answer.

Picture Quizzes
Look out for the picture quizzes with the blue backgrounds. These are pages dedicated to photographic quizzes.

Quiz Numbers
Each quiz is clearly numbered. There are 249 quizzes in total.

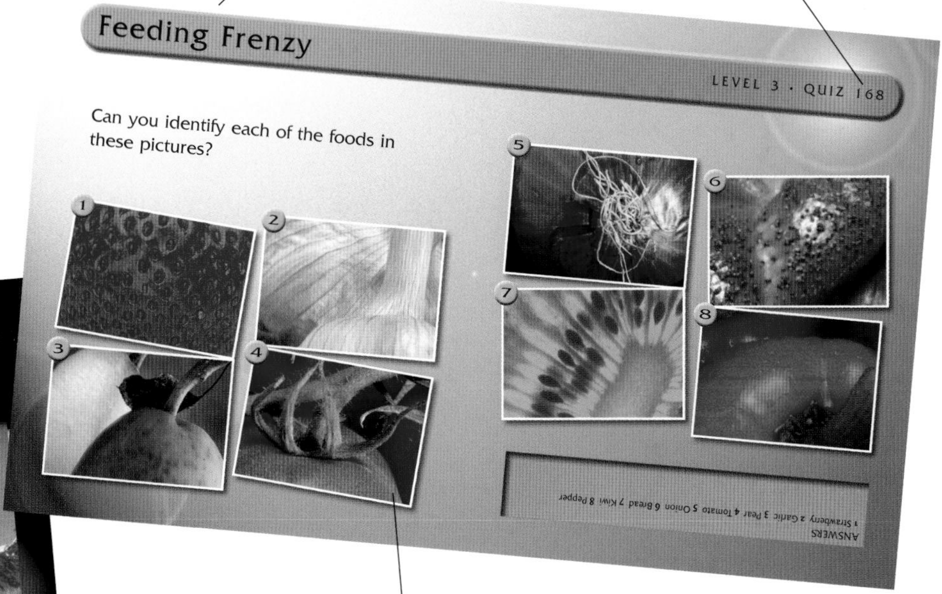

Feeding Frenzy
LEVEL 3 · QUIZ 168
Can you identify each of the foods in these pictures?
ANSWERS
1 Strawberry 2 Garlic 3 Pear 4 Tomato 5 Onion 6 Bread 7 Kiwi 8 Pepper

Picture Quiz Clues
The picture quizzes are made up of eight close-up shots of anything from animals to everyday objects. They can be tricky!

Answers
The answers to each quiz are positioned upside down on the right-hand pages.

Total Trivia

1 What work did the Seven Dwarfs do?

2 What is mutton: calf meat, sheep meat or lamb meat?

3 In which country is the city of Bombay situated?

4 Are modern British fire engines green, red or black?

5 Which magical character emerged from Aladdin's lamp?

6 Cirrus and cumulus are examples of what kind of natural feature?

Q 5

7 What natural substance is chocolate made from?

8 What does a thermometer measure?

9 What is the modern name of the Roman port of *Londinium*?

10 Is a cello a stringed or a wind instrument?

ANSWERS

1 They worked in a mine **2** Sheep meat **3** India **4** Red **5** A genie **6** Clouds
7 Cocoa beans **8** Temperature **9** London **10** Stringed

Natural Selection

BACKGROUND BONUS

What kind of animal is a gannet?

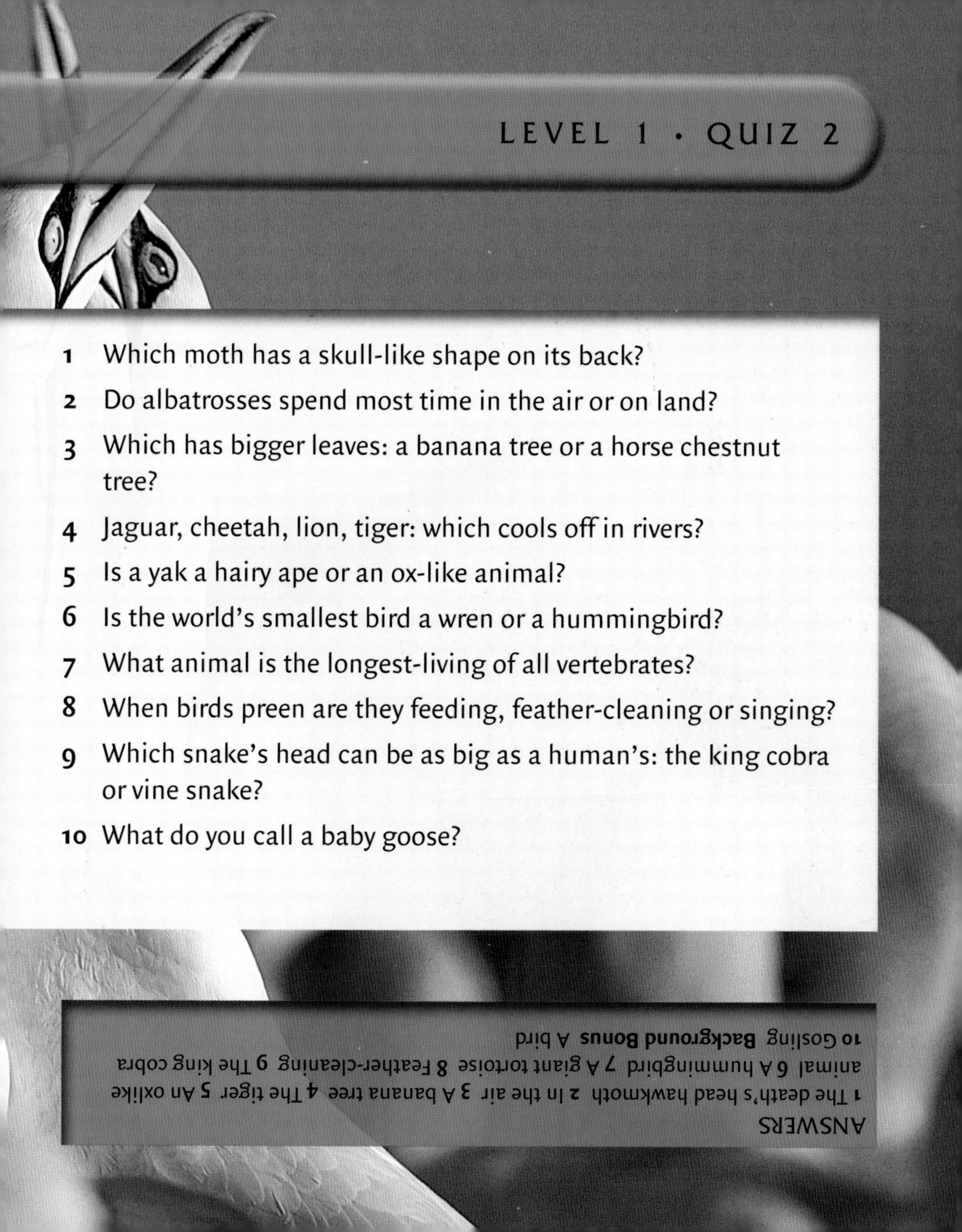

LEVEL 1 • QUIZ 2

1 Which moth has a skull-like shape on its back?

2 Do albatrosses spend most time in the air or on land?

3 Which has bigger leaves: a banana tree or a horse chestnut tree?

4 Jaguar, cheetah, lion, tiger: which cools off in rivers?

5 Is a yak a hairy ape or an ox-like animal?

6 Is the world's smallest bird a wren or a hummingbird?

7 What animal is the longest-living of all vertebrates?

8 When birds preen are they feeding, feather-cleaning or singing?

9 Which snake's head can be as big as a human's: the king cobra or vine snake?

10 What do you call a baby goose?

ANSWERS

1 The death's head hawkmoth **2** In the air **3** A banana tree **4** The tiger **5** An oxlike animal **6** A hummingbird **7** A giant tortoise **8** Feather-cleaning **9** The king cobra **10** Gosling **Background Bonus** A bird

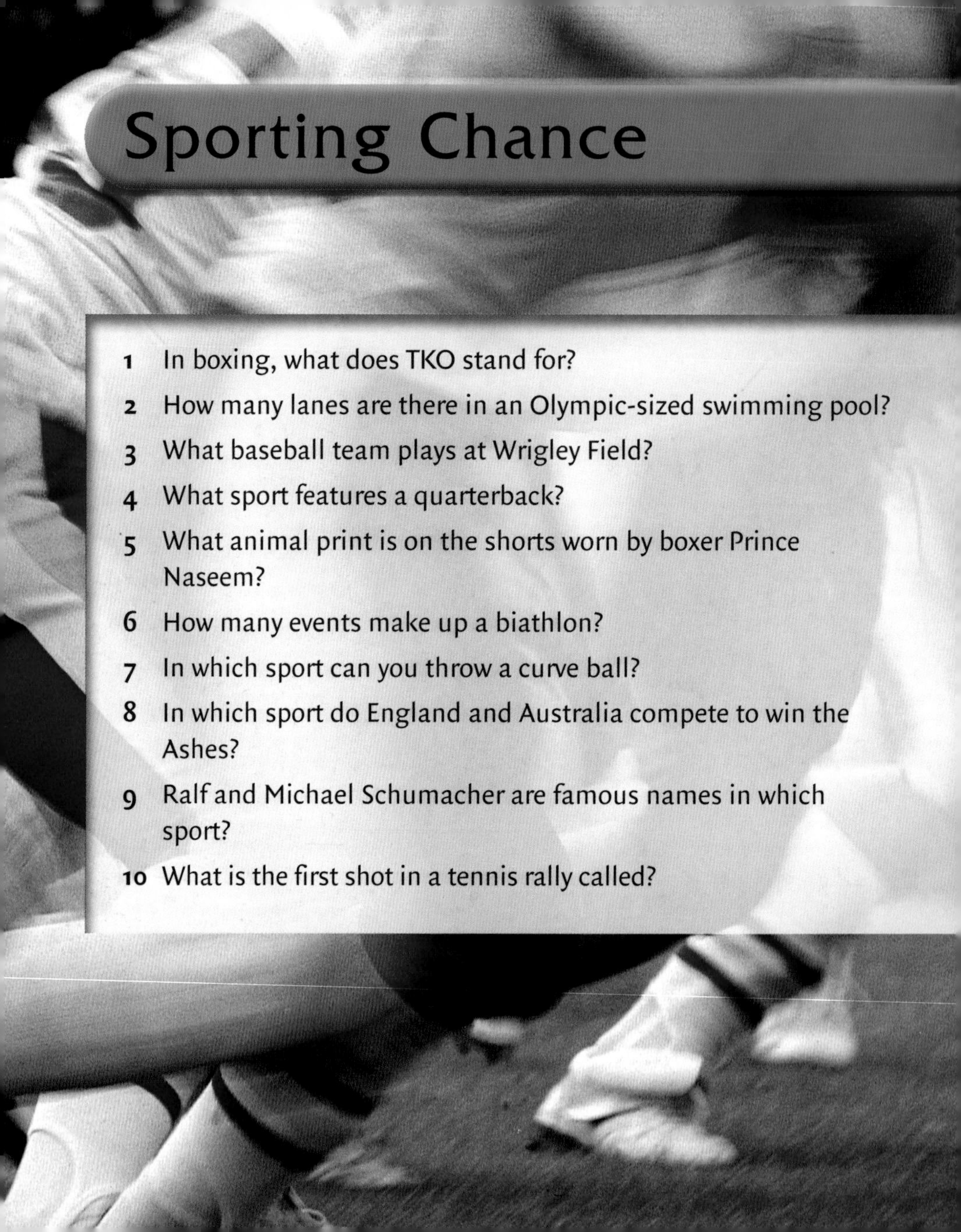

Sporting Chance

1 In boxing, what does TKO stand for?

2 How many lanes are there in an Olympic-sized swimming pool?

3 What baseball team plays at Wrigley Field?

4 What sport features a quarterback?

5 What animal print is on the shorts worn by boxer Prince Naseem?

6 How many events make up a biathlon?

7 In which sport can you throw a curve ball?

8 In which sport do England and Australia compete to win the Ashes?

9 Ralf and Michael Schumacher are famous names in which sport?

10 What is the first shot in a tennis rally called?

LEVEL 1 • QUIZ 3

ANSWERS
1 Technical Knockout **2** Eight **3** Chicago Cubs **4** American Football **5** Leopard's spots **6** Two **7** Bowling **8** Cricket **9** Motor racing **10** Serve

Making History

1 What was the Colosseum in Rome used for?

2 Which World War II German general was nicknamed The Desert Fox?

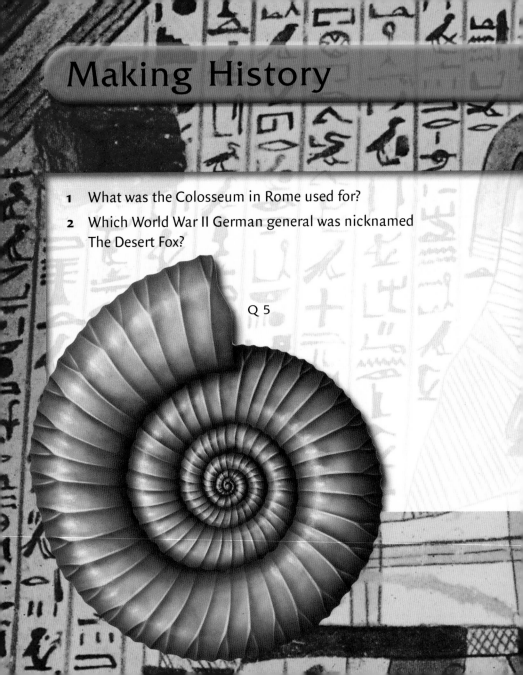

Q 5

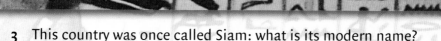

3 This country was once called Siam: what is its modern name?

4 Explorers in South America caught and ate cavies: what are cavies?

5 What is an ammonite: a metal, a fossil or a kind of tree?

6 What were U-boats?

7 What were pieces of eight?

8 Which country used Zero fighters during World War II?

9 Who is the odd one out of these three leaders: Truman, Macmillan, Bush?

10 Against whom did Richard the Lionheart fight in the Crusades?

ANSWERS

1 Gladiator games **2** Rommel **3** Thailand **4** Guinea pigs **5** A fossil **6** German submarines **7** Silver coins **8** Japan **9** Macmillan (British prime minister not U.S. president) **10** Saladin

Sporting Chance

1 On what surface is the Wimbledon Tennis Championship played?
2 What does a boxing referee count to, to signify a knockout?
3 Which sport is sometimes called ping-pong?
4 What is Canada's national sport?
5 In which sport do you wear either quad or in-line skates?
6 What kind of race is the Tour de France?
7 What shape is a boxing ring?
8 In which sport do you putt the ball?
9 On a chessboard, what piece is also a member of the clergy?
10 In tennis, what is the score when an umpire calls deuce?

Q 5

ANSWERS

1 Grass **2** Ten **3** Table tennis **4** Ice hockey **5** Rollerblades **6** Cycling **7** Square **8** Golf **9** Bishop **10** 40–40

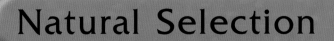

Natural Selection

1 Rockhopper, macaroni and emperor are all types of which bird?

2 What is a squirrel's nest called?

3 Bactrian and dromedary are types of what?

Q 4

4 Which dog is known as a sausage dog?

5 Sponge, coral, kelp: which is the plant?

6 What is a group of leopards called: a pod or a leap?

7 Tent-building, vampire and hog-nosed are all types of which animal?

8 Which large bird builds an eyrie as a nest?

9 What do you call a female goat?

10 Do herons nest in trees or in floating plants?

ANSWERS

1 Penguin **2** A drey **3** Camel **4** A dachshund **5** Kelp (it is a seaweed) **6** A leap **7** Bats **8** An eagle **9** A nanny goat **10** In trees

Scientifically Speaking

1 What is the name for the curved glass in spectacles?

2 What black powder did the Chinese invent to make fireworks?

3 What is 50 percent of 80?

4 Which G word describes the force that pulls objects to the midle of the Earth?

Q 9

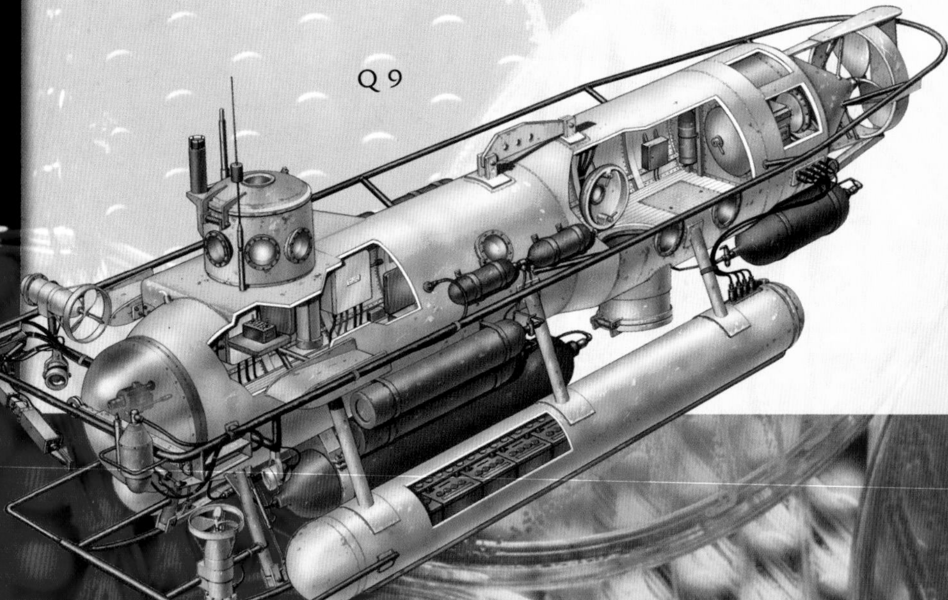

5 Which of these numbers is not exactly divisible by 7: 7, 17, 21, 14, 28?

6 What would you lose if you had laryngitis?

7 What in space is an enormous collection of stars?

8 Is crimson deep red or light blue?

9 Is a bathyscaphe used to explore underground, under the sea or outer space?

10 What is the remainder when 26 is divided by 3?

ANSWERS

1 A lens **2** Gunpowder **3** 40 **4** Gravity **5** 17 **6** Your voice **7** A galaxy **8** Deep red **9** Under the sea **10** Two

Making History

Q 8

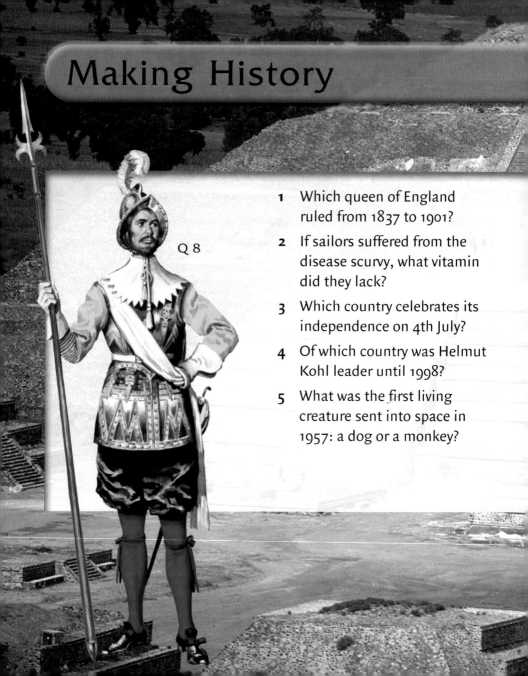

1 Which queen of England ruled from 1837 to 1901?

2 If sailors suffered from the disease scurvy, what vitamin did they lack?

3 Which country celebrates its independence on 4th July?

4 Of which country was Helmut Kohl leader until 1998?

5 What was the first living creature sent into space in 1957: a dog or a monkey?

6 What did Caligula, Augustus and Titus all have in common?

7 Was Columbus born in Spain or Italy?

8 Was a pike a long, spearlike weapon or a helmet with a spike on top?

9 In 1642, Abel Tasman landed on a new island that he called Van Diemen's Land. What is it called now?

10 Which Indian leader was known as the Mahatma or "Great Soul"?

BACKGROUND BONUS

What kind of places of worship were built by some ancient American civilizations?

ANSWERS

1 Queen Victoria **2** Vitamin C **3** The United States **4** Germany **5** A Russian dog named Laika **6** They were all Roman emperors **7** Italy **8** A long, spearlike weapon **9** Tasmania **10** Gandhi **Background Bonus** Pyramids

Total Trivia

1 What does Popeye eat for strength?

2 Which part of an aircraft is the fuselage?

3 How many blackbirds were baked in a pie?

4 Which limbs of the *Venus de Milo* sculpture are missing?

5 Which animal is usually ridden in the desert?

6 What is agoraphobia a fear of?

7 Which of these numbers can be divided by both 3 and 4: 9, 12, 15, 16?

8 Joseph Barbera and William Hannah created which cat and mouse duo?

9 What is the missing number: 18 x ? = 180

10 Is Robin Hood associated with blue or green?

Q 5

ANSWERS
1 Spinach **2** The body **3** 24 **4** The arms **5** The camel **6** Open or public spaces **7** 12 **8** Tom and Jerry **9** Ten **10** Green

Scientifically Speaking

1 What do vaccinations protect you from?

2 Does electricity flow through metal or rubber?

3 Which children's toy uses a spring to make it jump out of its box?

4 What is 532 + 629 + 423?

5 Are the letters on a computer keyboard lower case or upper case?

6 What do we call the imaginary points at either end of the Earth?

7 Which part of your body has a palm?

8 In which continent would you find zebras and elephants?

9 What is 0.25 as a fraction?

10 What is the name of the unit used for measuring the loudness or intensity of sound?

BACKGROUND BONUS

What natural occurrence is called a tsunami?

LEVEL 1 • QUIZ 10

Q 3

ANSWERS

1 Infectious diseases **2** Metal **3** A jack-in-the-box **4** 1,584 **5** Upper case **6** North and South Poles **7** Your hand **8** Africa **9** 1/4 **10** Decibels (dB)

Background Bonus A very large wave

Written Word: The Bible

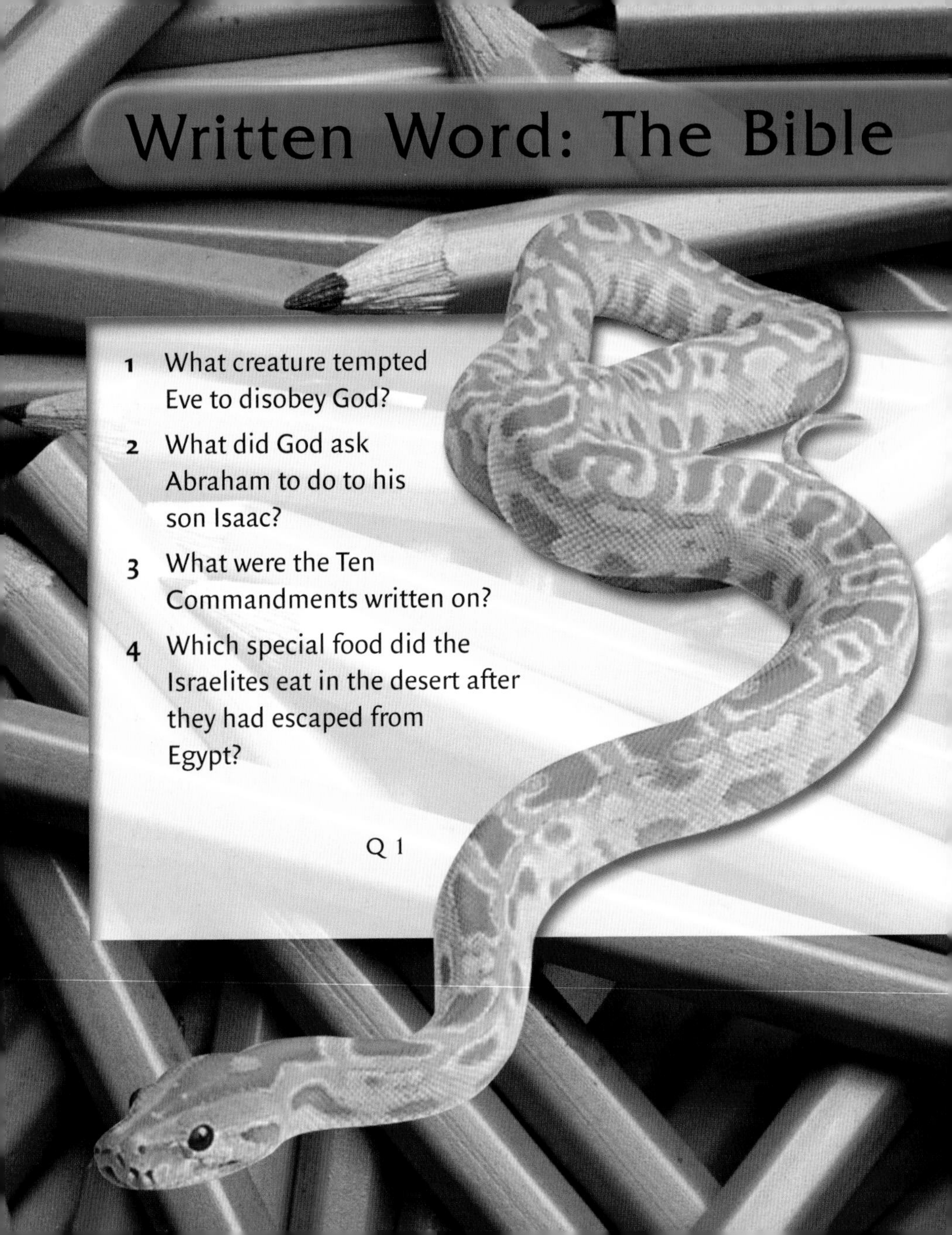

1 What creature tempted Eve to disobey God?

2 What did God ask Abraham to do to his son Isaac?

3 What were the Ten Commandments written on?

4 Which special food did the Israelites eat in the desert after they had escaped from Egypt?

Q 1

5 What did Jesus do with five loaves and two small fishes?

6 What is the name of the town where Jesus grew up?

7 Who climbed a tree so that he could get a better view of Jesus?

8 What was King Solomon famous for?

9 Who ruled Palestine at the time of Jesus?

10 How many Gospels are there?

ANSWERS

1 A serpent 2 Kill him as a sacrifice to God 3 Tablets of stone 4 Manna
5 Fed 5,000 people 6 Nazareth 7 Zacchaeus 8 His wisdom 9 The Romans 10 Four

Spot the Sport

Can you identify the sports that these objects relate to?

1

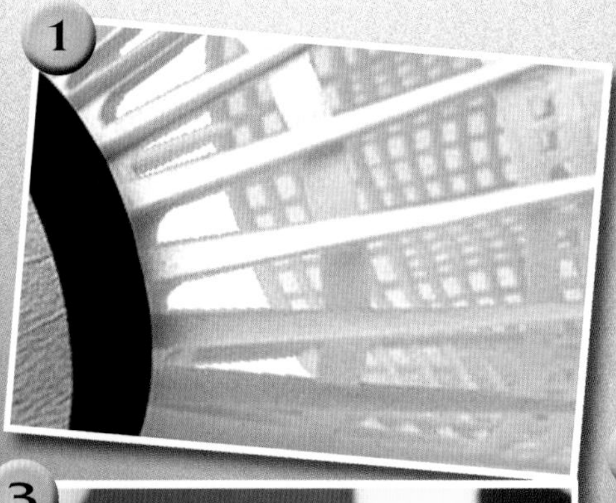

2

3

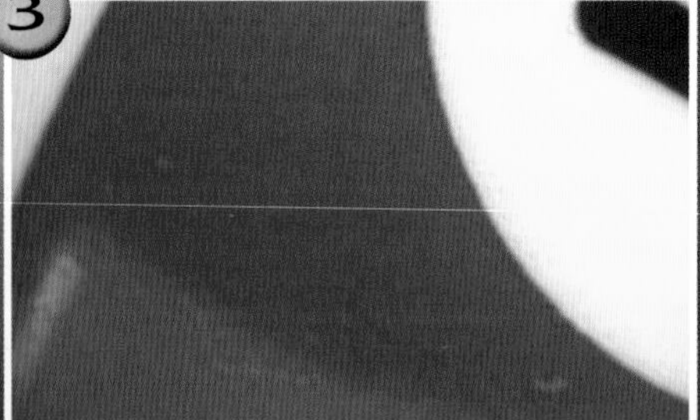

4

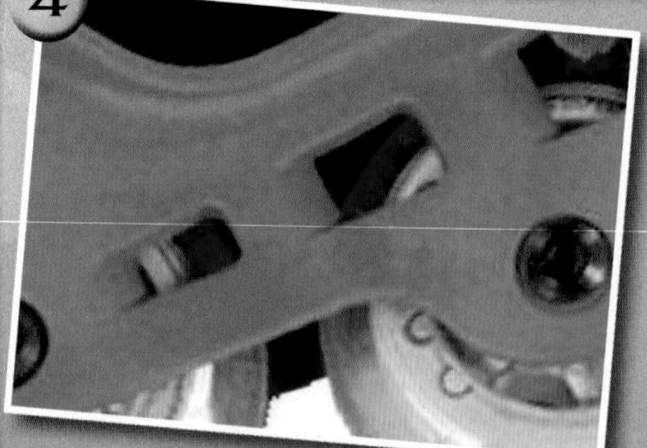

LEVEL 1 • QUIZ 12

5

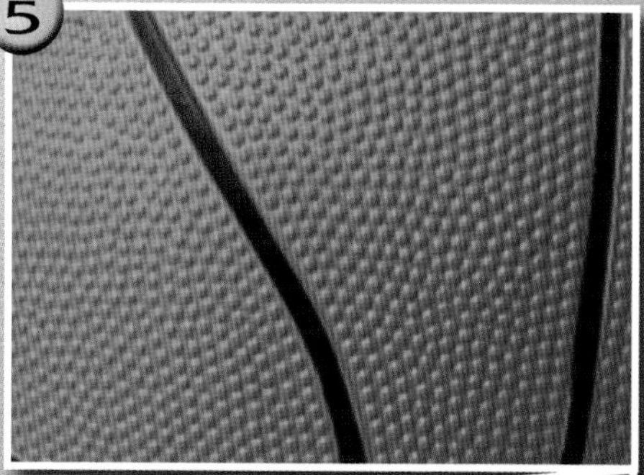

6

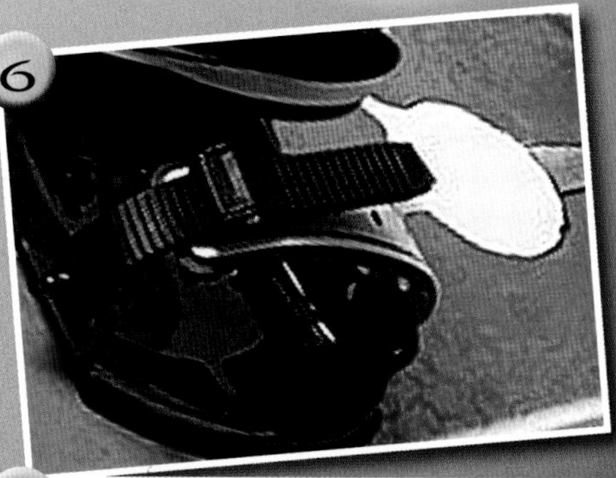

7

8

ANSWERS
1 Badminton **2** Baseball **3** Pool **4** Rollerblading **5** Basketball **6** Snowboarding
7 American Football **8** Table tennis

Great and Famous

Q 8

1 Was the composer Frédéric Chopin English, French, Italian or Polish?

2 For which sport did Michael Jordan become famous?

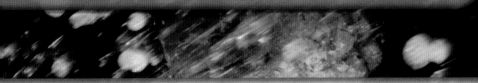

3 Thor Heyerdahl sailed on a raft from Polynesia to which country: Peru, Australia or the United States?

4 By what nickname is Emma Bunton better known?

5 Who wrote the music for *The Lion King*: George Michael, Sheryl Crow, Andrew Lloyd-Webber or Elton John?

6 Which Italian dictator was known as *Il Duce*?

7 Jacques Cousteau is associated with what sort of exploration: undersea or rainforest?

8 Stanley Gibbons was a dealer in which collectable item?

9 Which Judy played Dorothy in the movie version of *The Wizard of Oz*?

10 Annie Mae Bullock is the real name of which hugely successful U.S. singer?

ANSWERS

1 Polish 2 Basketball 3 Peru 4 Baby Spice 5 Elton John 6 Benito Mussolini 7 Undersea 8 Stamps 9 Judy Garland 10 Tina Turner

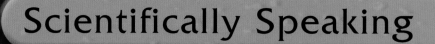

Scientifically Speaking

1 What does not have a tail: a kite, a boat or a jet?

2 What instrument is used for drawing circles?

3 Does a meteorologist study meteorites, the ocean or the weather?

Q 9

4 Which planet is nearest the Sun?

5 How many seconds in three minutes?

6 What is the joint that lets you bend your arm?

7 What part of your body wrinkles when you frown?

8 In which direction does a compass needle point?

9 If you had hayfever, what would you be allergic to?

10 Where would you find your calf muscle?

ANSWERS

1 A boat **2** A compass **3** The weather **4** Mercury **5** 180 **6** Elbow **7** Your forehead **8** North **9** Pollen **10** The bottom of your leg

Global Matters

1 What is the alternative name for the Netherlands?
2 In which continent does the country of Croatia lie?
3 What is the capital city of Peru: Bogotá, Lima or Quito?
4 AK is the abbreviation for which U.S. state?
5 What does the D stand for in Washington D.C.?
6 What is the highest mountain in the United Kingdom?
7 What is the world's largest island?
8 In which country are the cities Seville and Madrid?
9 Which gemstone provides part of Ireland's nickname?
10 Is Greenland north or south of the Equator?

BACKGROUND BONUS

What is the name of the steplike terrain on which rice is grown?

LEVEL 1 • QUIZ 15

Q 7

ANSWERS

1 Holland **2** Europe **3** Lima **4** Alaska **5** District (of Columbia) **6** Ben Nevis (Scotland) **7** Greenland **8** Spain **9** Emerald (The Emerald Isle) **10** North

Background Bonus A terrace

Natural Selection

1 Was the dodo a bird or a kind of deer?

2 Do snakes have two teeth or many teeth?

3 Is ivy a tree, a climber or a bush?

4 Do leopards store prey in trees or underground?

5 What common natural event can cause forest fires?

6 Does the praying mantis chase its prey or ambush it?

7 Which tree-living rodent with a fluffy tail mainly eats conifer seeds?

8 With which part of their body do anteaters collect termites?

9 Does the European wildcat live in thick woodlands or open meadows?

10 Which of these is the largest cat: bobcat, cougar or tiger?

Q 6

ANSWERS

1 A bird **2** Many teeth **3** A climber **4** In trees **5** Lightning **6** It ambushes it **7** The squirrel **8** Their tongue **9** In thick woodlands **10** The tiger

Total Trivia

Q 3

BACKGROUND BONUS

Grevy's and Burchell's are two species of what kind of animal?

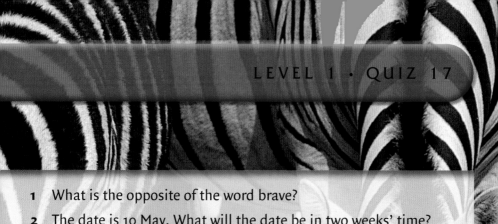

LEVEL 1 • QUIZ 17

1 What is the opposite of the word brave?

2 The date is 10 May. What will the date be in two weeks' time?

3 What does the French word *légume* mean in English?

4 What is one-quarter of a half?

5 What does a biologist study?

6 What is the plural of sheep?

7 Frog spawn, tadpole. What comes next?

8 By what title is the Bishop of Rome also known?

9 What does the Roman numeral V equal?

10 Which sport would you learn on nursery slopes?

ANSWERS

1 Cowardly **2** 24 May **3** Vegetable **4** One-eighth **5** Plants and animals **6** Sheep **7** Frog **8** The Pope **9** Five **10** Skiing

Background Bonus Zebra

Scientifically Speaking

1 What has hands, a face and wheels?
2 What did Clarence Birdseye invent in 1924?
3 What is the name of a giant block of ice floating in the sea?
4 Why is blinking good for your eyes?
5 What are the two passages in your nose called?
6 What is the layer of air around the Earth called?
7 On a compass, which direction is opposite east?
8 What is the name for walls of rock that go down to the sea?
9 How many seconds are there in one and a half minutes?
10 What is the total of three 3s and seven 4s?

LEVEL 1 • QUIZ 18

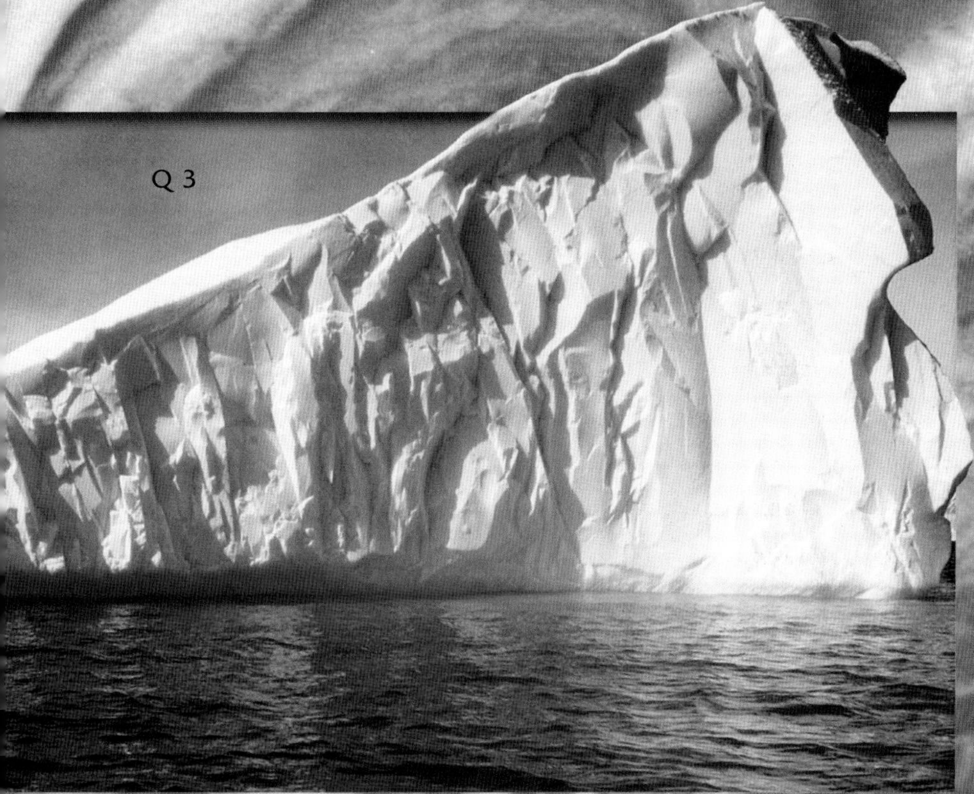

Q 3

ANSWERS

1 A clock **2** Frozen food **3** An iceberg **4** It keeps them clean **5** Nostrils
6 The atmosphere **7** West **8** Cliffs **9** go **10** 37

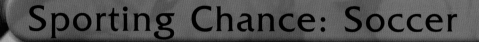

Sporting Chance: Soccer

Q 2

1 Which Scottish soccer club does Rangers play in the Old Firm derby?

2 In which country does the soccer team Bordeaux play its home matches?

LEVEL 1 · QUIZ 19

3 Which Paulo pushed a soccer referee over: Di Canio, Maldini or Wanchope?

4 What is the name of the only Scottish soccer league team beginning with K?

5 In a soccer penalty shoot-out, how many penalties does each side take before sudden death begins?

6 In which English city does the soccer team Aston Villa play its home matches?

7 In which European country are the headquarters of FIFA?

8 What country, which shares its name with a bird, was knocked out of the 2002 World Cup semi-finals?

9 In which Scottish city does Celtic play its home matches?

10 Royal and Woolwich were formerly part of the name of which London soccer club?

ANSWERS

1 Celtic 2 France 3 Paulo di Canio 4 Kilmarnock 5 Five 6 Birmingham 7 Switzerland 8 Turkey 9 Glasgow 10 Arsenal

Natural Selection

LEVEL 1 · QUIZ 20

1 Which of these fish is striped: herring, mackerel or trout?

2 Do grasshoppers jump and fly, or only jump?

3 Shark, dolphin, salmon: which breathes in air using lungs?

4 Cookie-cutter and basking are types of which animal?

5 Which part of a tree dies in winter?

6 The blue poison-dart is what kind of animal?

7 Thrush, pheasant, goose: which is the smallest?

8 What creature sat down beside Little Miss Muffet?

9 Do dogs keep cool by panting or sweating?

10 Where do giant squid live?

Q 6

ANSWERS

1 The mackerel **2** They jump and fly **3** The dolphin **4** Shark **5** The leaves **6** Frog **7** The thrush **8** A spider **9** Panting **10** In the ocean

Making History

1 The people of which ancient classical civilization wore togas?

2 Which composer went deaf in his later years?

3 Which ancient peoples devised the 365-day calendar?

4 How many voyages did Columbus make to the Americas: one, two, three or four?

5 What country did Napoleon invade in 1812?

6 When did Euclid write *Elements of Geometry*, one of the most influential mathematics books ever: 1300BC, 300BC or AD12?

7 What was the nickname of the U.S. Confederate General, Thomas Jackson?

8 When was gunpowder first used in battle in Europe: 1346, 1446 or 1546?

9 Which Scottish king killed King Duncan, but was himself killed by Duncan's son, Malcolm III?

10 Which king ordered the Domesday Book to be made in England?

Q 5

ANSWERS

1 Rome **2** Beethoven **3** Ancient Egyptians **4** He made four **5** Russia **6** 3000BC **7** Stonewall **8** 1346 **9** Macbeth **10** William the Conqueror

Lights, Camera, Action!

BACKGROUND BONUS

Which Los Angeles district is central to the TV and movie industries?

1 Which sport featured in the movie *The Natural*?

2 Name the title of the 1990 movie sequel to *Three Men and a Baby*?

3 Who plays the Malcolm in the TV show *Malcolm in the Middle*?

4 According to Mary Poppins, how much did it cost to feed the birds?

5 Name Mickey Mouse's pet dog.

6 In the *Bugs Bunny* cartoons, is Yosemite Sam's beard black, red or white?

7 What type of creature is Willy in the *Free Willy* movies?

8 Which onions are also the name of the central family in *Rugrats*?

9 Who played Cruella de Vil in the 1996 movie *One Hundred and One Dalmatians*?

10 In the movie *Jimmy Neutron*, what piece of kitchen equipment is made into a satellite?

ANSWERS

1 Baseball **2** *Three Men and a Little Lady* **3** Frankie Muniz **4** Tuppence a bag **5** Pluto **6** Red **7** Killer whale **8** Pickles **9** Glenn Close **10** Toaster

Background Bonus Hollywood

Total Trivia

1 Is a mandolin a stringed instrument or a keyboard instrument?

2 How many fiddlers had Old King Cole?

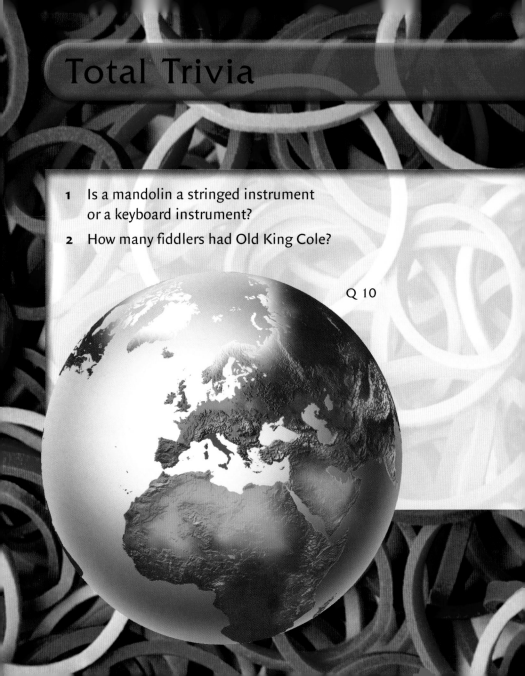

Q 10

3 What is claustrophobia a fear of?

4 In 1993 who became the 42nd president of the United States?

5 Where is the bow of a ship?

6 Which bird lays the largest egg?

7 *Costa* is the Spanish word for what?

8 What is Holland's national flower?

9 In which African country is Tripoli?

10 Where is the city of Turin?

ANSWERS

1 Stringed 2 Three 3 It is the fear of enclosed spaces 4 Bill Clinton 5 At the front
6 The ostrich 7 Coast 112 8 Tulip 9 Libya 10 Italy

Flower Power

Can you give the common name for each of these flowers?

1

2

3

4

5

6

7

8

ANSWERS

1 Tulips **2** Daisies **3** Crocuses **4** Primroses **5** Roses **6** Snowdrops **7** Pansies **8** Poppies

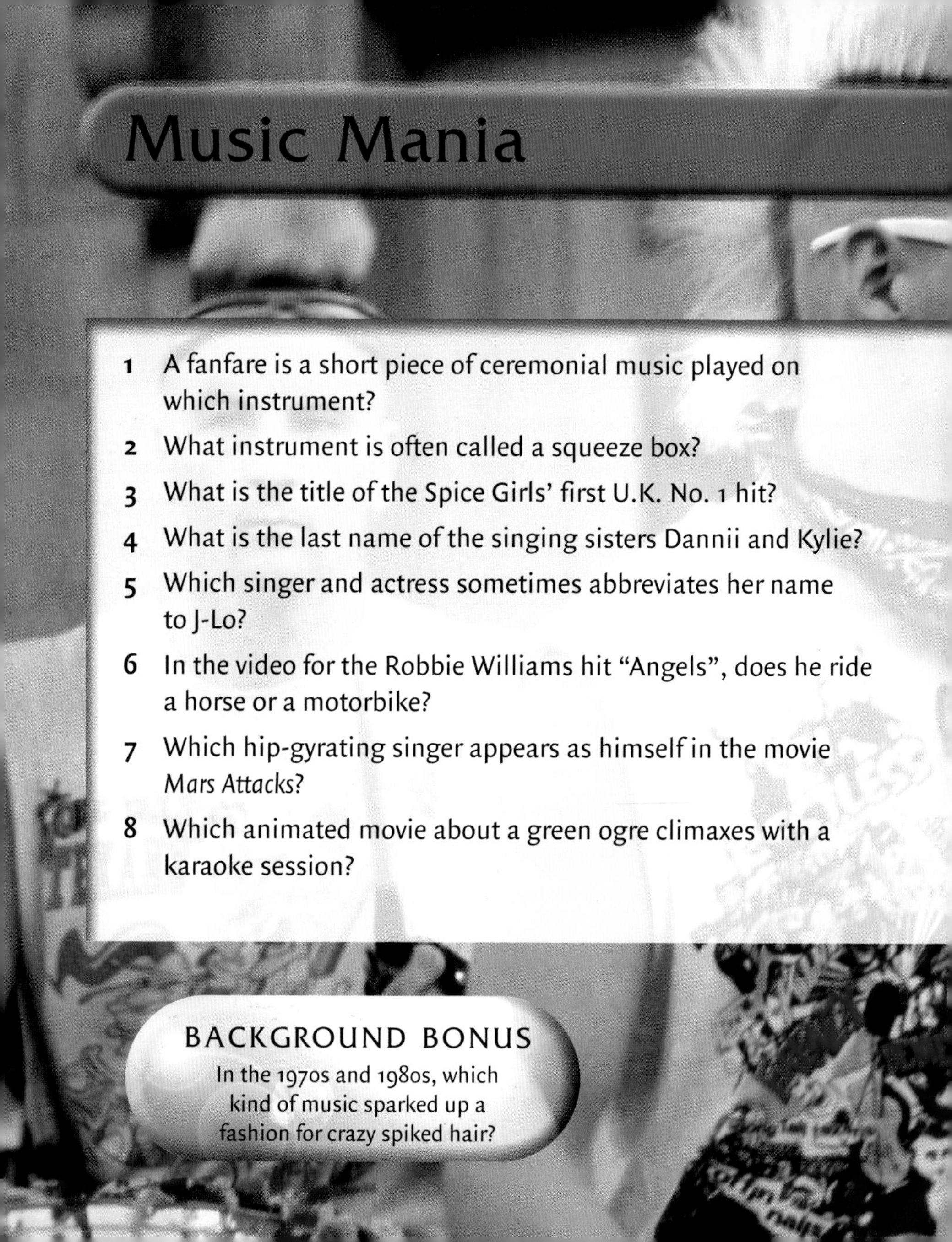

Music Mania

1 A fanfare is a short piece of ceremonial music played on which instrument?

2 What instrument is often called a squeeze box?

3 What is the title of the Spice Girls' first U.K. No. 1 hit?

4 What is the last name of the singing sisters Dannii and Kylie?

5 Which singer and actress sometimes abbreviates her name to J-Lo?

6 In the video for the Robbie Williams hit "Angels", does he ride a horse or a motorbike?

7 Which hip-gyrating singer appears as himself in the movie *Mars Attacks*?

8 Which animated movie about a green ogre climaxes with a karaoke session?

BACKGROUND BONUS

In the 1970s and 1980s, which kind of music sparked up a fashion for crazy spiked hair?

Q 2

9 What is the first name of John Travolta's character in the movie *Grease*?

10 Are cymbals a percussion or brass instrument?

ANSWERS

1 The trumpet **2** The accordion **3** "Wannabe" **4** Minogue **5** Jennifer Lopez **6** Motorbike **7** Tom Jones **8** Shrek **9** Danny **10** Percussion

Background Bonus Punk rock

Sporting Chance

1 How many minutes long is a round in boxing?

2 In which sport do athletes throw a spearlike object?

3 Which watersport was originally called soccer-in-water?

4 Which fruit is traditionally eaten with cream at the Wimbledon Tennis Championships?

5 In which of the following sports is a volley not allowed: tennis, table tennis or badminton?

6 In what park does the New York Marathon finish?

7 From where does kendo originate?

8 In which sport do competitors travel on a skeleton?

9 In baseball, what is a "dinger"?

10 Describe the flag that is waved in Formula One racing when a driver crosses the finishing line.

ANSWERS

1 Three minutes **2** Javelin **3** Water polo **4** Strawberries **5** Table tennis **6** Central Park **7** Japan **8** Tobogganing **9** A home run **10** Black-and-white chequered

Total Trivia

1 What currency is used in France?
2 Which tree does an acorn come from?
3 What are forget-me-nots and marigolds examples of?
4 What is another name for a microprocessor in a computer?
5 What is 7 less than 3,000?
6 What is an ingot?
7 Which dinosaur had large, upright plates on its back?
8 Which games, held every four years, first took place in ancient Greece?
9 What are winkle-pickers: farmers, a type of shoe or a type of food?
10 Handel, Mozart and Brahms were all what?

Q 7

ANSWERS

1 The euro **2** The oak **3** Flowers **4** A microchip or a silicon chip **5** 2,993 **6** A brick-shaped bar of gold **7** *Stegosaurus* **8** The Olympic Games **9** A type of shoe **10** Composers

Making History

1 Which country built the *Nautilus*, the world's first nuclear submarine?

2 When was the first microscope invented: 1230, 1590 or 1750?

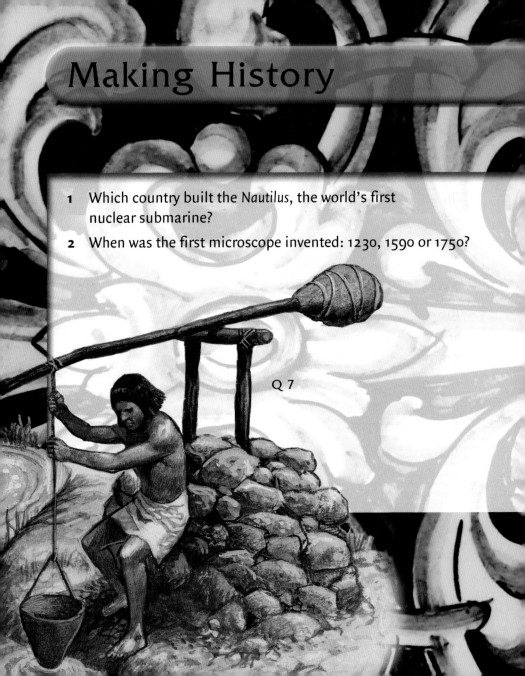

Q 7

3 Which Italian artist painted the roof of the Sistine Chapel in Italy?

4 In which year was the first pistol made: 1540, 1680 or 1810?

5 The mythical monster, the minotaur, is a man with the head of what: a lion, a bull or an eagle?

6 What weapon did jousting knights use when on horseback?

7 For what did the ancient Egyptians use a *shaduf*: moving stones or raising water?

8 What was a dragoon: a foot-soldier or a horse-soldier?

9 Which Greek conqueror founded the Egyptian city of Alexandria?

10 What was the name of the winged horse in Greek legend?

ANSWERS
1 The United States 2 1590 3 Michelangelo 4 1540 5 A bull 6 A lance
7 Raising water 8 Horse-soldier 9 Alexander the Great 10 Pegasus

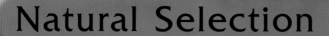

Natural Selection

1 What is the name given to a female pig?

2 Which big cat lives the longest: the lion, the panther or the tiger?

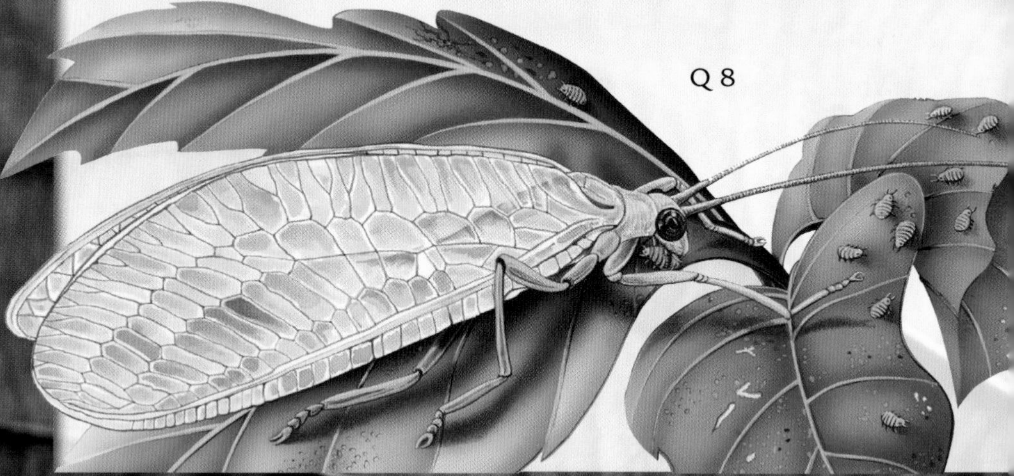

Q 8

3 What do we call the claw of a bird of prey?

4 In which part of its body does a koala keep its young?

5 What body part does a fish breathe through?

6 What is a great bustard: a bird or a fish?

7 Which creature has the largest eye in the animal kingdom?

8 What is a lacewing: a bird or an insect?

9 Which horse-like animal has a reputation for being stubborn?

10 Do sand vipers live on beaches or in deserts?

ANSWERS

1 A sow **2** The lion **3** A talon **4** In its pouch **5** Its gills **6** A bird (the heaviest flying bird) **7** The giant squid **8** An insect **9** The mule **10** In deserts

Total Trivia

1 Which fleet of ships tried to invade England in 1588?

2 What is the name of Donald Duck's girlfriend?

3 The tubing of which brass instrument is curved into circles?

4 In a desert, what is an area where water is found and plants grow called?

Q 3

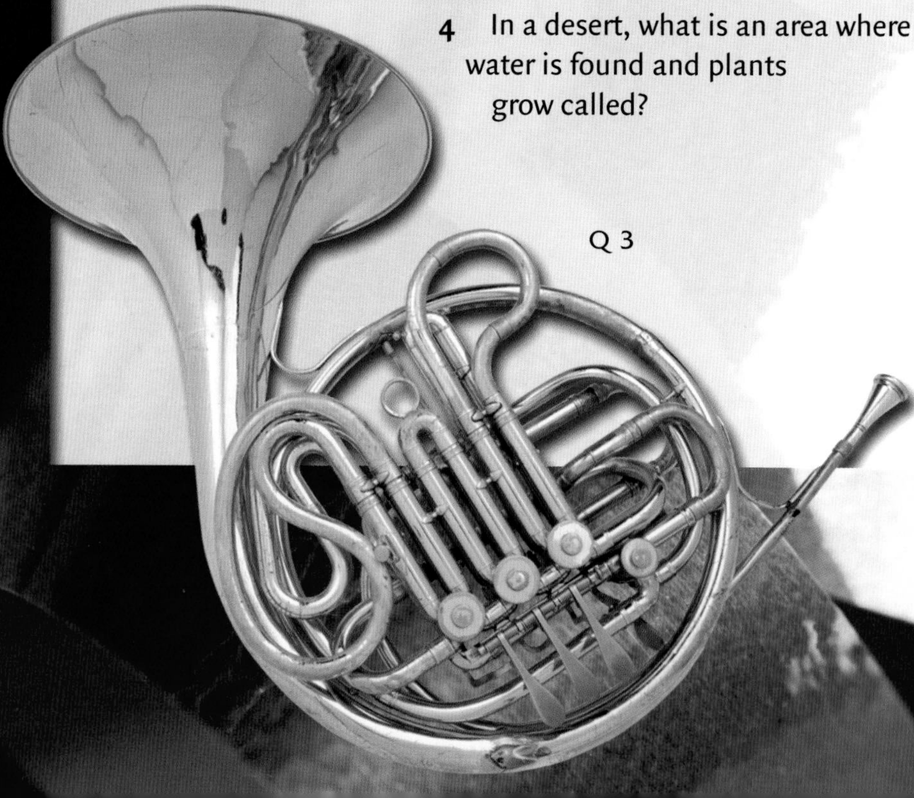

LEVEL 1 · QUIZ 30

5 What is a thatched roof made from?

6 What shape is the base of a pyramid?

7 Which country has the largest population in the world?

8 What kind of bird is Captain Flint in *Treasure Island*?

9 Is a chameleon a mammal, marsupial or reptile?

10 What is a group of lions called?

ANSWERS

1 The Spanish Armada 2 Daisy Duck 3 The French horn 4 An oasis 5 Straw or reed 6 A square 7 China 8 Parrot 9 Reptile 10 Pride

Making History

1 Where was the empire ruled by Akbar the Great?

2 Which planet, also the Roman god of the sea, was first seen in 1846?

3 On which river was Rome built?

4 What was a penny farthing?

5 Was a Tin Lizzie an early car or an early washing machine?

6 Which ocean did explorers cross to reach India from East Africa?

7 What was a Roman soldier in charge of 100 men called?

8 In 1868, which European country held the first cycle race?

9 In World War I, what was a Sopwith Camel?

10 Who was the king of the Roman gods?

LEVEL 1 • QUIZ 31

Q 4

ANSWERS

1 India **2** Neptune **3** The Tiber **4** An early bicycle **5** An early car **6** The Indian Ocean **7** A centurion **8** France **9** A fighter plane **10** Jupiter

Sporting Chance

Q 6

BACKGROUND BONUS

In which popular British game must players first pot 15 red balls?

LEVEL 1 • QUIZ 32

1 How many players are in a beach volleyball team?

2 At which horse and ball sport have British princes, William and Harry, been team mates of their father Prince Charles?

3 What do the letters PB next to an athlete's time indicate?

4 Which medal is awarded for third place in an Olympic final?

5 What name is given to a golfer's assistant who carries the clubs?

6 What is passed from runner to runner in a relay race?

7 In tennis, what is the line at the back of the court called?

8 On a yacht, what are sheets?

9 What is the duration of a basketball match?

10 What is worn in the mouth by boxers to protect their teeth?

ANSWERS

1 Two **2** Polo **3** Personal best **4** Bronze **5** Caddy **6** A baton **7** Baseline **8** Ropes **9** 60 minutes **10** A gum shield

Background Bonus Snooker

Total Trivia

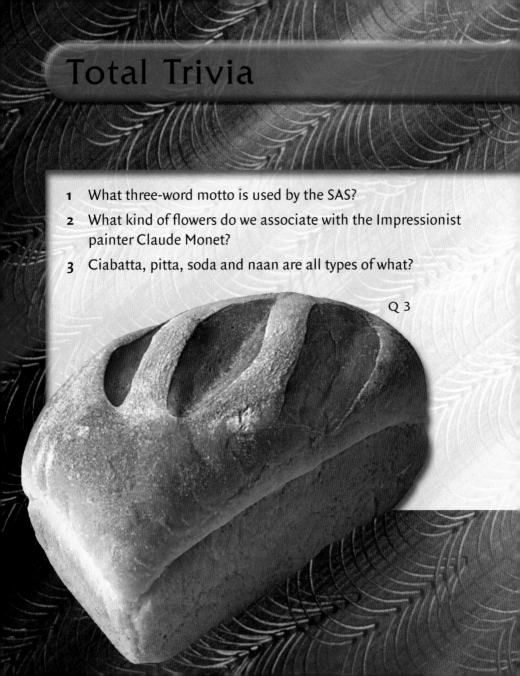

1 What three-word motto is used by the SAS?
2 What kind of flowers do we associate with the Impressionist painter Claude Monet?
3 Ciabatta, pitta, soda and naan are all types of what?

Q 3

4 What is sometimes referred to as Adam's ale?

5 Closely associated with Count Dracula, in which country is Transylvania?

6 Was *Indiana Jones and the Temple of Doom* the first or second movie in the series?

7 Judogi is the cotton outfit worn by competitors in which martial art?

8 A seal is a pinniped. What does this mean?

9 The Caspian Sea is the world's largest what?

10 What insects are kept in an apiary?

ANSWERS

1 Who dares wins **2** Water lilies **3** Bread **4** Water **5** Romania **6** Second **7** Judo **8** It has flippers **9** Lake **10** Bees

Natural Selection

1 Seagull, kingfisher: which can swim best?

2 Do crocodiles hold their mouths open to cool off or to trap insects?

3 Which grasshopper relative feeds in enormous swarms?

4 Do male deer shed their antlers every year or every five years?

5 Red admiral and cabbage white are types of what?

6 What type of creature is a redback?

7 What is the name used for a male swan?

8 Do scorpions lay eggs or give birth to live young?

9 Which animal has the biggest ears?

10 Which North American animal is the largest member of the deer family?

BACKGROUND BONUS

The okapi is related to which African animal?

LEVEL 1 • QUIZ 34

Q 6

ANSWERS

1 The seagull **2** To cool off **3** The locust **4** Every year **5** Butterflies **6** A spider (in Australia) **7** A cob **8** They give birth to live young **9** The African elephant **10** Moose **Background Bonus** Giraffe

Total Trivia

Q 7

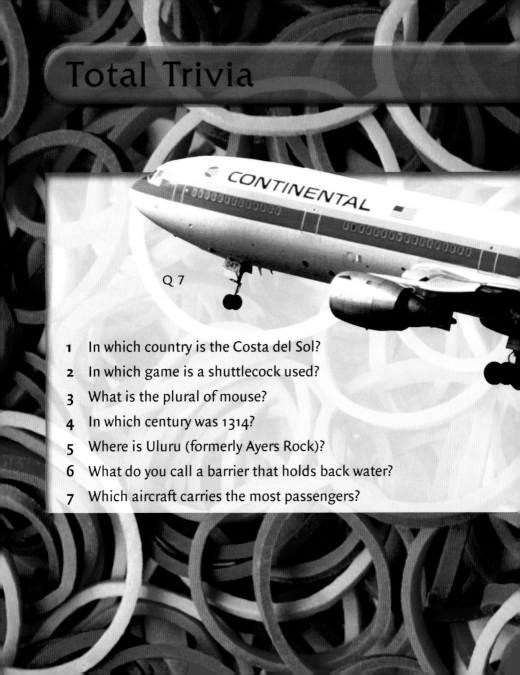

1 In which country is the Costa del Sol?
2 In which game is a shuttlecock used?
3 What is the plural of mouse?
4 In which century was 1314?
5 Where is Uluru (formerly Ayers Rock)?
6 What do you call a barrier that holds back water?
7 Which aircraft carries the most passengers?

8 Where are your incisors?

9 How many wives did King Henry VIII have?

10 What is the past tense of eat?

ANSWERS

1 Spain 2 Badminton 3 Mice 4 14th 5 Australia 6 A dam 7 Jumbo jet
8 In your mouth (they are teeth) 9 Six 10 Ate

Eye Spy

Can you identify these animals by their eyes?

1

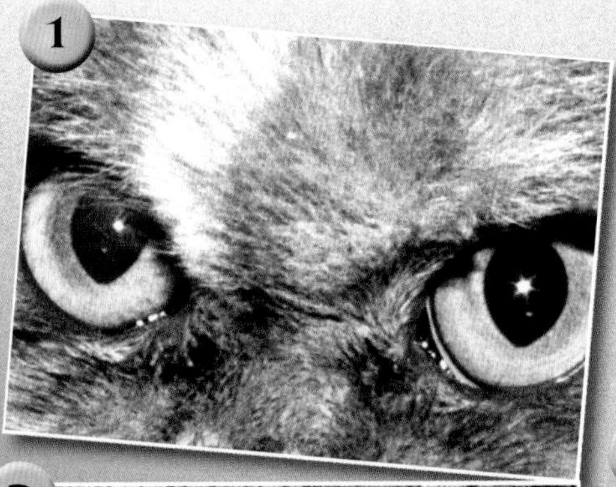

2

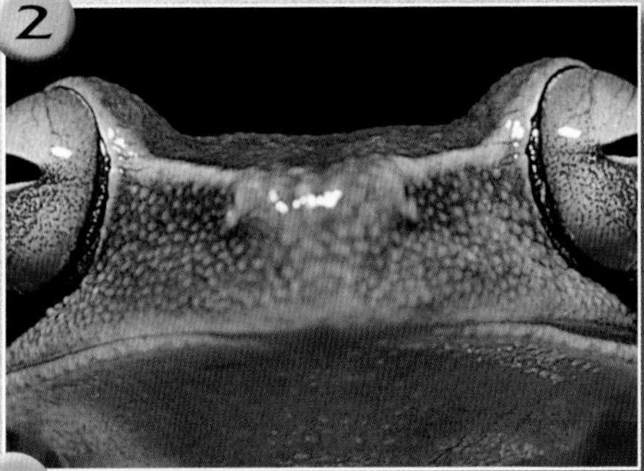

3

4

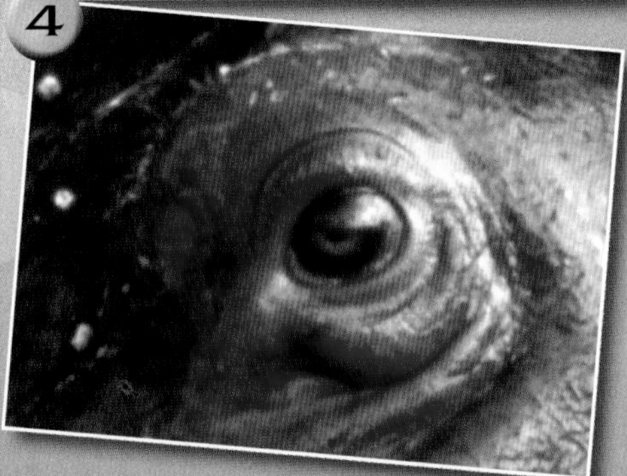

5

6

7

8

ANSWERS

1 Cat **2** Frog **3** Crocodile **4** Hippo **5** Flamingo **6** Tortoise **7** Seal **8** Dog

Lights, Camera, Action!

1 Which Hollywood actress starred in the movie *Notting Hill*?

2 Which brick road did the characters follow in *The Wizard of Oz*?

3 Where does Bart Simpson live?

4 Which cartoon movie tells the story of a lost Russian princess?

5 What U.S. state shares its name with Dr. Jones' first name?

6 Which cartoon duck was 65 years old in 1999?

7 What is the profession of the main characters in the movie *Top Gun*?

8 Which capital city did the Rugrats venture to in the 2000 movie?

9 What does the A stand for in the Steven Spielberg movie AI?

10 What kind of animal is Maid Marian in the Disney cartoon version of Robin Hood?

BACKGROUND BONUS

In which Italian city is a world famous movie festival held every year?

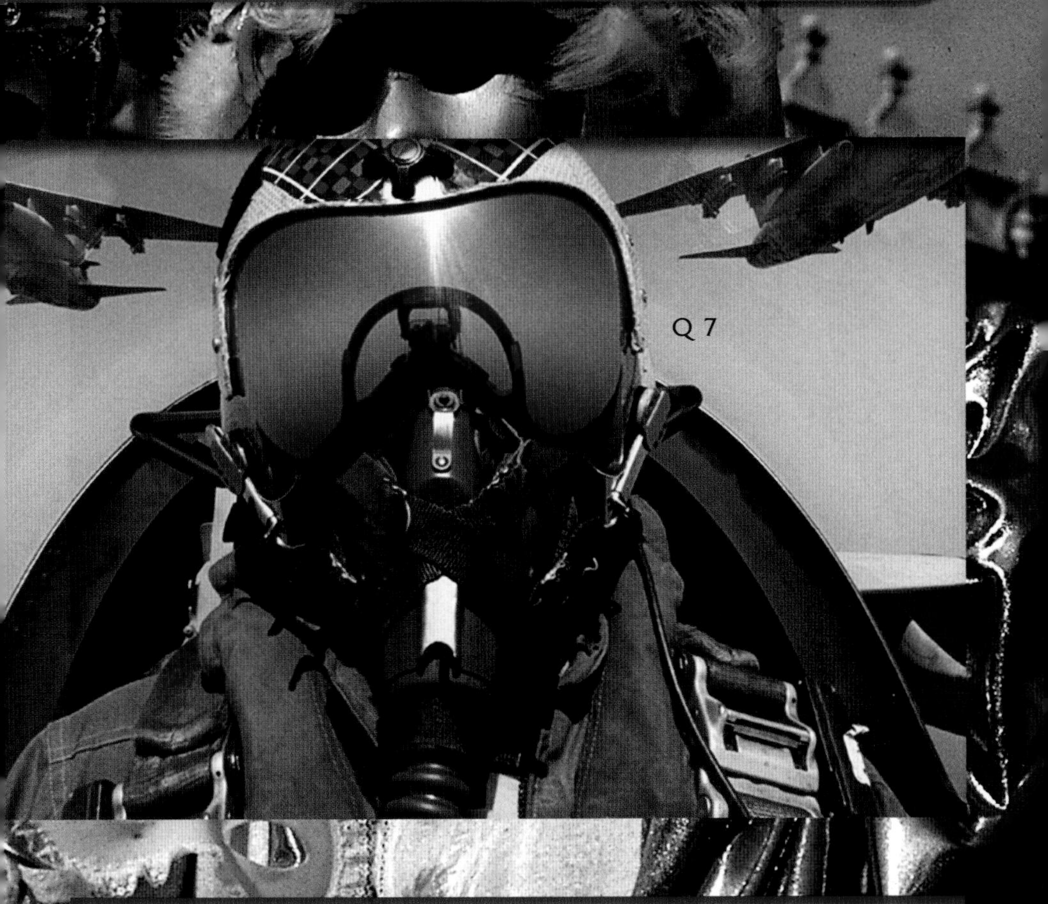

Q 7

ANSWERS
1 Julia Roberts **2** The Yellow Brick Road **3** Springfield **4** *Anastasia* **5** Indiana
6 Donald Duck **7** Jet fighter pilots **8** Paris **9** Artificial **10** Fox
Background Bonus Venice

Natural Selection

1 What do you call a baby eagle: an eagling or an eaglet?

2 Which is the smallest of these dinosaurs: *Triceratops*, *Compsognathus*, *Tyrannosaurus*?

3 What is the name given to a male giraffe?

4 How many arms does a starfish usually have?

5 Which is the biggest fish: the sea horse, whale shark or squirrelfish?

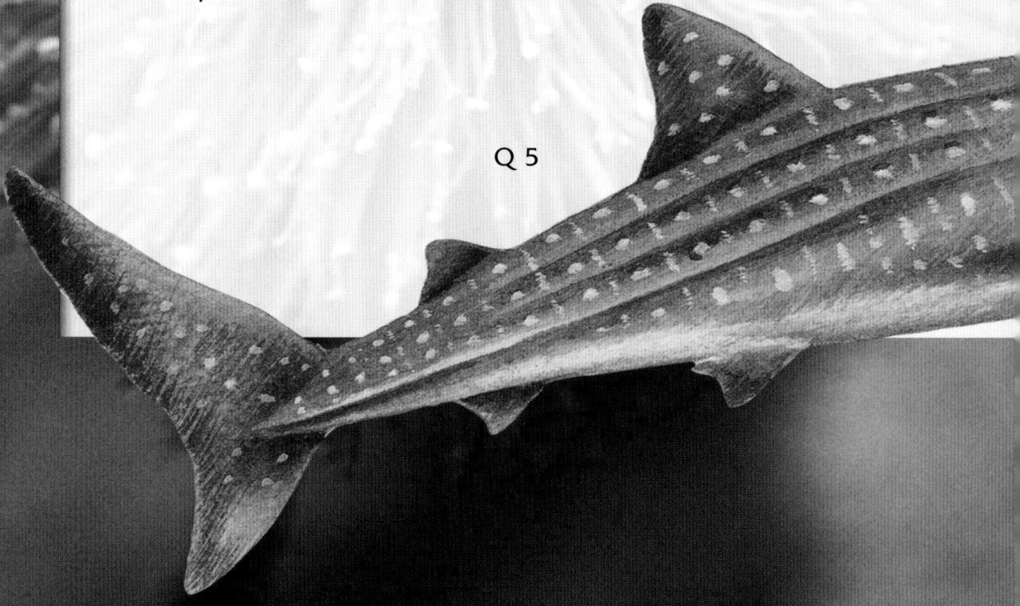

Q 5

6 Do parrots live in tropical forest or coastal sand dunes?

7 Fish, snake, toad: which does not have scales?

8 Can a sea urchin move along the seabed?

9 Is the peacock's cry very loud or very quiet?

10 Do grapes grow on trees or vines?

ANSWERS

1 An eaglet **2** *Compsognathus* **3** A bull **4** Five **5** Whale shark **6** Tropical forests **7** The toad **8** Yes, it "walks" on its spines **9** Very loud **10** On vines

Lights, Camera, Action!

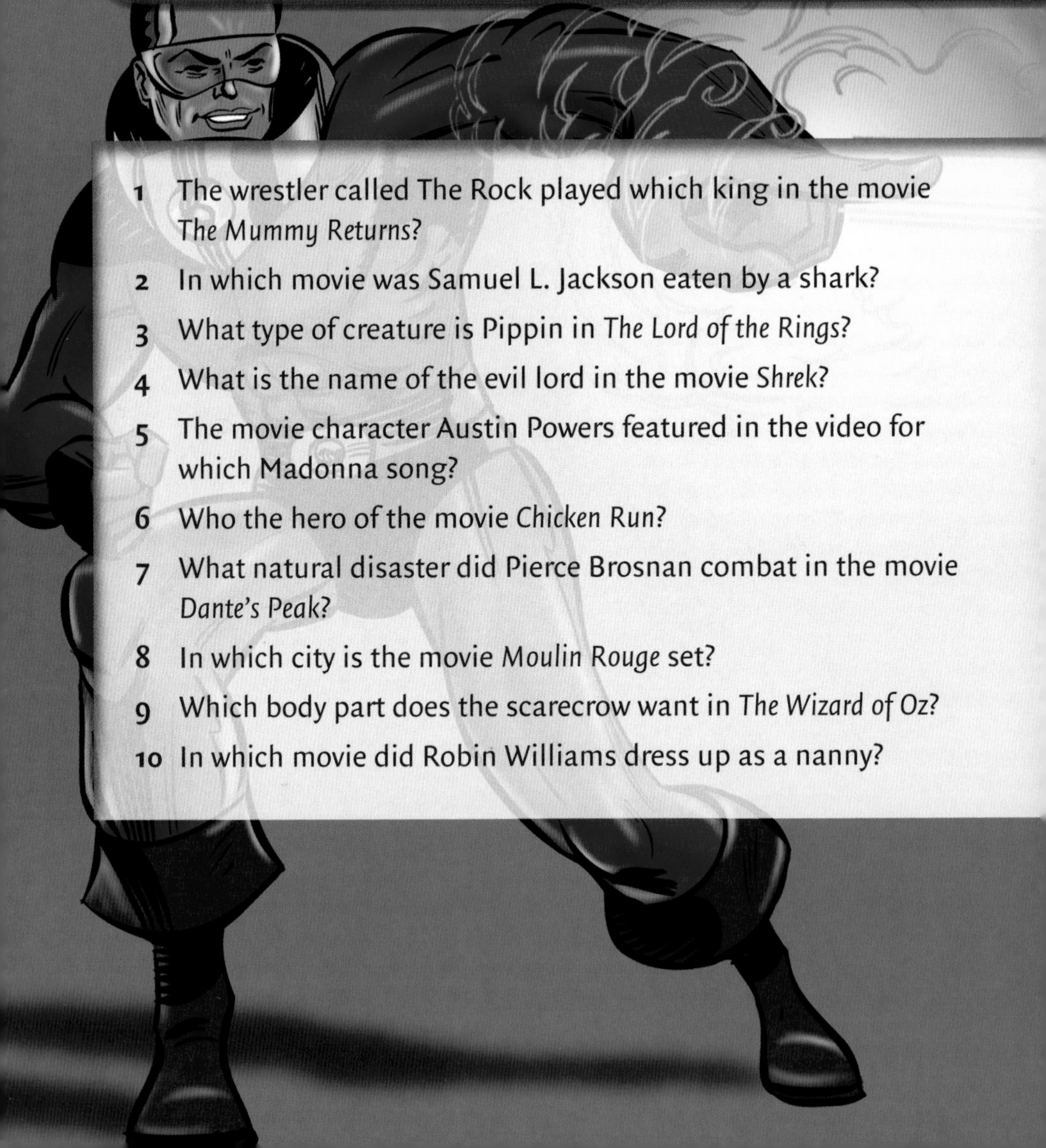

1 The wrestler called The Rock played which king in the movie *The Mummy Returns?*

2 In which movie was Samuel L. Jackson eaten by a shark?

3 What type of creature is Pippin in *The Lord of the Rings?*

4 What is the name of the evil lord in the movie *Shrek?*

5 The movie character Austin Powers featured in the video for which Madonna song?

6 Who the hero of the movie *Chicken Run?*

7 What natural disaster did Pierce Brosnan combat in the movie *Dante's Peak?*

8 In which city is the movie *Moulin Rouge* set?

9 Which body part does the scarecrow want in *The Wizard of Oz?*

10 In which movie did Robin Williams dress up as a nanny?

LEVEL 1 • QUIZ 39

Q8

ANSWERS

1 The Scorpion King **2** *Deep Blue Sea* **3** Hobbits **4** Lord Farquaad **5** "Beautiful Stranger" **6** Rocky **7** A volcanic eruption **8** Paris **9** Brain **10** Mrs. Doubtfire

Natural Selection

LEVEL 1 • QUIZ 40

1 Which weasel-like animal can be tamed as a pet?

2 What is a male bee without a sting called?

3 Is the dung beetle so-called because it smells of dung or because it collects it?

4 What does the swallow build its nest from?

5 Does rhubarb taste sweet or sour?

6 Which creature can contain a natural pearl inside its shell?

7 How long does a honey bee live for: six weeks, six months or six years?

8 Do bees swarm to find new nesting sites or to feed on nectar?

9 Which great ape beats its chest to scare enemies?

10 Are camels' feet best suited to sand, rock or marsh?

Q 9

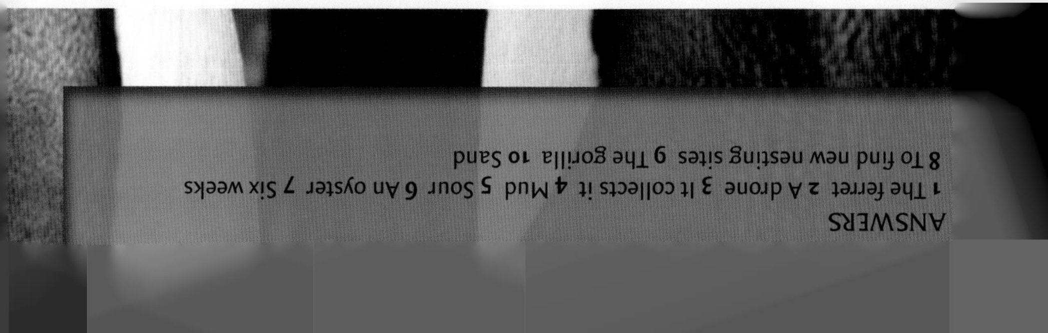

ANSWERS

1 The ferret 2 A drone 3 It collects it 4 Mud 5 Sour 6 An oyster 7 Six weeks 8 To find new nesting sites 9 The gorilla 10 Sand

Scientifically Speaking

1 When a dentist extracts teeth, what do they do?

2 What is titanium: a metal, a star or a part of the human body?

3 What is three-tenths as a decimal?

4 Which P word is the machine made of ropes and wheels used to lift heavy loads?

5 What shape is the Moon a few days after a New Moon?

6 What does your body need about eight hours of every day?

7 What is helium?

8 What is charcoal?

9 What is the name for any flat shape with three or more straight sides?

10 Does hot air travel up or down?

BACKGROUND BONUS

The optic nerve carries signals to the brain from which part of the body?

LEVEL 1 · QUIZ 41

Q 6

ANSWERS

1 Pull it out **2** A metal **3** 0.3 **4** A pulley **5** A crescent **6** Sleep **7** A gas **8** Partly burnt wood **9** A polygon **10** Up

Background Bonus The eye

Sporting Chance

1 How many kings are on a chessboard at the start of a game?

2 In baseball, what do the initials NL stand for?

3 What scores six points in a game of American Football?

4 In which sport might you perform a triple salchow?

Q 8

5 Where would you find a hoop, a backboard and a three point line?

6 How many shots would a golfer have taken if scoring a birdie on a par 4 hole?

7 How many players are there in a basketball team?

8 In which sport do the New York Yankees attempt to win the World Series?

9 Which animal takes part in point-to-point races and steeplechases?

10 Which jockey achieved the Magnificent Seven at Ascot in September 1996?

ANSWERS

1 Two **2** National League **3** Touchdown **4** Figure skating **5** A basketball court **6** Three shots **7** Five **8** Baseball **9** The horse **10** Frankie Dettori

Written Word

1 In *The Jungle Book*, is Bagheera a black panther or a brown bear?

2 What gas is an anagram of the word none?

3 What word can precede print, bottle and bell?

4 Where did the Lost Boys live in *Peter Pan*?

5 What is the first animal mentioned in the nursery rhyme *Hey Diddle Diddle*?

6 What kind of creature is Jeremy Fisher in the Beatrix Potter tales?

7 What is the name of the train that takes Harry Potter to the wizard's school?

8 Which capital city is an anagram of the word more?

9 Which literary doctor created *The Cat in the Hat*?

10 What is the fifth *Harry Potter* book called?

Q 2

LEVEL 1 • QUIZ 43

ANSWERS

1 A black panther **2** Neon **3** Blue **4** Never, Never Land **5** The cat **6** A frog **7** Hogwart's Express **8** Rome **9** Dr. Seuss **10** Harry Potter and the Order of the Phoenix

Lights, Camera, Action!

Q 4

1 In which movie does a sheep dog called Fly become a foster parent to a pig?

2 What type of animal was voiced by Eddie Murphy in *Shrek*?

3 Who stole Christmas in the 2000 movie?

4 Which character from *The Simpsons* has a teddy called Bobo?

5 Who plays Wanda in the movie *A Fish Called Wanda*?

6 What is Sid's dog in *Toy Story* called?

7 Which movie features hens called Ginger, Babs and Mac?

8 In the movie *A Bug's Life*, Flik hires circus performers to defend his colony from what?

9 Manfred, Sid and Diego are all characters from which movie?

10 What is the name of the bear who befriends Mowgli in *The Jungle Book*?

ANSWERS

1 Babe **2** Donkey **3** *The Grinch* **4** Mr. Burns **5** Jamie Lee Curtis **6** Scud **7** *Chicken Run* **8** Grasshoppers **9** *Ice Age* **10** Baloo

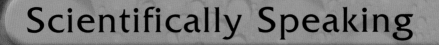

Scientifically Speaking

1 How many right angles does a right-angle triangle have?

2 Which machine is said to work like an electronic brain?

3 Which is the largest planet in our Solar System?

4 What is the smallest number divisible by both 3 and 4?

5 Which of your bones is shaped like a cage?

6 What silver metal is inside a thermometer?

7 Pb is the chemical symbol for which metal?

8 What material can you make from mixing newspaper, flour and water?

9 How many minutes long is the period of time starting at 6:15 and ending at 6:45?

10 What part of the Earth does a scuba diver explore?

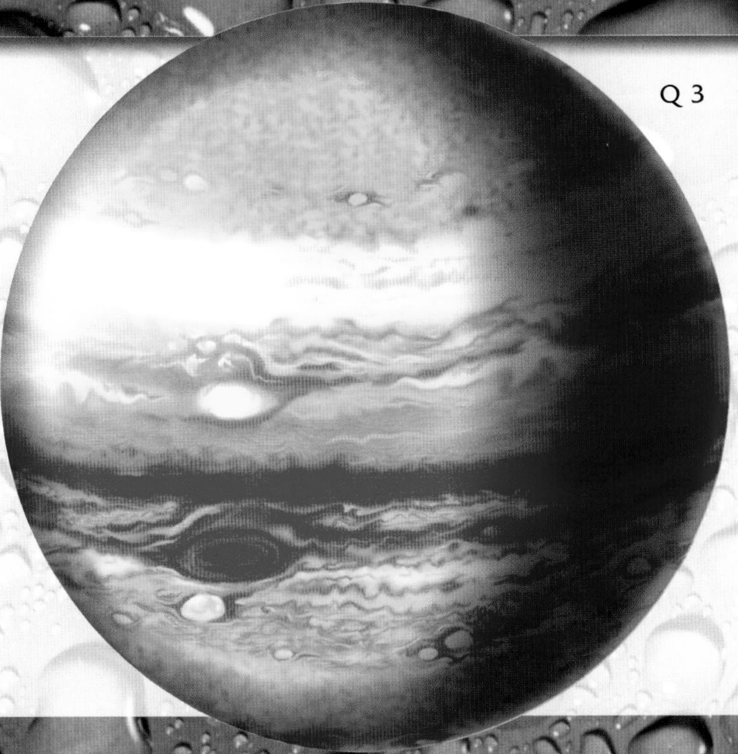

Q 3

ANSWERS

1 One **2** A computer **3** Jupiter **4** 12 **5** Ribs **6** Mercury **7** Lead **8** Papier-mâché **9** 30 minutes **10** Under the water

Total Trivia

1 Who is the younger tennis player: Serena or Venus Williams?
2 In which country did kung fu originate?
3 What type of creature is the movie and TV character Flipper?
4 Which TV show stars Blossom, Buttercup and Bubbles?
5 In which sport do you get three strikes before you are out?
6 In which sport are there categories of bantamweight, flyweight and featherweight?
7 Which is the shortest month of the year?
8 What kind of bird is Hedwig in the *Harry Potter* books?
9 Which two U.S. states beginning with M are part of New England?
10 What mechanical animal is chased by greyhounds in a greyhound race?

LEVEL 1 • QUIZ 46

Q 6

ANSWERS

1 Serena Williams **2** China **3** A dolphin **4** The Powerpuff Girls **5** Baseball **6** Boxing **7** February **8** Snowy owl **9** Maine and Massachusetts **10** The hare

Global Matters

1 Which two continents are natural homes to the elephant?

2 Which U.S. state is known as The Grand Canyon State?

3 How deep is the deepest part of the ocean: 1.6 km (1 mi), 4.8 km (3 mi) or 11.3 km (7 mi)?

4 If you ordered *tarte aux fraises* in a French restaurant, what would you get?

5 In which sea would you find the island country called Cyprus?

6 Which animal builds dams in North America and Europe?

7 In which U.S. state would you be if you were staying in Orlando?

8 What type of natural feature is K2?

9 What is the capital of Thailand?

10 Which of these Caribbean Islands isthe largest: Haiti, Cuba or Jamaica?

Q 6

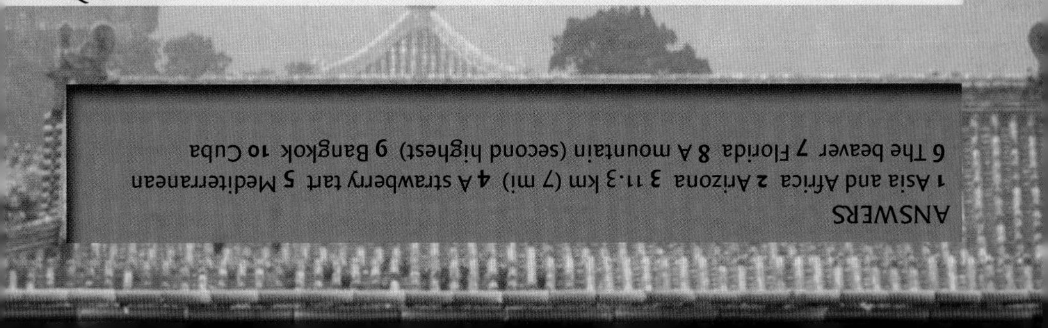

ANSWERS

1 Asia and Africa **2** Arizona **3** 11.3 km (7 mi) **4** A strawberry tart **5** Mediterranean **6** The beaver **7** Florida **8** A mountain (second highest) **9** Bangkok **10** Cuba

Famous Faces

Can you identify these famous people?

1

2

3

4

5

6

7

8

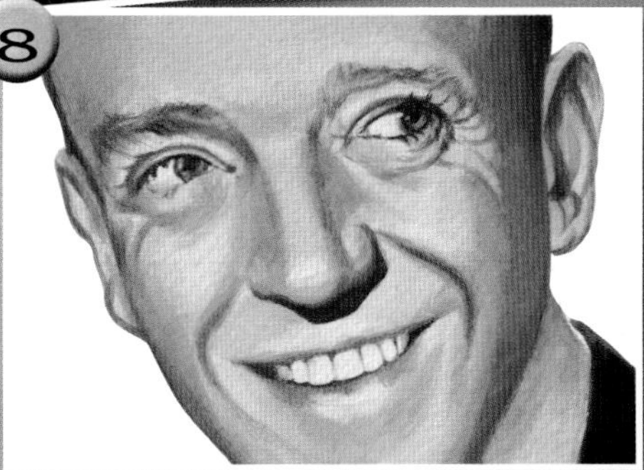

ANSWERS

1 Ché Guevara **2** Judy Garland **3** Nicole Kidman **4** William Shakespeare
5 Queen Elizabeth I **6** Salman Rushdie **7** Samuel L. Jackson **8** Fred Astaire

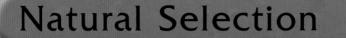

Natural Selection

1 Goose, albatross, cormorant: which can swim underwater?

2 Do poisonous frogs blend in well with their surroundings or stand out brightly?

3 Which insect product do humans often spread on bread?

4 Which animal is used to help herd sheep?

Q 7

LEVEL 1 • QUIZ 49

5 Are buttercups white or yellow?

6 Do fruit bats sleep in burrows or trees?

7 Is an armadillo a mammal or a reptile?

8 Do insects have two, three or four main body parts?

9 Do female rattlesnakes lay eggs or give birth to baby rattlers?

10 On which continent would you find llamas living in their natural habitat?

ANSWERS

1 Cormorant **2** Stand out brightly **3** Honey **4** A sheepdog **5** Yellow **6** In trees **7** A mammal **8** Three **9** Give birth to baby rattlers **10** South America

Sporting Chance: Soccer

1 Which soccer club did Dennis Wise captain to win the FA Cup?

2 What nationality is the soccer manager Alex Ferguson?

3 Which English soccer club is nicknamed “The Villains”?

4 How many minutes does each half last in a game of soccer?

5 What do the letters OG stand for in a soccer game?

6 Which Scottish soccer club has a five-letter name beginning with C, and is also a boy’s first name?

7 Which is the only English Football League team beginning with the letter I?

8 For which country do Nicolas Anelka and Patrick Vieira play?

9 Which is the only English Football League team beginning with the letter Q?

10 In the soccer Premiership, how many points do teams receive for winning a game?

BACKGROUND BONUS

What is the name for the peglike objects fixed to the sole of some sport footwear?

LEVEL 1 • QUIZ 50

Q 2

ANSWERS

1 Chelsea **2** Scottish **3** Aston Villa **4** 45 minutes **5** Own goal **6** Clyde **7** Ipswich Town **8** France **9** Queen's Park Rangers **10** Three

Background Bonus Studs

Written Word

1 Is the word fish a noun, a verb or both?

2 What is the silent letter in the word psychiatrist?

3 The cunning fox escaped from the hounds by hiding up a tree. Which word is the adjective?

4 How many vowels does the word vowels have?

Q 8

5 What is the past tense of the word shoot?

6 Which three-letter word can precede ring, stone and hole?

7 Which Shakespeare play is commonly referred to as the Scottish play?

8 In the Roald Dahl story, which giant fruit did James sail in?

9 Which five-letter M word is given to the grinding teeth at the back of your mouth?

10 What term is used for setting fire to property on purpose?

ANSWERS

1 Both 2 The letter P 3 Cunning (descriptive word) 4 Two (o and e) 5 Shot 6 Key 7 Macbeth 8 Peach 9 Molar 10 Arson

Natural Selection

1 Which has the keenest eyesight: eagle, duck or ostrich?

2 Which species of snake shares its name with a Cuban dance?

3 Does the sea anemone catch food with jaws or tentacles?

4 Is an albino animal white, black or brown?

5 Do vultures hover or soar in circles?

6 Which are taller: foxgloves or bluebells?

7 Leech, scorpion, chameleon: which is the reptile?

8 Which appeared first on Earth: spiders or dinosaurs?

9 Elephant, hippo, camel: which usually lives longest?

10 Are baby dolphins born on beaches or underwater?

BACKGROUND BONUS

What birds are pink due to the shrimps and algae that they eat?

Q 1

ANSWERS

1 The eagle **2** Mamba **3** Tentacles **4** White **5** Soar in circles **6** Foxgloves **7** The chameleon **8** Spiders **9** The elephant **10** Underwater

Background Bonus Flamingoes

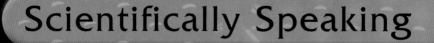

Scientifically Speaking

1 What kind of clock measures time by the Sun?

2 What is another name for perspiration?

3 What is the name for pieces of ice falling from clouds?

4 On a 24-hour digital clock, what numbers are displayed at 11:45 pm?

5 What is the name of our galaxy?

6 Which invention was first called a phonograph?

7 What part of your body works like a pump?

8 Which word describes how loud a sound is?

9 How many degrees is half a turn?

10 How many sides has an octagon?

Q 6

ANSWERS
1 A sundial **2** Sweat **3** Hail **4** 23:45 **5** The Milky Way **6** A gramophone **7** Your heart **8** Volume **9** 180 **10** Eight

Written Word

Q 8

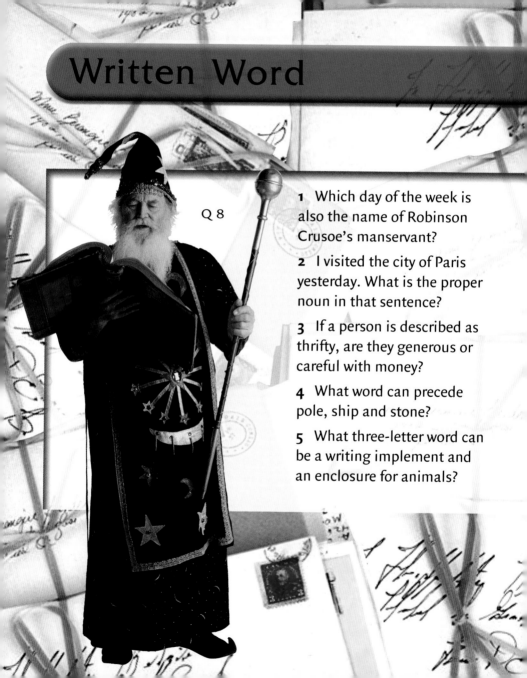

1 Which day of the week is also the name of Robinson Crusoe's manservant?

2 I visited the city of Paris yesterday. What is the proper noun in that sentence?

3 If a person is described as thrifty, are they generous or careful with money?

4 What word can precede pole, ship and stone?

5 What three-letter word can be a writing implement and an enclosure for animals?

6 How many books make up a trilogy?

7 The adjective equine refers to which animal?

8 In *The Lord of the Rings*, is Gandalf a witch, a wizard or a hobbit?

9 What is the name given to a young elephant, a young cow and a young whale?

10 What is the last vowel in the English alphabet?

ANSWERS

1 Friday 2 Paris 3 Careful with money 4 Flag 5 Pen 6 Three 7 Horse 8 Wizard 9 Calf 10 U

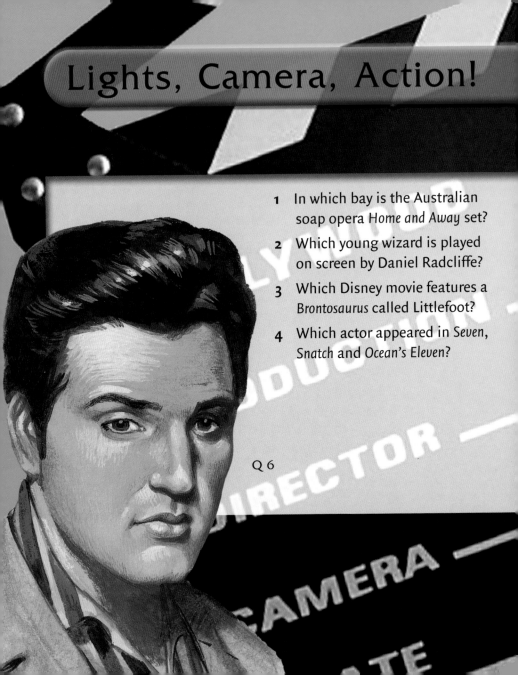

Lights, Camera, Action!

1 In which bay is the Australian soap opera *Home and Away* set?

2 Which young wizard is played on screen by Daniel Radcliffe?

3 Which Disney movie features a *Brontosaurus* called Littlefoot?

4 Which actor appeared in *Seven*, *Snatch* and *Ocean's Eleven*?

Q 6

5 Who is the cowboy character from *Toy Story?*

6 Which king of rock and roll starred in the movies *Jailhouse Rock* and *Blue Hawaii?*

7 What kind of animal is Kaa in the Disney movie *The Jungle Book?*

8 Who played one of Charlie's Angels and Mary in *There's Something About Mary?*

9 Name the actor who played the character of Neo in the movie *The Matrix.*

10 What is Batman's road vehicle called?

ANSWERS

1 Summer Bay **2** Harry Potter **3** *The Land Before Time* **4** Brad Pitt **5** Woody **6** Elvis Presley **7** Snake **8** Cameron Diaz **9** Keanu Reeves **10** The Batmobile

Scientifically Speaking

1 How many days are there in five weeks?

2 What is a monsoon?

3 Which kind of triangle has three equal sides?

4 You breathe air in through which two parts of your body?

5 What do you get if you mix red and blue?

6 What are constellations?

7 On a 24-hour digital clock, what numbers are displayed at 4 pm?

8 At what times of day can the sky become red?

9 What is the total of five 5s and ten 4s?

10 Which of the following will float in water: a cork, a nail, a coin?

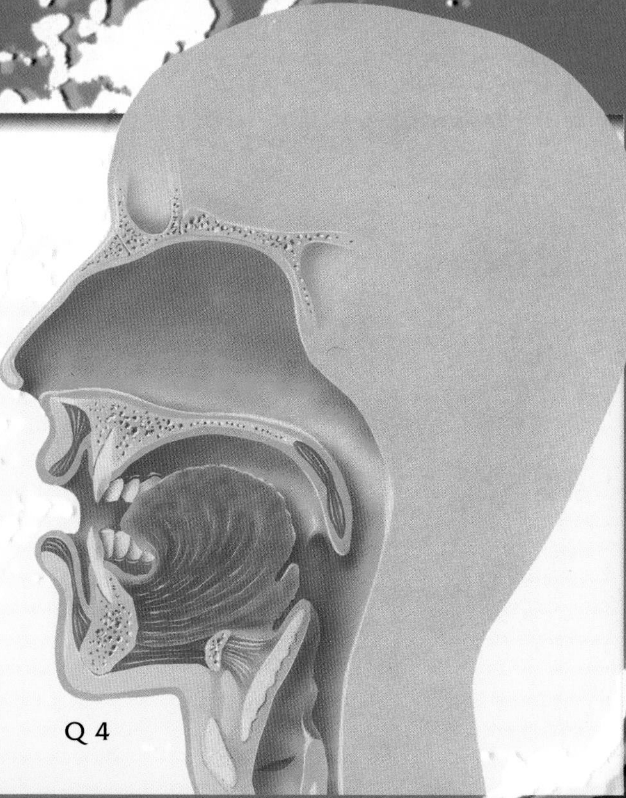

Q 4

ANSWERS

1 35 **2** A very heavy rainstorm **3** An equilateral triangle **4** Your mouth and nose **5** Purple **6** Patterns of stars in the sky **7** 16:00 **8** Sunrise and sunset **9** 65 **10** A cork

Written Word: The Bible

1 What did God create first, according to the words of Genesis, Chapter 1?

2 Who were Shem, Ham and Japheth?

3 What did Esau sell to his brother Jacob for a bowl of lentil stew?

4 What was Deborah's job?

Q 8

5 Who lived to be 969 years old?

6 What is a parable?

7 On which road did the events described in the story of the Good Samaritan take place?

8 Which bird returned to Noah's ark with an olive twig in its beak?

9 What kind of tree did Zacchaeus climb so he could see Jesus?

10 How did Jesus die?

ANSWERS

1 Light **2** The sons of Noah **3** His birthright (the rights as the eldest) **4** She was a judge **5** Methuselah **6** A story with a deeper meaning **7** The road from Jerusalem to Jericho **8** A dove **9** A sycamore tree **10** He was crucified

Total Trivia

1 Who are the Harlem Globe Trotters?

2 What is 15 divided by 2.5?

3 How many minutes are there between 10:15 and 11:05?

4 What is the singular of dice?

5 What title is given to the eldest son of an English sovereign?

6 Does a west wind blow from the west or to the west?

7 Who was the Roman god of the sea?

8 Which of these words is a noun: hopped, laughing, road, because?

9 What creature can unhinge its jaws?

10 How many legs has a quadruped?

ANSWERS

1 A basketball team **2** Six **3** 50 minutes **4** Die **5** Prince of Wales **6** It blows from the west **7** Neptune **8** Road **9** The snake **10** Four

Making History

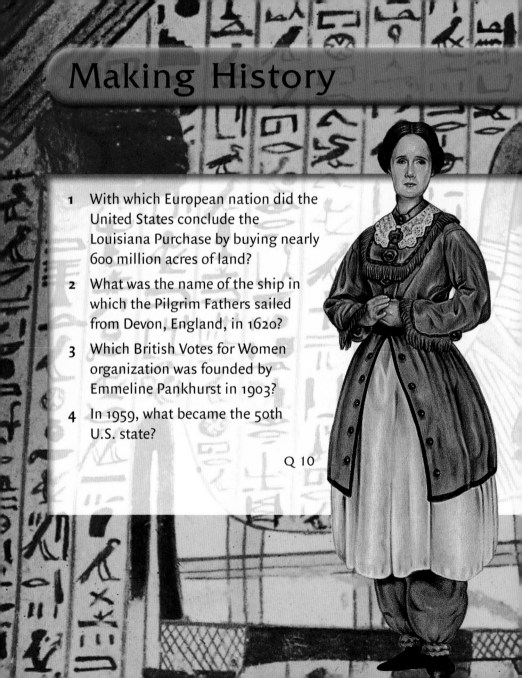

1 With which European nation did the United States conclude the Louisiana Purchase by buying nearly 600 million acres of land?

2 What was the name of the ship in which the Pilgrim Fathers sailed from Devon, England, in 1620?

3 Which British Votes for Women organization was founded by Emmeline Pankhurst in 1903?

4 In 1959, what became the 50th U.S. state?

Q 10

5 Anne Boleyn was the mother of which queen of England?

6 In what century did the astrologer Nostradamus live?

7 Who was the first U.S. president to resign from office?

8 Which Italian artist painted a mural of *The Last Supper* around 1495?

9 How many Scottish kings have been called Kenneth: one, two or three?

10 In the 1850s, which American woman invented a new kind of practical clothing for women?

ANSWERS

1 France 2 *The Mayflower* 3 The Suffragettes 4 Hawaii 5 Queen Elizabeth I 6 16th century 7 Richard Nixon 8 Leonardo da Vinci 9 Three 10 Amelia Bloomer

World Wonders

Can you identify these famous buildings and landmarks?

1

2

3

4

5

6

7

8

ANSWERS

1 Stonehenge 2 Angkor Wat 3 Notre Dame 4 Machu Picchu 5 Sydney Opera House 6 The Great Wall of China 7 Pyramids at Giza 8 Taj Mahal

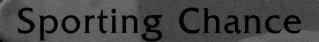

Sporting Chance

1 Which sport featured in the movie *Cool Runnings*, starring John Candy?

2 What is the only object that is thrown in the women's heptathlon?

3 In 1997, which 21-year-old became the youngest winner of golf's U.S. Masters?

4 Magic Johnson was named Most Valuable Player three times while playing for who?

5 What did Eddie Charlton carry in 1956 and Muhammed Ali in 1996?

6 Which ice hockey team had Stanley Cup victories in 1997 and 1998?

7 How many players are in a netball team?

BACKGROUND BONUS

What sport is played by the Cleveland Browns?

8 What side lost in four consecutive Superbowls in the early 1990s?

9 What is the national sport of Ireland?

10 What is not an event in the decathlon: 1,500 m, pole vault or triple jump?

Q 1

ANSWERS

1 Bobsleigh **2** Javelin **3** Tiger Woods **4** Los Angeles Lakers **5** Olympic torch **6** Detroit Red Wings **7** Seven **8** Buffalo Bills **9** Hurling **10** Triple jump

Background Bonus American football

Music Mania

1 "Never Ever" was a hit for which girl band?

2 Who couldn't get you out of her head in 2001?

3 Musician James Galway is associated with what instrument?

4 Which famous opera house was opened in 1973?

5 At what time of the day is a serenade traditionally sung?

6 Who had a hit with "It's Raining Men" in 2001?

7 In 1993, which chart topper sang "I'd Do Anything For Love, But I Won't Do That"?

8 Courtesy of the 1990 World Cup finals, who enjoyed a hit single with "Nessun Dorma"?

9 Which musical percussion instrument is named after its shape?

10 Gordon Sumner and Stuart Copeland were members of which 80s band?

Q 4

ANSWERS

1 All Saints **2** Kylie Minogue **3** Flute **4** Sydney Opera House **5** The evening
6 Geri Halliwell **7** Meatloaf **8** Luciano Pavarotti **9** Triangle **10** The Police

Scientifically Speaking

1 Which six-sided object does a group of snow crystals form?

2 How does a gyroscope move?

3 What are Orion, Cassiopeia and Virgo?

Q 2

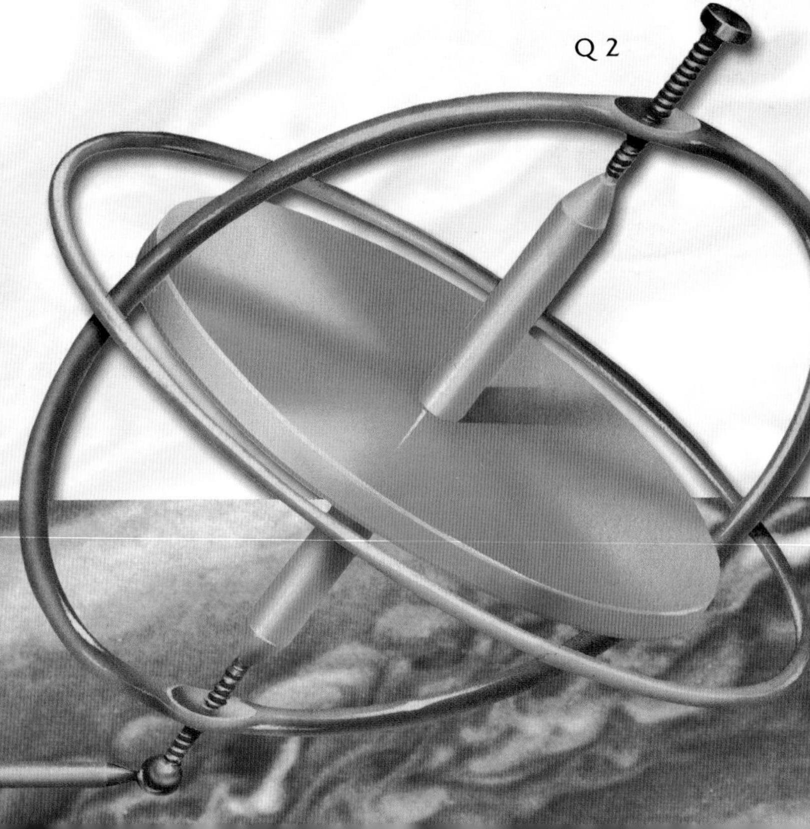

4 How long does it take for a meal to go through your digestive system: four hours, three days or one week?

5 The invention of what machine brought about the Industrial Revolution of the 1700s and 1800s?

6 What is a trawler?

7 How many equal sides has an isosceles triangle?

8 What metal is a mixture of copper and tin?

9 What would you measure with a hygrometer?

10 What gas do you breathe out: oxygen or carbon dioxide?

ANSWERS

1 Snowflake 2 It spins 3 Constellations 4 Three days 5 The steam engine 6 A fishing boat 7 Two 8 Brass 9 Humidity 10 Carbon dioxide

Total Trivia

1 Who are the Wallabies?

2 What country is the world's largest consumer of tea?

3 For what does G.M.T. stand?

4 How many noughts has a million?

5 In the Lewis Carroll story, which animal faded away leaving only its grin?

6 What might you find in an oyster?

7 In which sport do you do butterfly or crawl?

8 Who was William Gladstone?

9 What is a Camberwell beauty?

10 Which U.S. civil rights leader was assassinated in 1968?

Q 9

ANSWERS

1 The Australian rugby union team **2** Ireland **3** Greenwich Mean Time **4** 6 **5** The Cheshire Cat **6** A pearl **7** Swimming **8** A British prime minister **9** A butterfly **10** Martin Luther King

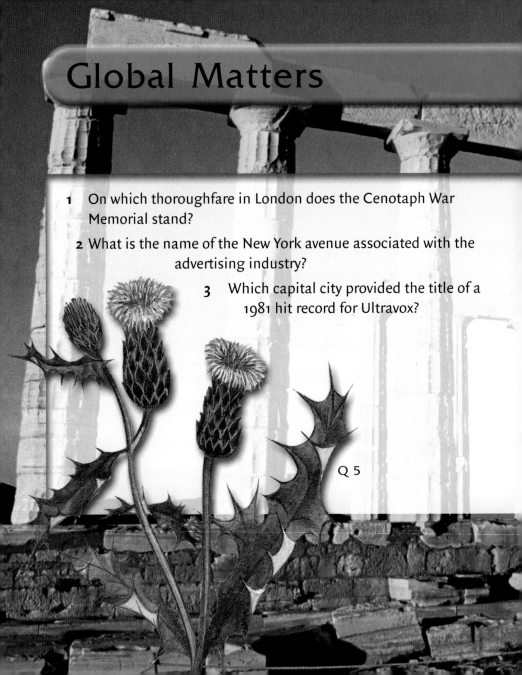

Global Matters

1 On which thoroughfare in London does the Cenotaph War Memorial stand?

2 What is the name of the New York avenue associated with the advertising industry?

3 Which capital city provided the title of a 1981 hit record for Ultravox?

Q 5

4 Which is the only U.S. state that begins with the letter P?

5 What is the national flower of Scotland?

6 On which river does the city of New Orleans stand?

7 Which Scottish city gave its name to a type of cake?

8 In France, what kind of vehicle is the T.G.V.?

9 Which Mediterranean island's flag includes an image of the George Cross?

10 On which Caribbean island is the resort of Montego Bay?

ANSWERS

1 Whitehall 2 Madison Avenue 3 Vienna 4 Pennsylvania 5 Thistle 6 Mississippi 7 Dundee 8 High-speed (Train à Grande Vitesse) 9 Malta 10 Jamaica

Total Trivia

1 What does the spine protect?
2 Which navigational instrument is named for its shape?
3 How many seconds in ten minutes?
4 What type of energy is made up of electrons?
5 Is kinetic energy movement or heat energy?
6 In a manual car, what pedal do you press to change gear?
7 What protects the Earth from the heat of the Sun?
8 Is an alloy a pure metal or a mixture of metals?
9 Do you grow more when you are awake or asleep?
10 What kind of vehicle was a Lanchester?

LEVEL 2 • QUIZ 66

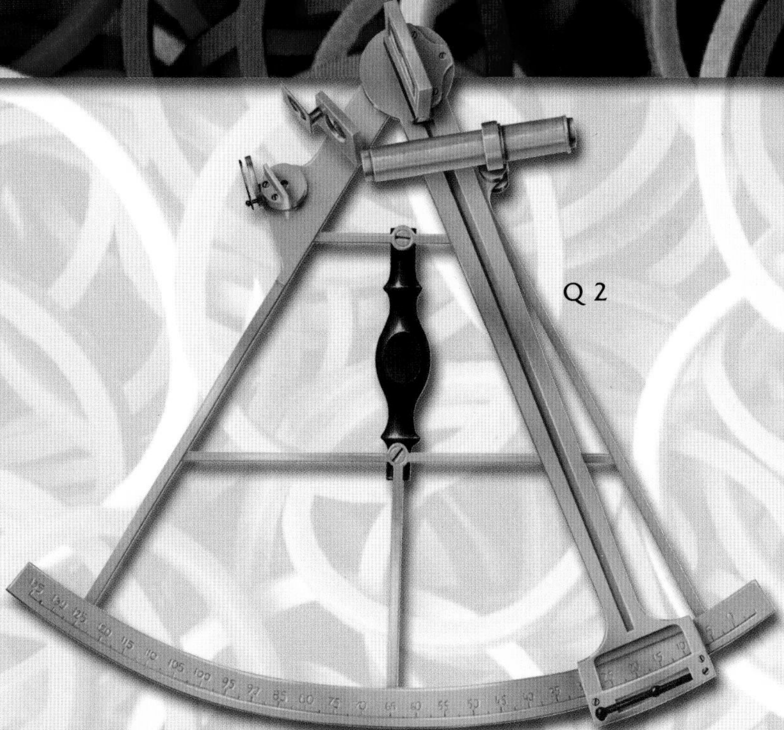

Q 2

ANSWERS
1 The spinal cord **2** The sextant **3** 600 **4** Electricity **5** Movement energy
6 The clutch pedal **7** The atmosphere **8** A mixture **9** Asleep **10** Car

Lights, Camera, Action!

LEVEL 2 • QUIZ 67

1 In which movie did Richard Harris play Emperor Aurelius?

2 Who played oil driller Harry Stamper in the movie *Armageddon*?

3 To which decade did Marty McFly travel back in the 1985 movie *Back to the Future*?

4 The 2001 movie, *Planet of the Apes*, is a remake of a 1968 movie starring which Hollywood star?

5 Which 1997 movie that features a talking pug dog called Frank?

6 Trinity, Tank and Mouse are all characters in which 1999 movie?

7 What was the world's top box office movie of the 1970s?

8 In which 1993 movie is Dr. Richard Kimble wrongly accused of murdering his wife?

9 *Thelma and Louise* starred which two famous actresses?

10 Which 1991 movie sequel is subtitled *Judgment Day*?

ANSWERS

1 *Gladiator* **2** Bruce Willis **3** The 1950s **4** Charlton Heston **5** *Men in Black* **6** *The Matrix* **7** *Star Wars* **8** *The Fugitive* **9** Susan Sarandon and Geena Davis **10** Terminator II

Sporting Chance

1. What nationality is motor racing star Jacques Villeneuve?
2. Which Korean city hosted the 1988 Summer Olympics?
3. With what sport would you associate the promoter Don King?
4. Name the first athlete to jump over 18 m in the triple jump.
5. What was won four times by Brazil in the 20th century, in 1958, 1962, 1970 and 1994?
6. In what century were the Wimbledon Tennis Championships first contested?
7. Which Derby-winning horse was kidnapped in 1983?
8. What sport is played by the San Antonio Spurs?
9. What sport uses balls with blue, white, red and yellow dots?
10. What is the maximum number of clubs a golfer is allowed to take onto the course?

LEVEL 2 · QUIZ 68

Q 2

ANSWERS
1 Canadian **2** Seoul **3** Boxing **4** Jonathan Edwards **5** Soccer's World Cup **6** The 19th century **7** Shergar **8** Basketball 9. Squash **10** 14

Making History

1 In which country were rockets probably invented over 700 years ago?
2 Who was the first woman to swim the English Channel?
3 What country was reformed by Kemal Atatürk during the 1920s?
4 Which short cut did Magellan take from the Atlantic to the Pacific?
5 How was the longbow a better weapon than the crossbow?
6 Of which country did Fidel Castro become leader in 1959?
7 What was the job of a knight's squire?
8 Who was the youngest ever president of the United States?
9 Who is the patron saint of Scotland?
10 What powered steamships before the invention of the screw propeller?

LEVEL 2 • QUIZ 69

Q 10

ANSWERS

1 China **2** Gertrude Ederle **3** Turkey **4** The straits that are now named after him **5** It could be loaded more quickly **6** Cuba **7** He was the knight's servant **8** John F. Kennedy **9** St. Andrew **10** Paddle wheels

Total Trivia

1 What are a clove hitch and a reef?

2 The world's fourth largest island lies off the east coast of Africa. What is it called?

Q 10

3 What made the craters on the Moon?

4 What vegetable is sauerkraut made from?

5 Which boy didn’t want to grow up?

6 Who were the Boers?

7 Why does water flow downhill?

8 What country was led by General de Gaulle?

9 Name the four citrus fruits.

10 What is a male chicken called?

ANSWERS

1 Types of knot **2** Madagascar **3** Meteorites **4** Cabbage **5** Peter Pan **6** Dutch settlers in South Africa **7** Because it is pulled by gravity **8** France **9** Oranges, lemons, limes grapefruits **10** A cockerel

Lights, Camera, Action!

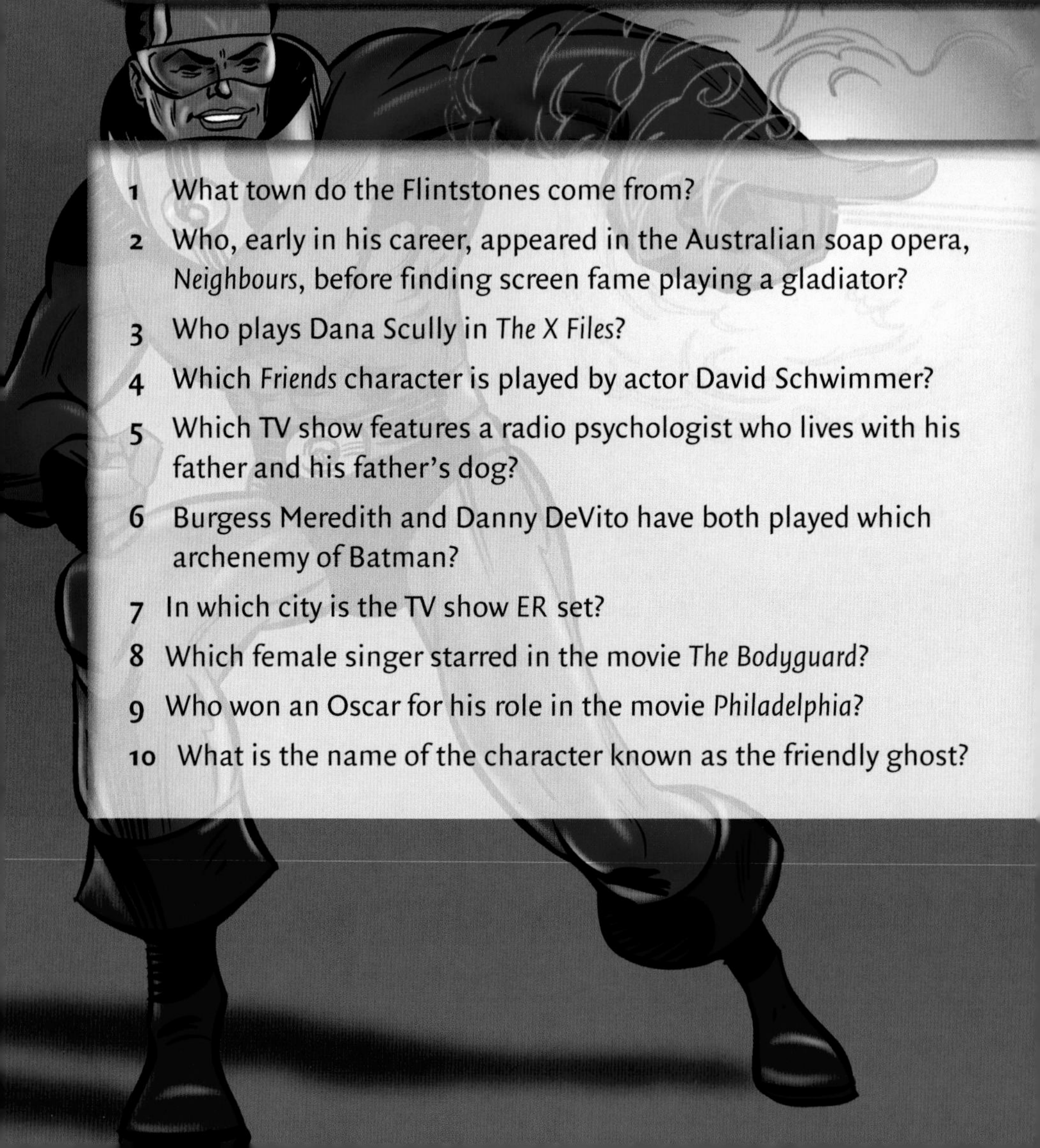

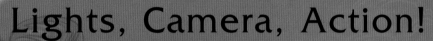

1 What town do the Flintstones come from?

2 Who, early in his career, appeared in the Australian soap opera, *Neighbours*, before finding screen fame playing a gladiator?

3 Who plays Dana Scully in *The X Files*?

4 Which *Friends* character is played by actor David Schwimmer?

5 Which TV show features a radio psychologist who lives with his father and his father's dog?

6 Burgess Meredith and Danny DeVito have both played which archenemy of Batman?

7 In which city is the TV show ER set?

8 Which female singer starred in the movie *The Bodyguard*?

9 Who won an Oscar for his role in the movie *Philadelphia*?

10 What is the name of the character known as the friendly ghost?

Q 7

ANSWERS

1 Bedrock **2** Russell Crowe **3** Gillian Anderson **4** Ross **5** Frasier **6** The Penguin **7** Chicago **8** Whitney Houston **9** Tom Hanks **10** Casper

Music Marvels

Can you identify these singers and musicians?

1

2

3

4

5

6

7

8

ANSWERS

1 Elton John **2** Jimi Hendrix **3** Jay Kay (Jamiroquai) **4** Nat King Cole **5** Missy Elliott **6** Justin Timberlake **7** Prince **8** Pink

Sporting Chance

1 What type of ball has three holes and weighs 7.25 kg (16 lb)?

2 The Anaheim Angels beat what side to win their first World Series in 2002?

3 What athlete broke Bob Beamon's 23-year-old long jump world record in 1991?

Q 9

4 Larry Bird is a NBA legend for what side?

5 What game developed from wooden balls being hit through hoops of willow?

6 Who was No. 1 seed in the men's singles at the 2002 Wimbledon Tennis Championships?

7 What golfer won the U.S. Open in 2002?

8 In table tennis, after how many points do the players change serve?

9 In which game do you use a tolley?

10 What is longer: a baseball bat or a tennis racket?

ANSWERS

1 Tenpin bowling ball 2 San Francisco 49ers 3 Mike Powell 4 Boston Celtics 5 Croquet 6 Lleyton Hewitt 7 Tiger Woods 8 Five 9 Marbles 10 A baseball bat

Making History

1 In the Middle Ages, what job did a spinster do?

2 What planet did William Herschel discover in 1781?

3 What nationality is Pope John Paul II?

4 Who wrote *The Invisible Man* in 1897?

5 Which common tool is associated with the Swiss army?

6 Which Himalayan peak is named after the man who mapped the area?

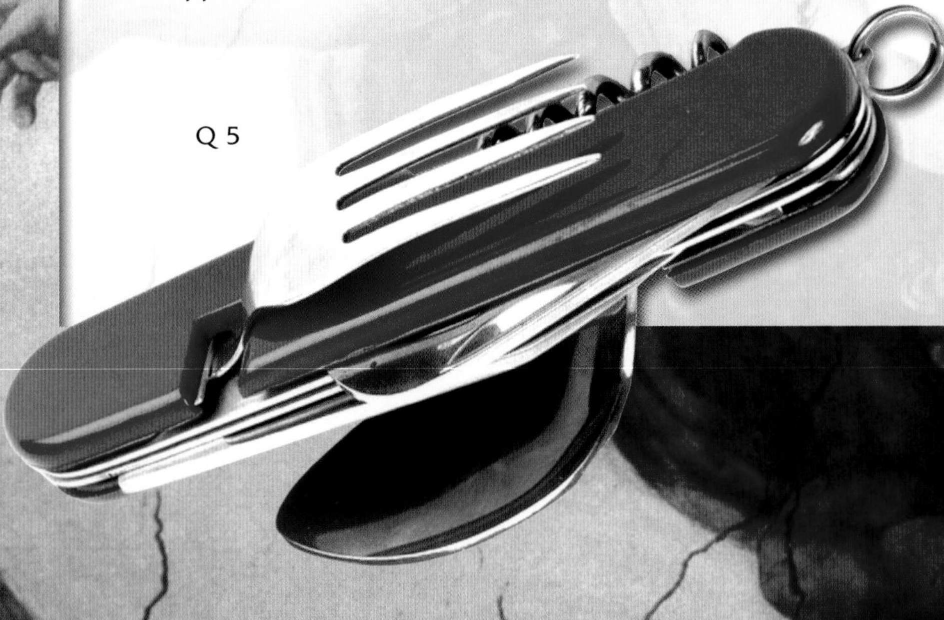

Q 5

7 Who were the Fauves: a group of artists, poets or jazz musicians?

8 In what year was the CD invented: 1959, 1979 or 1999?

9 Which Italian city minted its own gold coins called "florins"?

10 What was the name of the ruling council in ancient Rome?

BACKGROUND BONUS

Is a fresco a Renaissance wallpainting or an Impressionist outdoor painting technique?

ANSWERS

1 Spinning wool thread on a spindle **2** Uranus **3** Polish **4** H.G. Wells **5** Swiss army knife **6** Everest **7** Artists **8** 1979 **9** Florence **10** The Senate

Background Bonus A Renaissance wall painting

Total Trivia

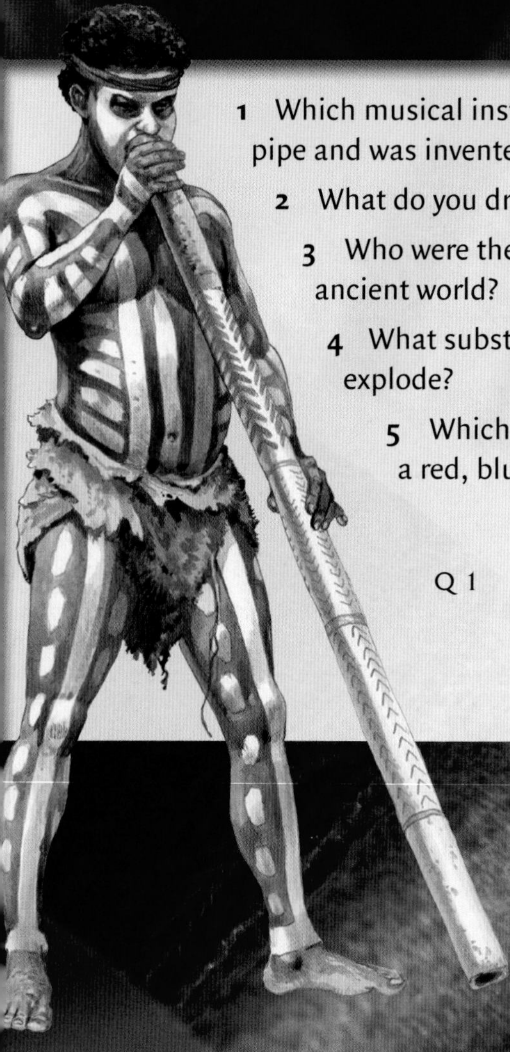

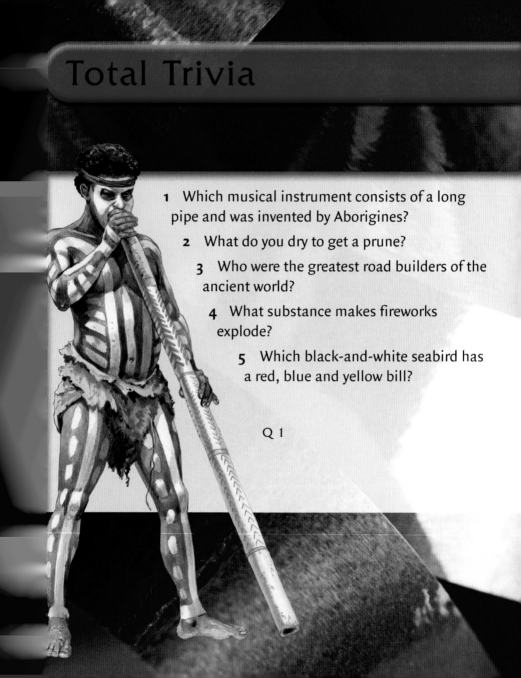

1 Which musical instrument consists of a long pipe and was invented by Aborigines?

2 What do you dry to get a prune?

3 Who were the greatest road builders of the ancient world?

4 What substance makes fireworks explode?

5 Which black-and-white seabird has a red, blue and yellow bill?

Q 1

6 What are the four cavities in the bones of your skull called?

7 What is the name for a high female singing voice?

8 What does it mean to nip something in the bud?

9 What religion did the Romans adopt in the AD300s?

10 What is an egress?

ANSWERS

1 The didgeridoo 2 A plum 3 The Romans 4 Gunpowder 5 The puffin 6 Sinuses 7 Soprano 8 To stop something before it begins 9 Christianity 10 It is an exit

Lights, Camera, Action!

1 What is the name of the tomb raider played on screen by Angelina Jolie?

2 Which *Friends* actress married her *Scream* co-star David Arquette in 1999?

3 Which man of steel is weakened when exposed to kryptonite?

4 In the movie *Grease*, does Danny fall in love with Sindy, Sandy or Mandy?

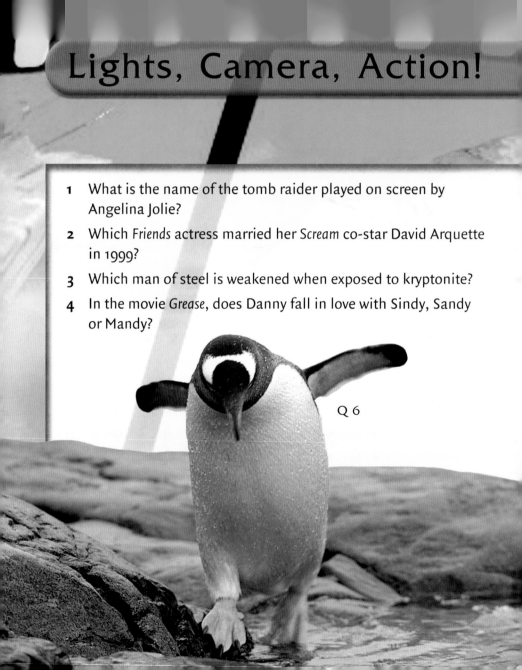

Q 6

5 Which sport features in the movie *The Bad News Bears*?

6 What kind of toy bird is Wheezy in *Toy Story II*?

7 What is the name of Popeye's girlfriend?

8 Which movie opens with the words: "A long time ago, in a galaxy far, far away..."?

9 In which country was Arnold Schwarzenegger born?

10 In which 1998 movie did Lindsay Lohan play twin sisters?

ANSWERS

1 Lara Croft **2** Courtney Cox **3** Superman **4** Sandy **5** Baseball **6** Penguin **7** Olive Oyl **8** *Star Wars* **9** Austria **10** *The Parent Trap*

Sporting Chance

1 Which new American Football team fought the 2000 Superbowl against the Rams?

2 In which country did speedskating originate?

3 Which player holds the major league baseball record for most home runs?

4 Which British athlete broke the javelin world record in 1990?

5 Which sporting body has the initials WBO?

6 Bernard Hinault is a national hero in France for which sport?

7 Who holds the major league baseball record for most strikeouts?

8 In which sport might you achieve a strike or a spare?

9 Who became Formula One World Champion in October 1996?

10 British Ice Dance champions Torvill and Dean are associated most with which piece of music?

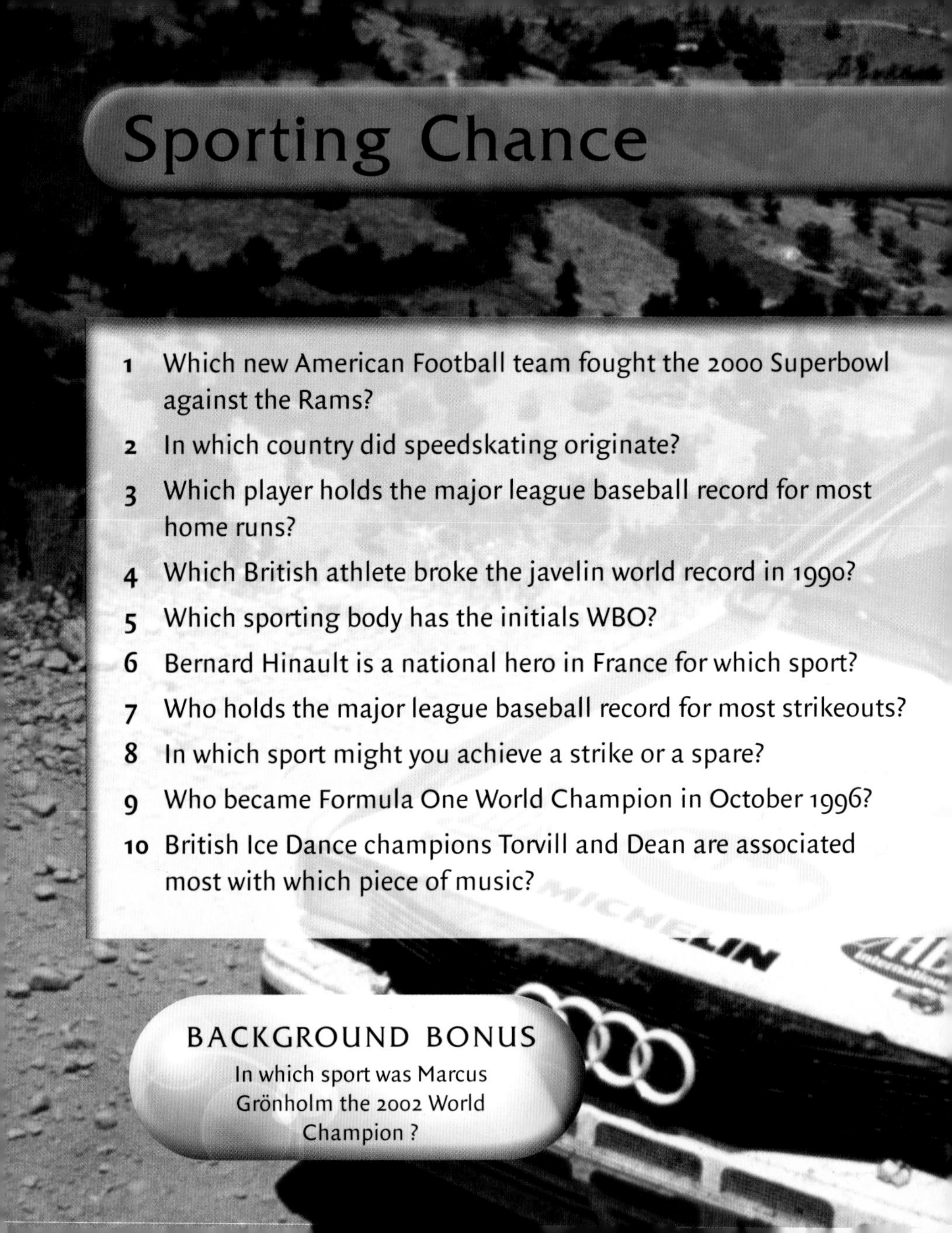

BACKGROUND BONUS

In which sport was Marcus Grönholm the 2002 World Champion ?

Q 5

ANSWERS

1 Tennessee Titans **2** The Netherlands **3** Hank Aaron (755) **4** Steve Backley **5** World Boxing Organization **6** Cycling **7** Nolan Ryan **8** Tenpin bowling **9** Damon Hill **10** Ravel's Bolero **Background Bonus** Rally

Lights, Camera, Action!

1 The 1999 teen movie, *10 Things I Hate About You*, was based on which Shakespeare play?

2 Which 1996 movie is based on the life of pianist David Helfgott?

3 What movies featured terrifying creatures called raptors?

4 Which movie, starring Jane Fonda, was based on a comic strip by Jean Claude Forest?

Q 10

5 What actress played the leading lady alongside Bob Hope and Bing Crosby in the *Road To...* movies?

6 Who played the clumsy inspector in the 1968 movie, *Inspector Clouseau?*

7 The 1970 movie, *The Music Lovers*, was based on the life of which classical composer?

8 What was the title of the first sound movie that featured Mickey Mouse?

9 Which 1953 movie starring Richard Burton was the first ever to be filmed in cinemascope?

10 In which 1995 movie did Sophie Marceau play Princess Isabelle?

ANSWERS

1 *The Taming of the Shrew* 2 *Shine* 3 *Jurassic Park* 4 *Barbarella* 5 Dorothy Lamour 6 Alan Arkin 7 Tchaikovsky 8 *Steamboat Willie* 9 *The Robe* 10 *Braveheart*

Natural Selection

1 Which bird, native to the island of Mauritius, became extinct in 1681?

2 A painted lady and monarch are both species of what?

3 From what animal is the meat venison obtained?

4 Which B word is the name given to whale fat?

Q 10

5 How many stomachs does a cow have?

6 What is the world's tallest bird?

7 What is stored in a camel's hump?

8 What shape are honeycomb cells in a beehive?

9 What kind of leaves provide the silkworm's staple diet?

10 A male pig and a male bear share the same name. What is it?

BACKGROUND BONUS

Which is the fastest land mammal?

ANSWERS

1 Dodo **2** Butterfly **3** Deer **4** Blubber **5** Four **6** Ostrich **7** Fat **8** Hexagonal **9** Mulberry **10** Boar

Background Bonus The cheetah

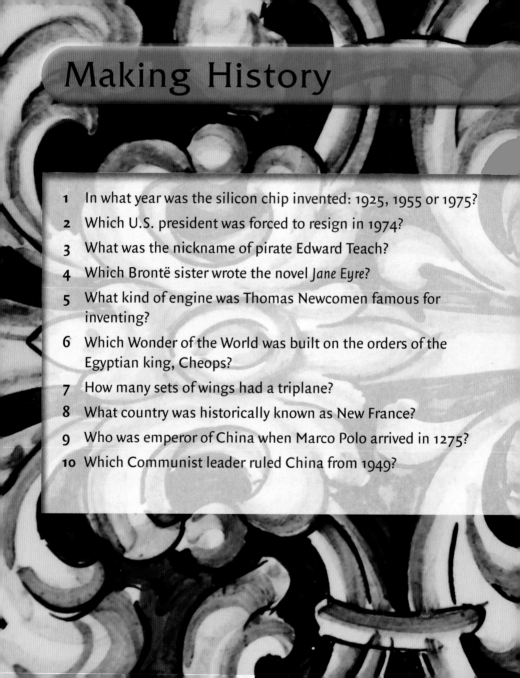

Making History

1 In what year was the silicon chip invented: 1925, 1955 or 1975?

2 Which U.S. president was forced to resign in 1974?

3 What was the nickname of pirate Edward Teach?

4 Which Brontë sister wrote the novel *Jane Eyre*?

5 What kind of engine was Thomas Newcomen famous for inventing?

6 Which Wonder of the World was built on the orders of the Egyptian king, Cheops?

7 How many sets of wings had a triplane?

8 What country was historically known as New France?

9 Who was emperor of China when Marco Polo arrived in 1275?

10 Which Communist leader ruled China from 1949?

LEVEL 2 · QUIZ 80

Q 8

ANSWERS

1 1975 **2** Richard Nixon **3** Blackbeard **4** Charlotte Brontë **5** Steam engine **6** The Great Pyramid **7** Three **8** Canada **9** Kublai Khan **10** Mao Tse-tung

Sporting Chance: Soccer

Q 4

1 In which tournament did Paul Gascoigne become famous for crying?

2 Robbie Fowler was a Liverpool supporter as a boy: true or false?

3 With which French club did Thierry Henry and Emmaunuel Petit begin their careers?

4 What nationality is Nwankwo Kanu?

5 Who scored the winner for Arsenal in the 1994 European Cup-Winners' Cup final?

6 With which British club did John Barnes begin his career?

7 Who was manager of Leeds when they won the League title in 1992?

8 What team lost both the 1993 League Cup and FA Cup finals to Arsenal?

9 What club did Eric Cantona play for before he joined Manchester United?

10 Which U.K. Division One side achieved a record number of points in the 1998 to 1999 season?

ANSWERS

1 The 1990 World Cup **2** False, he supported Everton **3** Monaco **4** Nigerian **5** Alan Smith **6** Watford **7** Howard Wilkinson **8** Leeds United **9** Sheffield Wednesday **10** Sunderland

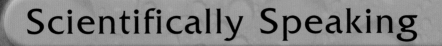

Scientifically Speaking

1 What instrument would a scientist use to see a micro-organism?

2 Which of these foods is not protein: meat, eggs, cabbage or cheese?

3 When it is summer in Europe, what season is it in Australia?

4 Do the north poles on two magnets pull together or push apart?

5 Does an astrologer or an astronomer study the effect of the stars on human lives?

6 What are the factors of 22?

7 Do things look larger or smaller through a convex lens?

8 What does a food chain always begin with: green plants, insects or animals?

9 What is the name of an angle between 90° and 180°?

10 What numbers show on a 24-hour digital clock at a quarter to nine in the evening?

Q 1

ANSWERS

1 A microscope **2** Cabbage **3** Winter **4** They push apart **5** An astrologer **6** 11 and 2 **7** Larger **8** Green plants **9** Obtuse **10** 20:45

Natural Selection

1 What animal is a cross between a mare and an ass?

2 Is the saki a type of rat, fish or monkey?

3 What is a stinkhorn?

4 What name is given to a male horse or pony that is less than four years old?

5 What part of a flower produces pollen?

6 What is the alternative name for a cranefly?

7 Is a young seal called a kitten, a pup or a cub?

8 What is the only bird that has nostrils?

9 What is a Manx cat missing?

10 From what flowers do we obtain opium?

Q 5

ANSWERS

1 Mule 2 Monkey 3 A kind of fungus 4 Colt 5 Stamen 6 Daddy-longlegs 7 Pup 8 Kiwi 9 A tail 10 Poppies

Animal Habitats

Can you match the animals listed with the habitats shown?

(a) Carp (b) Sun bear (c) Manta ray (d) Oyster catcher
(e) Puma (f) Cheetah (g) Kangaroo rat (h) Alligator

5

6

7

8

ANSWERS
1 (g) **2** (b) **3** (d) **4** (e) **5** (f) **6** (h) **7** (c) **8** (a)

Total Trivia

1 Dates, coconuts and raffia all come from what?

2 Who wrote the operas *Don Giovanni* and *The Magic Flute*?

3 Where is the volcano Mount Etna?

4 What game has knights, castles and bishops?

5 Which two sea creatures squirt out inky fluid to escape from an enemy?

6 What have taken the place of glass valves in radios?

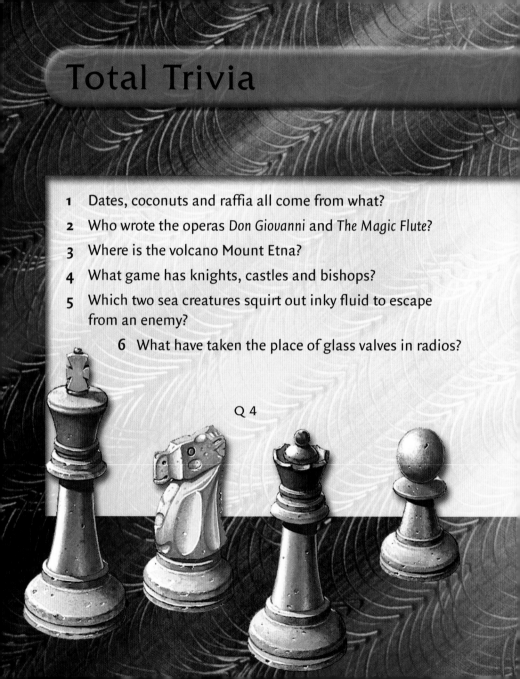

Q 4

7 Which large sea mammal has two long tusks?

8 What cereal grain is grown in paddies?

9 How often in 24 hours does the tide rise and fall?

10 In what year did World War I begin?

ANSWERS

1 Palm trees **2** Mozart **3** Italy (on the island of Sicily) **4** Chess **5** The octopus and squid **6** Transistors **7** The walrus **8** Rice **9** Twice **10** 1914

Sporting Chance

1 Which sport begins with a storke-off?

2 Cobi, mascot of the 1992 Olympics, was what type of animal?

3 On what shape of pitch is Australian Rules Football played?

4 What did Thomas Burgess become the second man to do ?

5 What was first achieved by Edmund Hillary and Tenzing Norgay in May 1953?

6 In tennis, what is the score in a set when the tie-break comes into play?

7 On what side of a yacht is the starboard side?

8 In which event did Bonfire win gold at the 2000 Olympics?

9 In which sport can competitors use the Western Roll?

10 Which nationality was the long distance runner Ingrid Kristiansen?

BACKGROUND BONUS

In which sport would players deliver a combination of jabs, hooks and uppercuts?

Q 5

ANSWERS

1 Bandy **2** A dog **3** Oval **4** Swim the English Channel **5** The first to climb Mount Everest **6** 6–6 **7** Right side **8** Dressage **9** High jump **10** Norwegian

Background Bonus Boxing

Total Trivia

1 Woodwind, percussion and brass are three sections of an orchestra. What is the fourth?

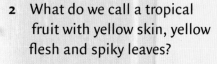

2 What do we call a tropical fruit with yellow skin, yellow flesh and spiky leaves?

3 If you go aft in a boat, where do you go?

4 Which jazz singer was known as "Lady Day"?

Q 2

5 Which garment, worn mainly by Hindu women, is made by wrapping cloth around the body?

6 What part of the body is affected by conjunctivitis?

7 If you were in Cuzco visiting the sites of the Incas, In which country would you be?

8 What sport is Le Mans famous for?

9 Which king of England was called The Lionheart?

10 What is the name of Moscow's chief square?

ANSWERS

1 Strings **2** The pineapple **3** To the stern (the back) **4** Billie Holiday **5** The sari **6** The eye **7** Peru **8** Motor racing **9** Richard I **10** Red Square

Natural Selection

Q 9

1 What is the world's largest amphibian?

2 Do frogs have dry scales or a thin, damp skin?

3 Do butterflies eat small insects, plant nectar or green leaves?

4 Is a haddock a type of octopus, oyster or fish?

5 Do all zebras have exactly the same stripe pattern or are they all different?

6 Do burrowing owls nest in pine trees, abandoned prairie dog burrows or hollow logs?

7 Does a newt egg hatch into a little newt or a tadpole?

8 Which animal from the American plains was almost hunted to extinction in the 19th century?

9 Is vanilla a member of the orchid, rose or lily family?

10 Which part of a radish do we eat: the leaf, the flower or the root?

ANSWERS

1 The giant salamander 2 Thin, damp skin 3 Plant nectar 4 Fish 5 They are all different 6 In abandoned prairie dog burrows 7 It is a tadpole at first 8 Buffalo 9 Orchid family 10 The root

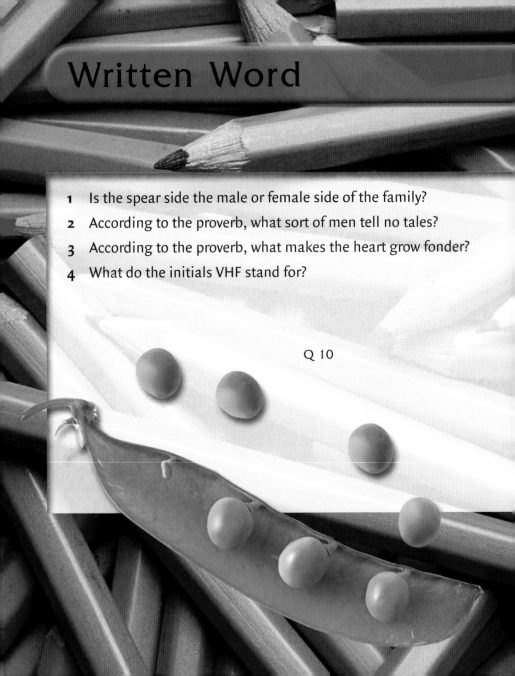

Written Word

1 Is the spear side the male or female side of the family?
2 According to the proverb, what sort of men tell no tales?
3 According to the proverb, what makes the heart grow fonder?
4 What do the initials VHF stand for?

Q 10

5 Which C word is the name given to an official in charge of a museum?

6 On a ship, which instrument, used for showing direction, is housed in a binnacle?

7 Which H word is the name given to the small stroke separating two words, as in re-enter?

8 The Penny Black was the first what in the world?

9 In Roman numerals, what is D: 50, 500 or 5,000?

10 What is the shared name for a natural container for peas and a group of dolphins?

ANSWERS

1 Male side 2 Dead men 3 Absence 4 Very High Frequency 5 Curator 6 Compass
7 Hyphen 8 A postage stamp 9 500 10 Pod

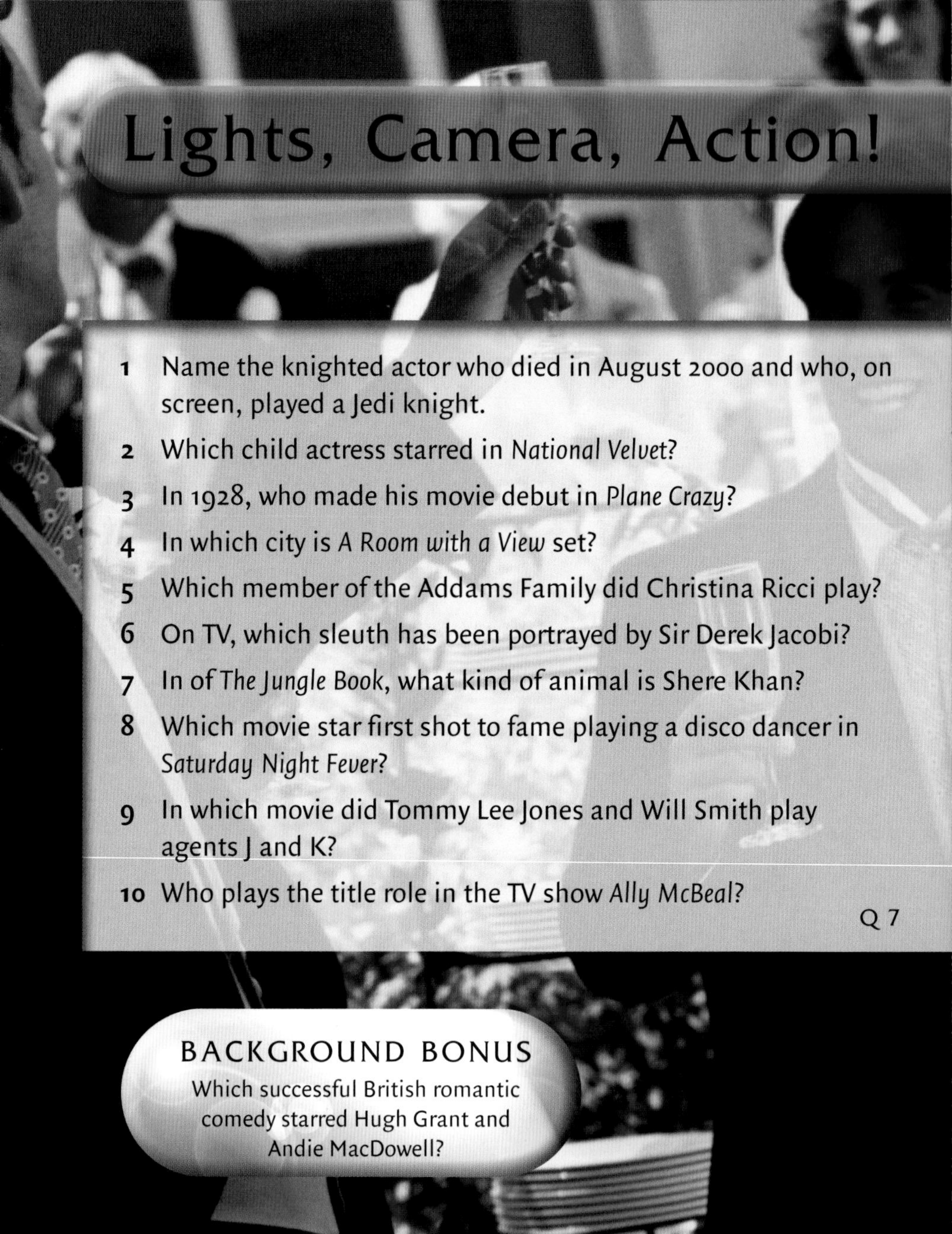

Lights, Camera, Action!

1 Name the knighted actor who died in August 2000 and who, on screen, played a Jedi knight.

2 Which child actress starred in *National Velvet*?

3 In 1928, who made his movie debut in *Plane Crazy*?

4 In which city is *A Room with a View* set?

5 Which member of the Addams Family did Christina Ricci play?

6 On TV, which sleuth has been portrayed by Sir Derek Jacobi?

7 In of *The Jungle Book*, what kind of animal is Shere Khan?

8 Which movie star first shot to fame playing a disco dancer in *Saturday Night Fever*?

9 In which movie did Tommy Lee Jones and Will Smith play agents J and K?

10 Who plays the title role in the TV show *Ally McBeal*?

Q 7

BACKGROUND BONUS

Which successful British romantic comedy starred Hugh Grant and Andie MacDowell?

ANSWERS

1 Sir Alec Guinness **2** Elizabeth Taylor **3** Mickey Mouse **4** Florence **5** Wednesday Addams **6** Cadfael **7** A tiger **8** John Travolta **9** *Men in Black* **10** Calista Flockhart **Background Bonus** *Four Weddings and a Funeral*

Making History

1 What kind of weapon was a ballista?

2 Who invented the phonograph, an early kind of record player?

3 Which planet in our Solar System was discovered in 1930?

4 What are teachers called in the Jewish religion?

5 Which famous structure was built by an Indian emperor as a tomb for his wife?

6 Which World War II fighter pilot had false legs?

7 Which U.S. state was founded by William Penn?

8 According to William Shakespeare who said, "Cry havoc and let slip the dogs of war"?

9 What do architects use a buttress for?

10 When did plastic surgery begin: 2,000 years ago, 100 years ago or 10 years ago?

Q 1

ANSWERS

1 A giant crossbow **2** Thomas Edison **3** Pluto **4** Rabbis **5** The Taj Mahal **6** Douglas Bader **7** Pennsylvania **8** Marc Anthony **9** To support a wall **10** 2,000 years ago

Global Matters

1 The timber wolf comes from what continent?

2 Which country produces more diamonds than all the world's nations put together?

3 If you were a Bruxellian, in which city would you live?

4 Captain James Cook was the first European to discover which U.S. islands?

5 Arthur's Seat and The Royal Mile are found in which British city?

Q 8

6 Did the Renaissance start in Poland, France or Italy?

7 What currency is used in Canada?

8 The U.S. city of St. Louis is famous for which monument?

9 Porto is a city in which European country?

10 In which two countries would you come across the region known as Patagonia?

ANSWERS

1 North America 2 South Africa 3 Brussels 4 Hawaii 5 Edinburgh 6 Italy 7 Canadian dollars 8 The Gateway Arch 9 Portugal 10 Argentina and Chile

Music Mania

1 Which member of defunct boy band Five was known by a single letter of the alphabet?

2 In 2001, which pop superstar released the album *Invincible*?

3 Whose music provided the score for the movie *The Sting*?

4 What is the alternative name for an English horn?

5 Which duo released the EP *Abba-esque* in 1992?

6 Which musical TV show featured Miss Sherwood, Leroy, Coco and Bruno?

7 What is the name of Kid Creole's backing singers?

8 Which boy band were the first Irish group to have five No. 1 hits in the U.K.?

9 A choir generally consists of four voice parts: soprano, alto, tenor and what?

BACKGROUND BONUS

Which musical instrument was invented in 1700 by German, Johann Christoph Denner?

10 Which British group produced a successful album in 1994 called *Parklife*?

Q 7

ANSWERS
1 J **2** Michael Jackson **3** Scott Joplin **4** Cor Anglais **5** Erasure **6** *Fame* **7** The Coconuts **8** Boyzone **9** Bass **10** Blur
Background Bonus The clarinet

Total Trivia

LEVEL 2 · QUIZ 94

1 Which English king reignedfrom 1660 to 1685?

2 Which dwarf could spinstraw into gold?

3 What is one third of 51?

4 What is a Jewish place of worship called?

5 Which crop does corn come from?

6 Who saw Cock Robin die?

7 Are cornflowers blue, white or yellow?

8 What is the climate like in a tropical forest: hot and dry or hot and wet?

9 Did the Crusades take place in the Middle Ages or the Dark Ages?

10 What fish makes spectacular leaps to return to its birthplace?

ANSWERS

1 Charles II **2** Rumpelstiltskin **3** 17 **4** A synagogue **5** Maize **6** The fly, with his little eye **7** Blue **8** Hot and wet **9** The Middle Ages **10** The salmon

Lights, Camera, Action!

1 Which actor battled with aliens in *Independence Day* and with dinosaurs in *Jurassic Park?*

2 Which singer won an Oscar for her role in the movie *Moonstruck?*

3 The James Bond movie, *A View to a Kill*, involves a scene set on which bridge ?

4 Which movie tells the story of Jim Garrison's investigation into a 1963 assassination?

5 What was Marilyn Monroe's first name in *Some Like it Hot?*

6 What is the third movie to feature the character of Indiana Jones?

7 Which actor was born Archibald Leach?

8 Which Hollywood legend was the subject of the 1983 movie *Mommie Dearest?*

9 What is the title of the 1991 movie in which Billy Crystal embarks upon a cattle-driving vacation?

10 In which 1976 movie did Jodie Foster play a gangster's moll?

Q 3

ANSWERS

1 Jeff Goldblum **2** Cher **3** Golden Gate Bridge **4** JFK **5** Sugar **6** Indiana Jones and the Last Crusade **7** Cary Grant **8** Joan Crawford **9** City Slickers **10** Bugsy Malone

Flying the Flag

Can you match the flags to these countries?

(a) Brazil (b) Turkey (c) Mexico (d) Japan (e) Argentina

(f) Australia (g) Denmark (h) Belgium

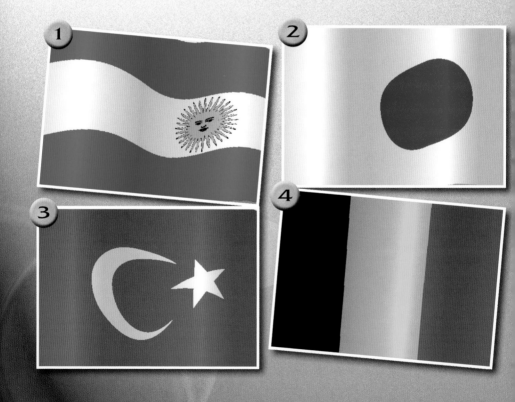

1

2

3

4

5

6

7

8

ANSWERS
1 (e) 2 (d) 3 (b) 4 (h) 5 (f) 6 (g) 7 (c) 8 (a)

Great and Famous

Q 4

1 Was Frank Sinatra once married to Mia Farrow, Lulu or Cher?

2 Who was the inventor of the *Peanuts* cartoon strip?

3 Which international statesman received the Nobel Peace Prize in 1990?

4 What did Mary Read do for a living?

5 What was George Bernard Shaw's profession?

6 Of which country was Archbishop Makarios the first president?

7 What nationality was Prince Henry the Navigator?

8 Which threatened author made a surprise appearance at a 1993 U2 concert?

9 What weapon was Sir Barnes Wallis famous for building?

10 In what year did Prince Charles and Diana marry?

BACKGROUND BONUS

Which inhospitable terrain was explorer Roald Amundsen the first to cross in 1911?

ANSWERS

1 Mia Farrow **2** Charles Schulz **3** Mikhail Gorbachev **4** She was a pirate **5** Playwright **6** Cyprus **7** Portuguese **8** Salman Rushdie **9** A bouncing bomb **10** 1981

Background Bonus Antarctica

Natural Selection

1 How did the cuckoo get its name?

2 Do lizards store fat in their legs, tails or heads?

3 Do caterpillars eat mainly leaves or fruit?

4 Which has tufted ears: the red squirrel or the grey squirrel?

5 Are the seeds of holly spread by wind or by birds?

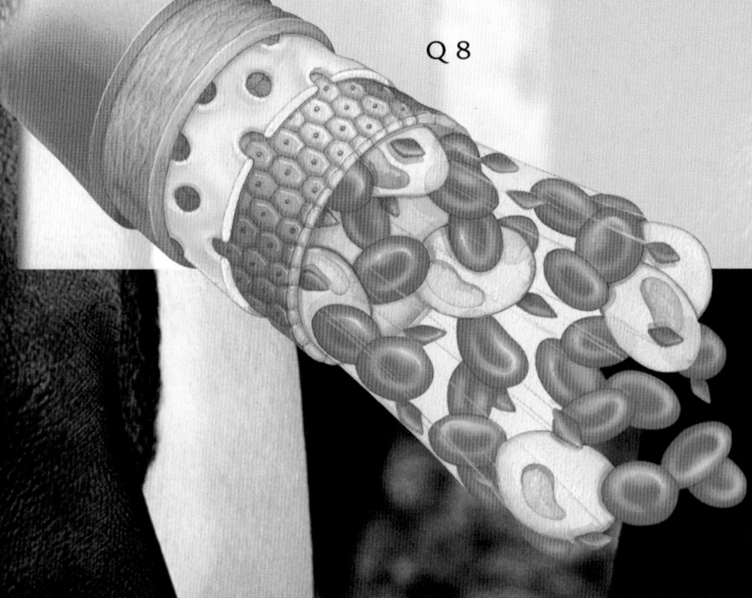

6 What does a bird have that no other animal has?

7 Snakes have voices: true or false?

8 What do mosquitoes, vampire bats and leeches have in common?

9 In summer, do caribou graze in the Arctic tundra or on southern prairies?

10 Do turtles have teeth or beaks?

ANSWERS

1 From the sound of its call **2** Tails **3** Leaves **4** The red squirrel **5** By birds **6** Feathers **7** True **8** They all feed on blood **9** In the Arctic tundra **10** Beaks

Making History

1 Who exhibited his painting *Impression: Sunrise* in 1874?

2 Which Scotsman made the first steam engine to use cranks and pistons in 1769?

3 Which Soviet leader called himself "Man of Steel"?

4 Who designed a helicopter and a parachute over 500 years ago?

5 Which Australian folk hero was hanged in Melbourne in 1880?

6 Which war was ended by the Treaty of Appomattox?

7 What birds live at the Tower of London?

8 Who became British prime minister in 1940?

9 Who was Queen Elizabeth I's mother?

10 Which South Seas volcano blew up in 1883?

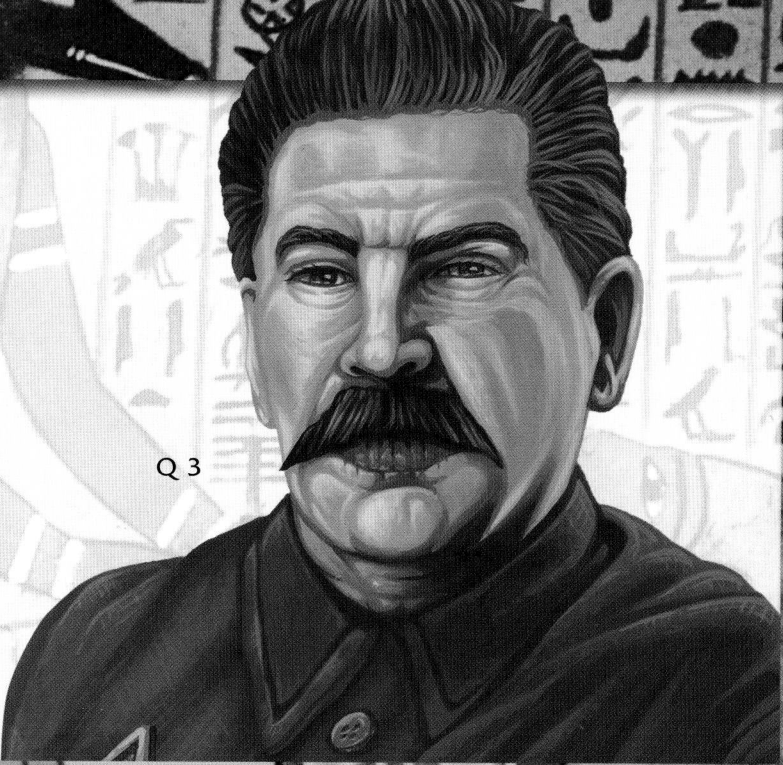

Q 3

ANSWERS
1 Claude Monet 2 James Watt 3 Josef Stalin 4 Leonardo da Vinci 5 Ned Kelly
6 The American Civil War 7 Ravens 8 Winston Churchill 9 Anne Boleyn 10 Krakatoa

Great and Famous

1 Who wrote the novel *The Great Gatsby*?

2 Who was the first person to meet Christ after the crucifixion?

3 Which pianist and composer wrote *Maple Leaf Rag*?

4 Whose famous art studio in the 1960s was called The Factory?

5 Which cartoonist's first job was drawing pictures for a barber, receiving 25 U.S. cents or a free haircut per picture?

6 Which Peter's biography, full of stories of his acting and writing days, was called *Just Me*?

7 Dashiell Hammett created which tough, fictional detective?

8 Which French painter co-created the style known as Cubism?

9 The novel *Brighton Rock* was written by which English author?

10 Which U.S. male tennis player was known as "Superbrat" and "Motormouth"?

ANSWERS
1 F. Scott Fitzgerald 2 Mary Magdalene 3 Scott Joplin 4 Andy Warhol 5 Walt Disney 6 Peter Ustinov 7 Sam Spade 8 Georges Braque 9 Graham Greene 10 John McEnroe

Total Trivia

1 Who led the Israelites out of captivity in Egypt?
2 What is the correct term for ancient Egyptian picture writing?
3 Which process for preserving food was named after Louis Pasteur?
4 Which fungus is used to make bread, beer and wine?
5 How many people are there in a quintet?
6 Which doglike animal makes an uncanny laughing noise?
7 What empire did Genghis Khan found?
8 Which animals shed their antlers and grow new bigger ones every year?
9 What proportion of the air is oxygen: one fifth, one eighth or one tenth?
10 What is 20 percent of 100?

Q 8

ANSWERS

1 Moses **2** Hieroglyphic script **3** Pasteurization **4** Yeast **5** Five **6** The hyena **7** The Mongol Empire **8** Deer **9** One-fifth **10** 20

Making History

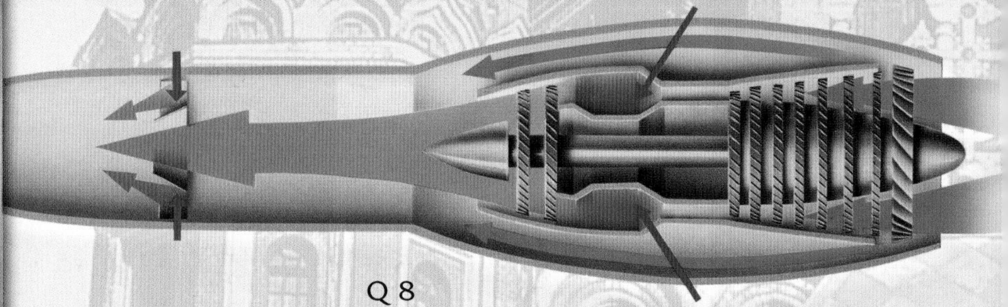

Q 8

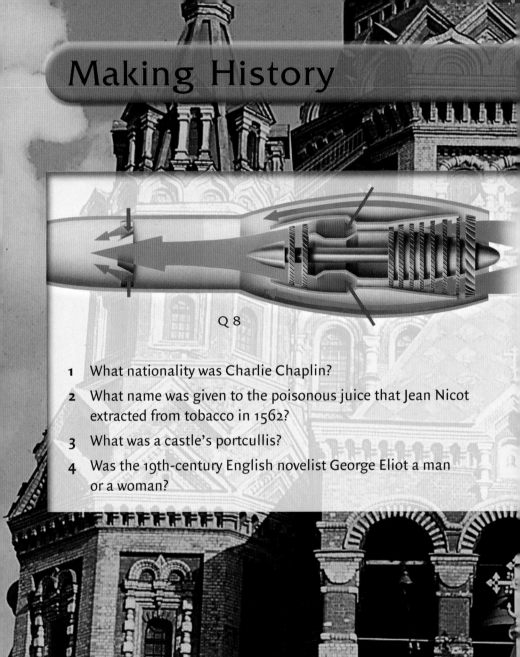

1 What nationality was Charlie Chaplin?

2 What name was given to the poisonous juice that Jean Nicot extracted from tobacco in 1562?

3 What was a castle's portcullis?

4 Was the 19th-century English novelist George Eliot a man or a woman?

5 What kind of weapon is a bayonet?

6 When did sailors first use the magnetic compass: 1000BC, AD1000 or AD1500?

7 How many British kings have been called Charles?

8 What new kind of aircraft engine was developed by Frank Whittle in the 1930s?

9 Who wrote the novel *Far From the Madding Crowd*?

10 Who tried to invade Russia in 1812?

BACKGROUND BONUS

In which cathedral is Peter the Great buried?

ANSWERS

1 British **2** Nicotine **3** A barrier fitted to a gateway **4** A woman (Mary Ann Evans) **5** A blade on a rifle **6** AD1000 **7** Two **8** The jet engine **9** Thomas Hardy **10** Napoleon

Background Bonus Cathedral of St. Peter and St. Paul

Sporting Chance

1. Roger Craig, Joe Perry and Ricky Watters all played for which NFL team?
2. What team holds the record for the least points scored in a Superbowl?
3. What did the basketball legend Lew Alcindor change his name to?
4. Which sport, popular in Ireland, is played using a ball called a sliothar?

Q 8

5 Who was the No. 1 seed in the women's singles at the 2002 Wimbledon Championships?

6 Along with the Buffalo Bills, which two other sides have lost in four Superbowls?

7 Which piece of sporting equipment has a maximum length of 96.5 cm (38 in) and a maximum width of 10.8 cm (4.25 in)?

8 What country was the host of the Olympic Games when Judo made its debut?

9 What nationality is skier Jean-Claude Killy?

10 How many hurdles does each runner negotiate in a 110 m hurdle race?

ANSWERS

1 San Francisco 49ers 2 Miami Dolphins 3 Kareem Abdul-Jabbar 4 Hurling 5 Venus Williams 6 Denver Broncos and Minnesota Vikings 7 A cricket bat 8 Japan 9 French 10 10

Scientifically Speaking

1 Do your back or front teeth grind up your food?

2 What is 2.3 + 0.7?

3 What is a vacuum?

4 What is the name for the study of points, lines and flat, solid shapes?

5 How many faces does an octahedron have?

6 What invention by Joseph Lister allowed him to reduce the number of deaths from surgery?

7 In what industry was William Caxton a pioneer?

8 On a cold day, from which part of your body does most heat escape?

9 Where in the body is the smallest muscle, the stapedius?

10 What does a geologist study?

BACKGROUND BONUS

Which C word describes the board on which electronic data is handled and arranged?

LEVEL 2 · QUIZ 104

Q 7

ANSWERS

1 Back **2** 3 **3** An empty space **4** Geometry **5** Eight **6** He introduced antiseptic **7** Printing **8** Your head **9** In your ear **10** Rocks and how Earth was formed

Background Bonus Circuit board

Total Trivia

1 Where might you find the Abominable Snowman?

2 What bear is called the Lord of the Arctic?

3 What mountains divide Spain from France?

4 Howard Carter discovered which Egyptian pharaoh's tomb in 1922?

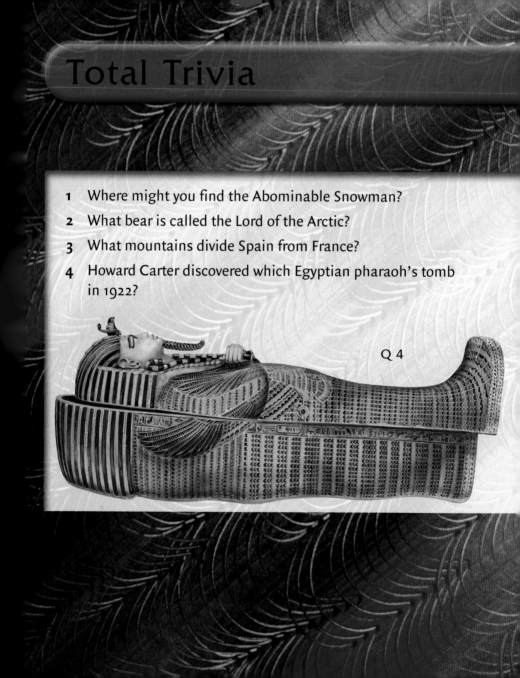

Q 4

5 How many players are there in an ice hockey team?

6 What is the name for a French castle or a large mansion?

7 What is a bream?

8 What instrument did Chopin play?

9 "Elementary, my dear Watson." Who said this?

10 Which speckled freshwater fish belongs to the salmon family?

ANSWERS

1 In the Himalaya Mountains 2 Polar bear 3 The Pyrenees 4 Tutankhamun
5 Six and the goalkeeper 6 A château 7 A fish 8 The piano 9 Sherlock Holmes
10 The trout

Making History

1 Who made the first successful wireless, in 1895?

2 What kind of instrument is a clavicord?

Q 1

3 Who brought the first horses to North America?

4 Why were canaries once taken down coal mines?

5 What kind of plane was a Stuka?

6 Which pack animal was known as "the ship of the desert"?

7 What is the companion story to Lewis Carroll's *Alice in Wonderland*?

8 The island of Réunion became a colony of what country in 1764?

9 James Cook's first ship was a collier. What kind of ship was this?

10 In 1769, a French priest designed a waistcoat filled with cork. What was it?

ANSWERS

1 Guglielmo Marconi **2** A keyboard instrument **3** The Spanish **4** To give warning of dangerous gases **5** A dive-bomber **6** The camel **7** *Alice Through the Looking Glass* **8** France **9** One made for carrying coal **10** The first lifebelt

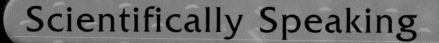

Scientifically Speaking

1 How many hours are there in a week?
2 What do builders use a spirit level for?
3 What kind of boat has wings called foils?
4 Which husband and wife team discovered radium?
5 How many degrees colder is $-5^{\circ}C$ than $1^{\circ}C$?
6 What do seismic waves travel through?
7 What shape is a volcano?
8 What kind of operation is used to give someone a new heart?
9 What does an angle of 180° look like?
10 Did *Thrust 2* break the land, water or air speed record?

LEVEL 2 · QUIZ 107

Q 10

ANSWERS

1 168 **2** To check if something is level **3** A hydrofoil **4** Pierre and Marie Curie **5** 6°
6 The Earth **7** A cone **8** A transplant **9** A straight line **10** Land

Name that Place

Can you identify these famous landmarks?

1

2

3

4

5

6

7

8

ANSWERS

1 The Giant's Causeway **2** Uluru (Ayers Rock) **3** Iguaçu Falls **4** Mount Kilimanjaro **5** The Grand Canyon **6** Rio de Janeiro **7** The Great Barrier Reef **8** Mount Fuji

Written Word

1. Semaphore is a system using arm signals and what else?
2. What do the initials CB in CB radio stand for?
3. Is an epilogue at the beginning or at the end of a book?
4. Choreography is the art of arranging what?
5. What do the initials I.C.U. stand for in a hospital?
6. Which four-letter word can come before ache, light and phone?
7. According to the grammatical rule, which letter comes before E except after C?
8. Which A word is the name given to a drug that counteracts a poison?
9. Is hypothermia when your body gets very hot or very cold?
10. What does the letter P stand for in POW?

Q 9

ANSWERS

1 Flags **2** Citizen's Band **3** At the end **4** Dance **5** Intensive Care **6** Head **7** The letter i **8** Antidote **9** Very cold **10** Prisoner (of War)

Total Trivia

1 Which ancient people invented paper?
2 What is the mongoose famed for killing?
3 What do three dots represent in the Morse Code?
4 What two countries make up the Iberian Peninsula?
5 Tibet is ruled by what country?
6 Which tropical bird has bright plumage and an enormous beak?
7 What is the capital of Turkey?
8 Where is urine made in your body?
9 What ocean lies between Africa, Asia, Australia and Antarctica?
10 What is the name for a male goose?

Q 6

ANSWERS
1 The Chinese 2 Snakes 3 The letter s 4 Spain and Portugal 5 China 6 The toucan 7 Ankara 8 In your kidneys 9 The Indian Ocean 10 Gander

Natural Selection

1 What flying insect is known for spreading malaria?

2 Do scorpions produce live young or lay eggs?

3 Which B word is the name given to the study of plants?

4 What is the more common name for a eucalyptus tree?

Q 9

5 What name is given to a female foal?

6 A Wessex Saddleback is a breed of which farm animal?

7 What kind of creature is a natterjack?

8 Which species of snake has varieties called green tree, reticulated, Indian and Burmese?

9 What breed of dog connects Beethoven, Schnorbits and the patron saint of mountaineers?

10 A rookery is the name given to a collection of which fast-swimming birds?

BACKGROUND BONUS

African tiger, blue coral and Cuban wood are all types of what creature?

ANSWERS

1 Mosquito **2** Live young **3** Botany **4** Gum tree **5** Filly **6** Pig **7** A toad **8** Python **9** St. Bernard **10** Penguins

Background Bonus Snake

Scientifically Speaking

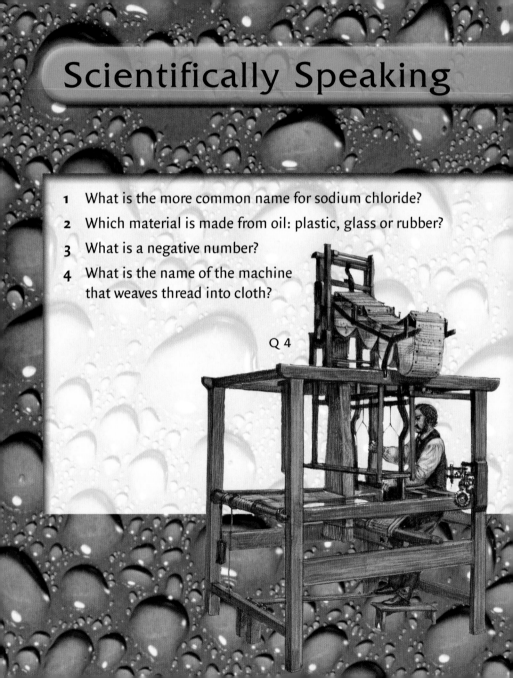

1 What is the more common name for sodium chloride?

2 Which material is made from oil: plastic, glass or rubber?

3 What is a negative number?

4 What is the name of the machine that weaves thread into cloth?

Q 4

5 Is ornithology the study of bones, birds or precious metals?

6 What happens to a boy's voice when it breaks?

7 What is another word for data?

8 Where on your body is your skin the thinnest?

9 Which of these shapes is not a polygon: triangle, decagon, tetrahedron, octagon?

10 What did Edmond Halley have named after him?

ANSWERS

1 Table salt **2** Plastic **3** A number less than zero **4** A loom **5** Birds **6** It sounds deeper **7** Information **8** Eyelids **9** Tetrahedron **10** A comet

Global Matters

Q 1

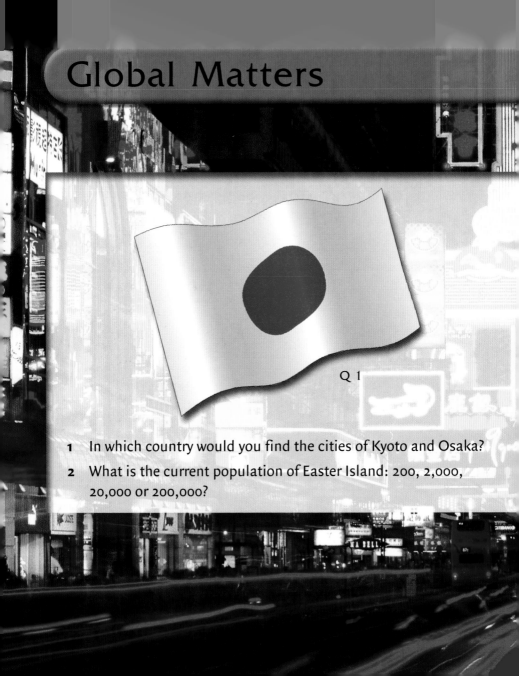

1 In which country would you find the cities of Kyoto and Osaka?

2 What is the current population of Easter Island: 200, 2,000, 20,000 or 200,000?

3 Would you find Hilo Bay in the English Channel, Hawaii or the Canary Islands?

4 The Olympic flame is found in which country?

5 If you were sitting in Wenceslaus Square, would you be in Warsaw, Prague or Budapest?

6 Is the Rila Monastry found in Bulgaria, Hungary or France?

7 Is a small, rounded hill called a knoll, a coll or a poll?

8 Was Montezuma a famous Aztec, Inca or Mongol leader?

9 The Sahara Desert is home to which nomadic tribe?

10 In which country would you find the Nazca Plains?

ANSWERS

1 Japan **2** 2,000 **3** Hawaii **4** Greece **5** Prague **6** Bulgaria **7** Knoll **8** Aztec **9** Tuareg **10** Peru

Total Trivia

1 In which city is the Louvre?

2 What rodent spread the Plague?

3 Alligators, crocodiles and snakes are all what?

Q 4

LEVEL 2 · QUIZ 114

4 Which rock is formed from grains of sand?

5 What is the most common animal in Australia?

6 What does supersonic mean?

7 What are your biceps?

8 What are you doing if you are performing the quickstep?

9 How many sides has a cube?

10 Which of the Seven Wonders of the World still stands?

ANSWERS

1 Paris **2** The rat **3** Reptiles **4** Sandstone **5** The sheep **6** Faster than the speed of sound **7** Muscles in your arms **8** Dancing **9** Six **10** The Great Pyramid, Egypt

Scientifically Speaking

1 What was the name of the first artificial satellite?
2 What did Charles Macintosh invent in 1823?
3 In your body, where would you find marrow?
4 In your home, which device breaks an electric circuit?
5 Do things look larger or smaller through a concave lens?
6 In which flying machine does the pilot hang below the wings?
7 How many right-angles are there in a rectangle?
8 Does it take more muscles to smile or to frown?
9 What foods give you vitamin C?
10 What does REM stand for?

BACKGROUND BONUS

Which gas of the chemical symbol, Ne, was named after the Greek word for new?

Q 3

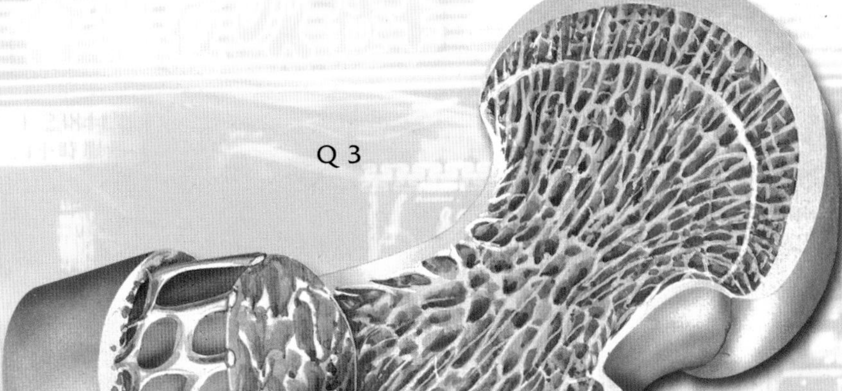

ANSWERS

1 Sputnik **2** Waterproof material **3** In your bones **4** A switch **5** Smaller **6** A hang glider **7** Four **8** To frown **9** Fruit and vegetables **10** Rapid Eye Movement

Background Bonus Neon

Sporting Chance: Soccer

Q 3

1 Which 1966 World Cup winner went on to manage the Republic of Ireland in the World Cup finals?

2 In which country did Gary Lineker play for Grampus 8?

LEVEL 2 · QUIZ 116

3 At the 1998 World Cup, which nation was known as "The Reggae Boys"?

4 Which Italian Chelsea star scored the quickest ever goal in the 1997 FA Cup final?

5 Which was the first British club that Eric Cantona played for?

6 Who was England's manager in the 1990 World Cup?

7 In the 1920s, which legendary Everton striker scored 60 goals in a single season?

8 Who were England's first opponents in the 2002 World Cup finals?

9 Who was the first soccer player to score 100 goals in England's Premiership?

10 Which soccer club was Brian Clough managing when he announced his retirement from the game?

ANSWERS

1 Jack Charlton 2 Japan 3 Jamaica 4 Roberto di Maggio 5 Leeds United 6 Bobby Robson 7 Dixie Dean 8 Sweden 9 Alan Shearer 10 Nottingham Forest

Global Matters

1 What was the island of Sri Lanka known as before 1948?

2 What design is on the flag of Canada?

3 Where did Quasimodo ring the bells?

4 What is the capital of Thailand?

5 In which European capital city could you visit the Tivoli Gardens?

6 The island of Zanzibar lies off the east coast of which continent?

7 What is the name of the straits that separate Anglesey from mainland Wales?

8 Which Israeli port gave its name to a variety of orange?

9 Palm trees are native to what kind of natural habitat?

10 What is the national bird of India?

BACKGROUND BONUS

In what industry would you use a subsoiler, windrower and baler?

Q9

ANSWERS

1 Ceylon **2** A maple leaf **3** Notre Dame **4** Bangkok **5** Copenhagen **6** Africa **7** Menai Straits **8** Jaffa **9** Subtropical coastal areas **10** Peacock

Background Bonus Farming

Sporting Chance

Q 8

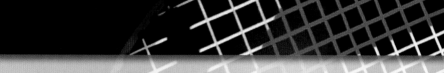

1 Johnny Weissmuller won five Olympic golds In which sport?

2 Wilt Chamberlain holds the NBA record for most points in a baseball game. How many points?

3 Who became World Heavyweight Boxing champion in 1986?

4 In which city did Australian Rules Football originate?

5 In gymnastics, what is a backward handspring known as?

6 What sport is played by the Doncaster Belles?

7 Where is the Happy Valley racecourse>

8 What piece of sporting equipment shares its name with a character from Shakespeare's *A Midsummer Night's Dream*?

9 In what type of car did Paddy Hopkirk and Henry Widden win the 1964 Monte Carlo Rally?

10 In polo, with what do you hit the ball?

ANSWERS

1 Swimming **2** 100 **3** Mike Tyson **4** Melbourne **5** A flic flac **6** Soccer **7** Hong Kong **8** Puck **9** A Mini **10** A mallett

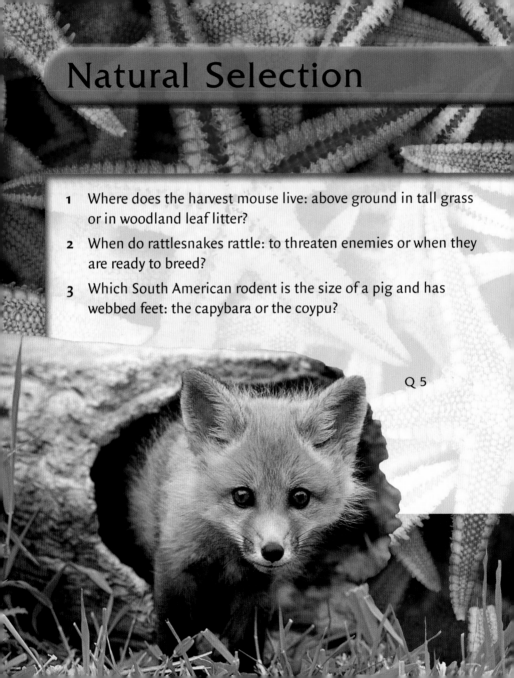

Natural Selection

1 Where does the harvest mouse live: above ground in tall grass or in woodland leaf litter?

2 When do rattlesnakes rattle: to threaten enemies or when they are ready to breed?

3 Which South American rodent is the size of a pig and has webbed feet: the capybara or the coypu?

Q 5

4 Which prickly American desert plant sometimes swells up when it rains: the cactus or the yucca?

5 Which wild, red-furred European member of the dog family lives in cities?

6 Which yellow, sausage-shaped fruit is grown throughout the Caribbean Islands?

7 Do turtles lay their eggs in underwater nests or on land?

8 Which seabird did sailors consider it bad luck to kill: the gannet, the tern or the albatross?

9 What proportion of all living species are made up by insects: one-tenth, one-quarter or over half?

10 Which creatures create the dawn chorus: mice, birds or insects?

ANSWERS

1 Above ground in tall grass (and other plants) **2** To threaten enemies **3** Capybara **4** Cactus **5** The red fox **6** The banana **7** They all lay their eggs on land **8** The albatross **9** Over half **10** Birds

Country Silhouettes

Study the country silhouettes and match them to the countries listed below:

(a) Brazil (b) Canada (c) Spain (d) Norway
(e) Wales (f) Japan (g) China (h) Germany

1

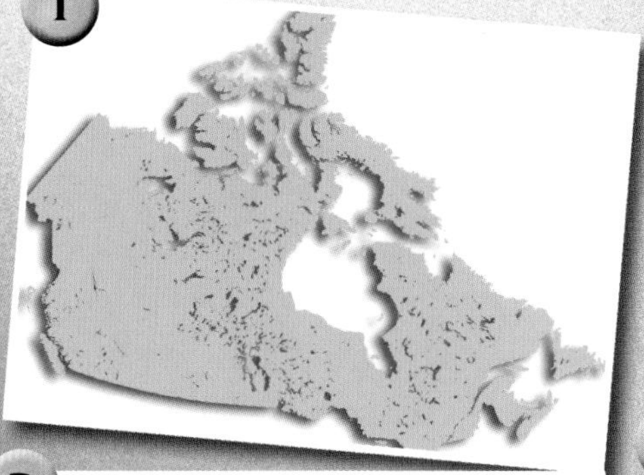

2

3

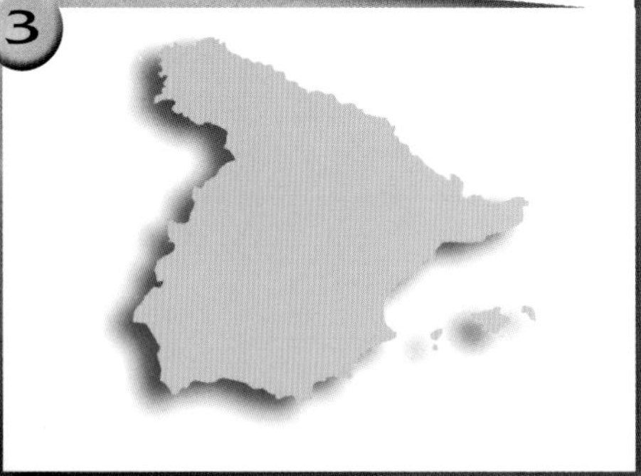

4

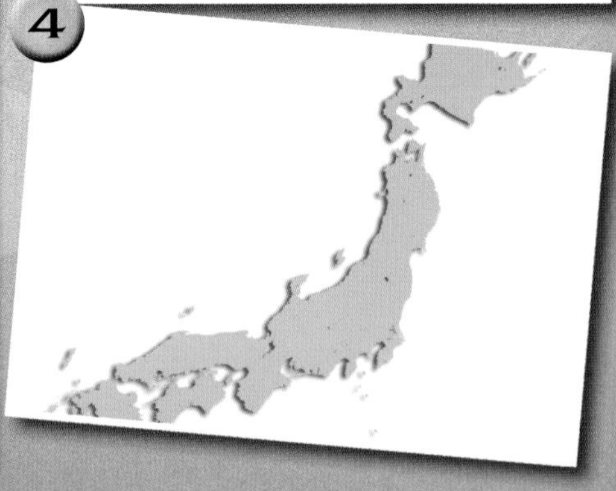

5

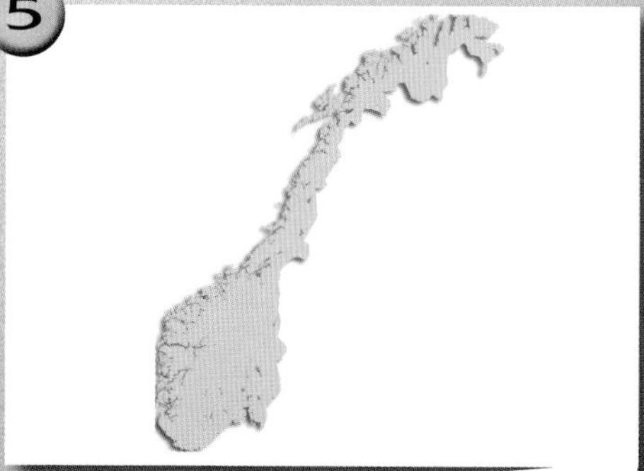

6

7

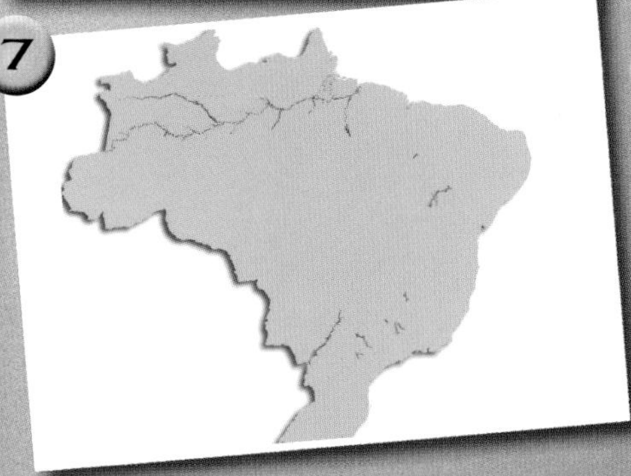

8

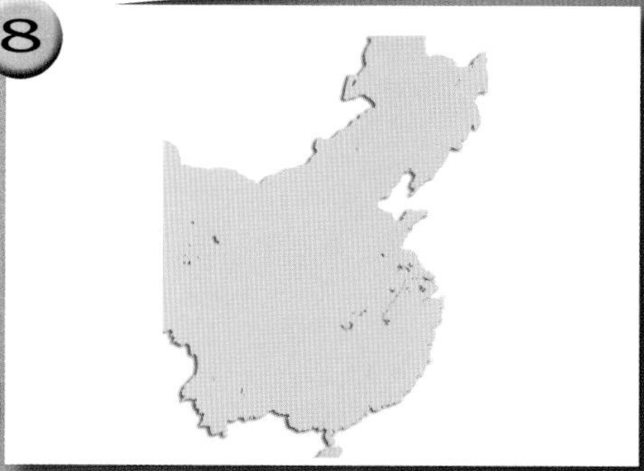

ANSWERS

1 (b) 2 (e) 3 (c) 4 (f) 5 (d) 6 (h) 7 (a) 8 (g)

Total Trivia

1 What rodent is covered with long, sharp, black-and-white spikes called quills?

2 What name is given to the text of an opera?

3 What is another name for ping-pong?

Q 9

4 What is the device for showing the movement of stars and planets on a curved ceiling?

5 According to the Christmas carol, when did King Wenceslas last look out?

6 Who invented radio?

7 What queen was called Bloody Mary?

8 What strait connects the Mediterranean Sea to the Atlantic Ocean?

9 Which prehistoric reptiles died out 65 million years ago?

10 Which is the highest mountain in Europe?

ANSWERS

1 The porcupine **2** Libretto **3** Table tennis **4** A planetarium **5** On the feast of St. Stephen **6** Guglielmo Marconi **7** Queen Mary I **8** The Strait of Gibraltar **9** Dinosaurs **10** Mt. Elbrus (in the Russian Federation)

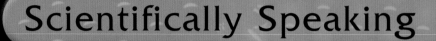

Scientifically Speaking

1. In which bodily substance is plasma found?
2. What part of the body is affected by conjunctivitis?
3. What paper is used to measure acids and alkalis?
4. How many decades are there in a millennium?
5. Which type of body tissue expands and relaxes in order to let you move?
6. What is produced by a solar cell?
7. What are the names of the three segments of an insect?
8. What are the three states of matter?
9. What term describes half of the diameter of a circle?
10. What word describes a region's average weather over a long period of time?

LEVEL 3 · QUIZ 122

Q 3

ANSWERS

1 Blood **2** The eye **3** Litmus paper **4** 100 **5** Muscle **6** Electricity **7** Head, thorax, abdomen **8** Solid, liquid, gas **9** The radius **10** Its climate

Natural Selection

1 What kind of animal is a tuatara?

2 Does the Australian thorny devil lizard get its water fromrain, rivers or dew?

3 Eel, mussel, oyster, clam: which is the odd one out?

Q 8

4 Which tail-less, furry and popular European pet is eaten by some people in South America?

5 Which nut, often ground into a sandwich spread, grows underground?

6 What is the smallest mammal baby?

7 Why is the mistle thrush also called the stormcock?

8 Which poisonous spider relative pulls its prey apart with its massive claws?

9 How does the golden wheel spider escape attack?

10 How many types of oak tree are there: 10, 150 or more than 400?

ANSWERS

1 A reptile **2** Dew (it lives in the desert) **3** The eel is the only fish **4** The guinea pig **5** The peanut **6** The baby mouse opossum **7** Because it sings during storms **8** The scorpion **9** By curling into a ball and rolling away **10** More than 400

Music Mania

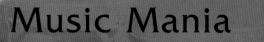

1 Which U.K. pop act had a Christmas hit with "Saviour's Day"?

2 Which U.S. musician is a direct descendant of Herman Melville?

3 Which country singer starred in the 1989 movie *Steel Magnolias*?

4 According to the song, what did Molly Malone sell in the streets of Dublin?

5 "Somethin' Stupid" was a U.K. hit in 2001 for Robbie Williams and Nicole Kidman. Who sang it originally?

6 Which Cuban singer enjoyed a 1992 festive hit with "Christmas Through Your Eyes"?

7 What kind of Christmas did Elvis Presley sing about in 1964?

8 What group did Paul McCartney form after the The Beatles?

9 Which Bond theme did Sheena Easton perform?

10 What is the last name of the punk princess Toyah? Q 8

BACKGROUND BONUS

Tico Torres is best-known for what?

ANSWERS
1 Cliff Richard **2** Moby **3** Dolly Parton **4** Cockles and mussels **5** Frank and Nancy Sinatra **6** Gloria Estefan **7** "Blue Christmas" **8** Wings **9** "For Your Eyes Only" **10** Wilcox **Background Bonus** Drumming for Bon Jovi

Making History

1 Michael Collins was a famous revolutionary In which country?

2 What is the large medieval catapult that was used to attack castles called?

3 Which Roman god was ruler of the Underworld?

4 In which country did samurai warriors live?

5 Which 1947 invention made pocket-sized radios possible?

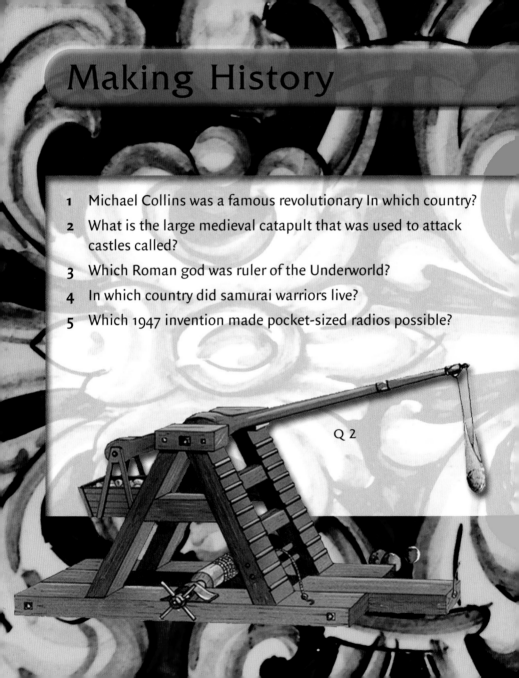

Q 2

6 Who ruled the Soviet Union from 1924 to 1953?

7 In ancient Egypt, what was a nilometer used for?

8 What year was the first digital computer made?

9 Which oath, taken by modern doctors, is named after a Greek physician?

10 How many kings of England have been called Henry?

ANSWERS

1 Ireland **2** Trebuchet **3** Pluto **4** Japan **5** The transistor **6** Stalin **7** Measuring the depth of the river Nile **8** 1946 **9** The Hippocratic oath (after Hippocrates) **10** Eight

Natural Selection

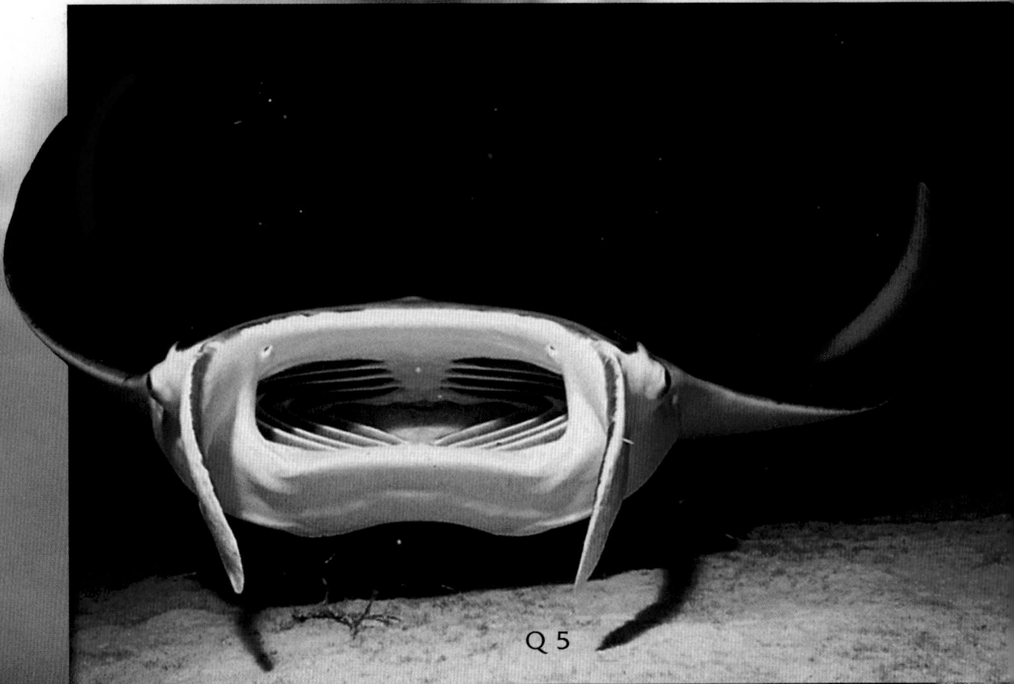

BACKGROUND BONUS

What is the name of the small ape sometimes referred to as the 'songbird' of the primate family?

LEVEL 3 • QUIZ 126

1 What came first: dinosaurs or crocodiles?

2 What spider has a hinged, flaplike entrance to its nest?

3 Which American mammal once roamed the prairies in enormous herds?

4 What ape is most closely related to humans?

5 Which is the largest member of the ray family?

6 What creatures live in groups called shoals?

7 How does the marine toad deter its enemies: by growling, squirting venom or biting?

8 Which is the largest land predator in Africa?

9 Where does the wombat live?

10 What is a skink?

ANSWERS

1 Crocodiles **2** The trapdoor spider **3** The bison **4** The chimpanzee **5** The manta ray **6** Fish **7** By squirting venom **8** The lion **9** Australia **10** A type of lizard

Background Bonus Gibbon

Lights, Camera, Action!

1 What lighter-than-air substance was invented by the Absent Minded Professor?

2 What actor connects the movies *Jurassic Park*, *The Omen*, and *The Final Conflict*?

3 In which 1989 movie did Daniel Day Lewis play the writer Christie Brown?

4 The 1993 movie *Backbeat* told the story of the early days of which superstar pop group?

5 What outlaw was played by Paul Newman in the movie *The Left Handed Gun*?

6 On which Greek island is *Zorba the Greek* set?

7 Which movie star played the title role in the 1998 historical drama, *Elizabeth*?

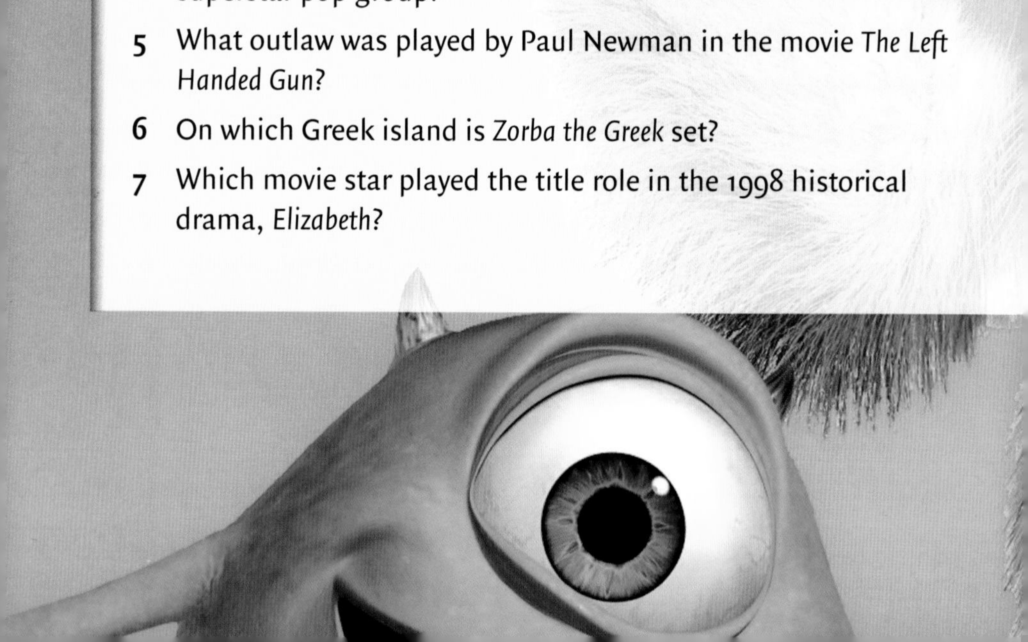

8 Which *Oliver* star also played a Sherwood Forest outlaw in *Robin Hood, Prince of Thieves*?

9 What is the only musical movie to win ten Oscars?

10 Which Disney character fell in love with a prince called Eric?

Q 5

ANSWERS
1 *Flubber* **2** Sam Neill **3** *My Left Foot* **4** The Beatles **5** Billy the Kid **6** Crete **7** Cate Blanchett **8** Jack Wild **9** *West Side Story* **10** Ariel, the Little Mermaid

Scientifically Speaking

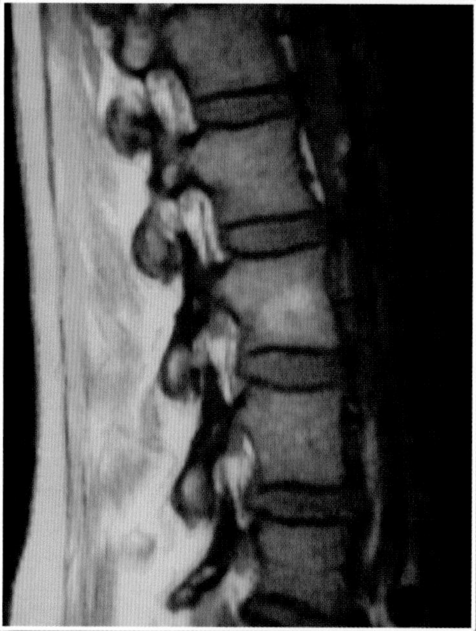

1 What is the name of the molten rock that is thrown up from a volcano?

2 The disease Rubella is also known by what other name?

3 How many weeks are there in five years?

4 What does a dermatologist study?

Q 6

LEVEL 3 • QUIZ 128

5 What fraction of a circle is a section measuring 270°?
6 What part of your body has vertebrae?
7 What comes in varieties called bar, horseshoe and electro?
8 At room temperature, is helium a gas, a liquid or a solid?
9 What is the name of the light-sensitive lining behind the eye?
10 Glass is mainly composed of what?

ANSWERS
1 Lava 2 German measles 3 260 4 The skin 5 Three-quarters 6 The backbone
7 A compass 8 A gas 9 The retina 10 Sand

Total Trivia

Q 10

1 In which country was the environmental organization Greenpeace, founded?

2 How long is a leap year?

3 What is the capital of Albania?

4 Which parts of a tree trap sunlight and make food for the tree?

5 What is pyrophobia a fear of?

6 What is the word fax short for?

7 What is India's main religion?

8 In which American state is Amarillo?

9 Which girl's first name is the Italian name for woman?

10 What does "long in the tooth" mean?

ANSWERS

1 Canada 2 366 days 3 Tirana 4 The leaves 5 Fire 6 Facsimile 7 Hinduism 8 Texas 9 Donna 10 Getting old

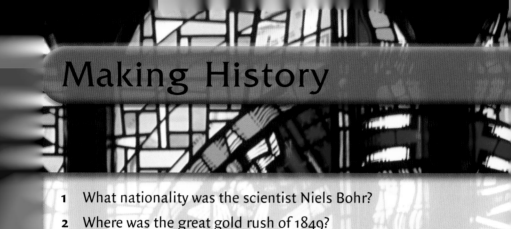

Making History

1 What nationality was the scientist Niels Bohr?

2 Where was the great gold rush of 1849?

3 What crop did Jimmy Carter grow before he became U.S. president?

4 Which two important metals were mined in England during Roman times?

5 Which science-fiction story caused a panic in the United States in 1938?

6 In which Asian country was the Khmer empire founded in about AD900?

7 Which British prime minister had the forenames Margaret Hilda?

8 Was the first globe of the Earth made in 1350, 1492 or 1796?

9 What land did Cartier claim for France in 1534?

10 What is the name of the pyramid-like platforms built in ancient Mesopotamia?

Q 5

ANSWERS

1 Danish 2 California 3 Peanuts 4 Lead and tin 5 *The War of the Worlds* 6 Cambodia 7 Margaret Thatcher 8 1492 9 Canada 10 Ziggurats

Music Mania

1 What opera is subtitled *The Lass That Loved a Sailor*?

2 In which city was the singer Gloria Estefan born?

3 Who performed the title song for the Bond movie *Never Say Never Again*?

4 Who wrote the Tina Turner hit "Private Dancer"?

5 Which best-selling song of the 20th century was written by Bernie Taupin?

Q 5

LEVEL 3 · QUIZ 131

6 Who replaced Keith Moon in The Who?

7 How old was Buddy Holly when he died?

8 On whose novel is the musical *Les Misérables* based?

9 On what island was Nana Mouskouri born?

10 With which musical instrument is Sonny Rollins associated?

ANSWERS

1 HMS *Pinafore* 2 Havana 3 Lani Hall 4 Mark Knopfler 5 "Candle in the Wind" 6 Kenny Jones 7 22 8 Victor Hugo 9 Crete 10 Saxophone

Remarkable Rhymes

Can you guess the names of these well-loved nursery rhymes?

1

2

3

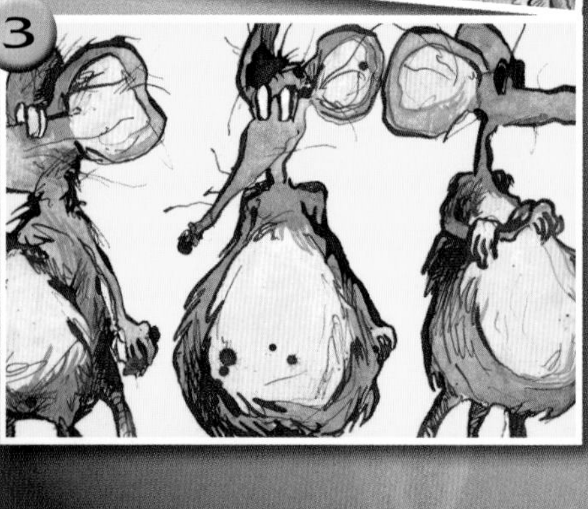

4

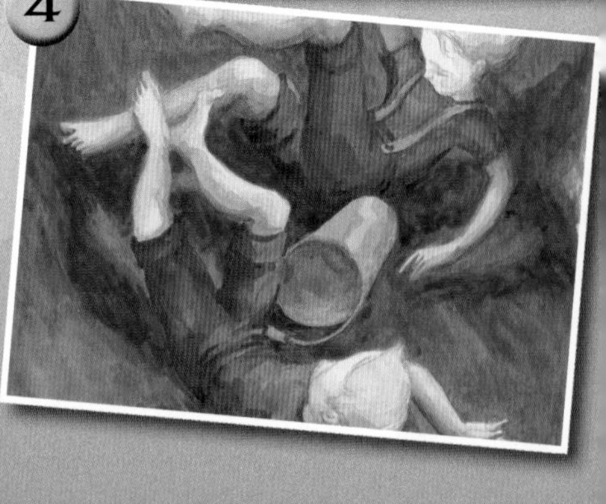

LEVEL 3 · QUIZ 132

5

6

7

8

ANSWERS

1 Rub a dub dub **2** *Jack be nimble* **3** Three blind mice **4** *Jack and Jill* **5** Humpty Dumpty **6** Hush a bye baby **7** *London bridge is falling down* **8** Row, row, row your boat

Lights, Camera, Action!

1 When were the Oscars first awarded?

2 In which country was the 1984 movie *The Killing Fields* set?

3 What is the first name of Baron Frankenstein?

4 What connects the movies *Raising Cain*, *Dead Ringers* and *The Man in the Iron Mask*?

5 In which 1985 movie comedy did Richard Pryor inherit millions of dollars?

6 In which movie, starring Nicholas Cage and John Travolta, did Archer "borrow" Troy's face?

7 What movie saw David Tomlinson "bobbing along on the bottom of the beautiful briny sea"?

8 Which of the Marx Brothers was born with the first name of Leonard?

BACKGROUND BONUS

In The Adventures of Rocky and Bullwinkle, what kind of animal is Bullwinkle?

9 In which 1995 movie did Michelle Pfeiffer play an ex-marine who becomes a schoolteacher at a tough inner city school?

10 The 1993 movie *Dragon* is a biopic of which martial arts hero?

Q 5

ANSWERS

1 1929 **2** Cambodia or Kampuchea **3** Victor **4** Twin brothers **5** *Brewster's Millions* **6** *Face/Off* **7** *Bedknobs and Broomsticks* **8** Chico **9** *Dangerous Minds* **10** Bruce Lee

Background Bonus Moose

Total Trivia

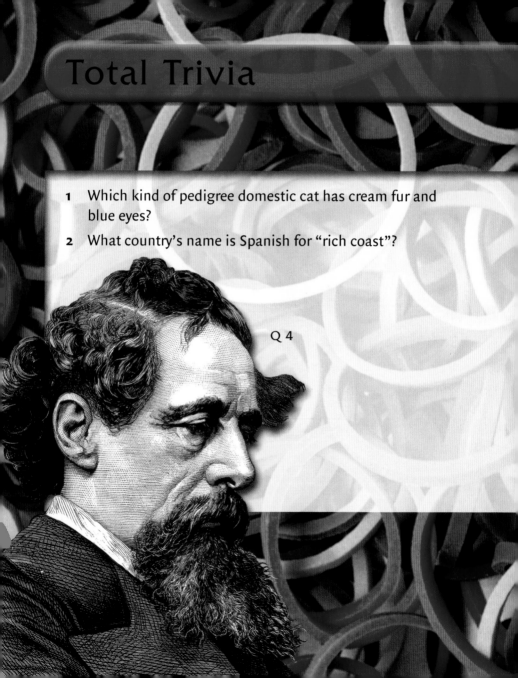

1 Which kind of pedigree domestic cat has cream fur and blue eyes?

2 What country's name is Spanish for "rich coast"?

Q 4

3 What do you call a toy with mirrors that creates random regular patterns?

4 Who wrote *David Copperfield*?

5 Which precious stone is purple?

6 Who is Mickey Mouse's girlfriend?

7 Which river flows through Paris?

8 Who led Britain for much of World War I?

9 *Papillon* is the French word for what?

10 What is the capital of Egypt?

ANSWERS

1 A Siamese cat 2 Costa Rica 3 A kaleidoscope 4 Charles Dickens 5 Amethyst 6 Minnie Mouse 7 The Seine 8 Lloyd George 9 Butterfly 10 Cairo

Scientifically Speaking

Q 10

BACKGROUND BONUS

In a laboratory, what is the name of the dish on which bacteria are grown?

LEVEL 3 • QUIZ 135

1. What is the body's largest joint?
2. How much water is there in urine: 10 percent, 60 percent or 95 percent?
3. Where would you find your femur bone?
4. Acoustics is the study of what?
5. Which vitamin, found in liver and green vegetables, helps with clotting blood?
6. What planet is known as the red planet?
7. Ancient scientists believed that there were only four elements: earth, fire, air and what else?
8. What is petrology the study of?
9. What is nausea?
10. What does a nutritionist specialize in?

ANSWERS

1 The knee **2** 95 percent **3** In your leg **4** Sound and how it travels **5** Vitamin K **6** Mars **7** Water **8** Rocks **9** The feeling that you need to be sick **10** Food and diet

Background Bonus Petri dish

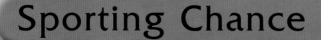

Sporting Chance

1 Who won Olympic gold medals for the long jump in 1984, 1988 and 1992?

2 In which country was the tennis star Monica Seles born?

3 Who moved to the New York Yankees from the Boston Red Sox in 1921 for afee of $125,000?

4 Who was World Professional Billiards champion from 1968 to 1980?

5 In which city did Allan Wells win an Olympic gold medal?

6 Who was ranked as Britain's No. 1 male tennis player in 2001?

7 From which wood were longbows traditionally made?

8 Which B word is the name of a form of hockey played on ice with a ball?

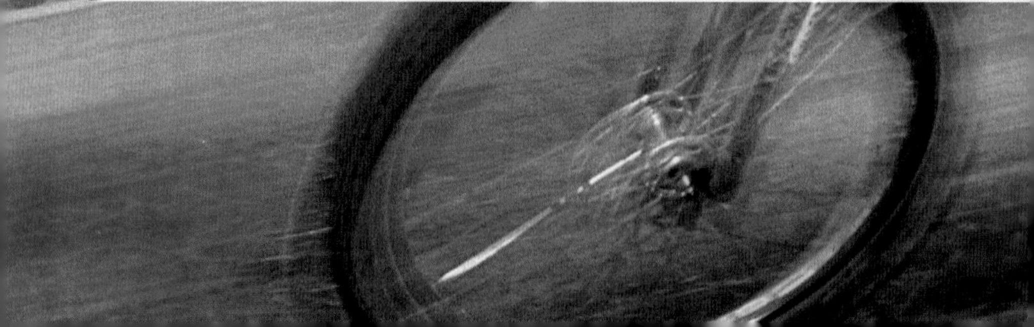

9 Who was the first South African golfer to win the U.S. Open?

10 What is swimmer Ian Thorpe's nickname?

Q 2

ANSWERS

1 Carl Lewis 2 Yugoslavia 3 Babe Ruth 4 Rex Williams 5 Moscow 6 Tim Henman
7 Yew 8 Bandy 9 Gary Player 10 "Thorpedo"

Music Mania

Q 3

1 Which group was Lionel Richie the lead singer of?

2 In which horror movie were extracts from Mike Oldfield's *Tubular Bells* used?

3 Falco had a hit with "Rock Me Amadeus" from the movie *Amadeus*. Where is Falco from?

4 "Stuck in the Middle with You" can be heard during a famous scene in which Quentin Tarantino movie?

5 Underworld's "Born Slippy" shot to No. 2 in the U.K. after featuring in which movie?

6 Which solo artist recorded the album *Listen Without Prejudice?*

7 Which group recorded the theme to the 1973 Bond movie *Live and Let Die?*

8 What movie helped Huey Lewis up the charts with "The Power of Love"?

9 Whose career was documented in *The Great Rock'n'Roll Swindle?*

10 *Desperately Seeking Susan* starred which female singer?

ANSWERS

1 The Commodores 2 *The Exorcist* 3 Austria 4 *Reservoir Dogs* 5 *Trainspotting* 6 George Michael 7 Wings 8 *Back to the Future* 9 The Sex Pistols 10 Madonna

Total Trivia

1 What is another name for the sea creature called an orca?

2 Managua is the capital of what country?

Q 4

3 Where can the Metropolitan Museum of Art be found?

4 Which president of the Soviet Union introduced Perestroika in the 1980s?

5 Which is the fastest-moving snake in the world?

6 Who composed "Air on a G String"?

7 What country makes more of the world's television sets than any other?

8 In which country is the Brenner Pass?

9 Khartoum is the capital of what country?

10 In what year was John Lennon shot?

ANSWERS

1 Killer Whale 2 Nicaragua 3 New York 4 Mikhail Gorbachev 5 Black mamba 6 J.S. Bach 7 Japan 8 Austria 9 Sudan 10 1980

Natural Selection

1 Where would you be most likely to find a hornets' nest?

2 What kind of fish is the halibut?

3 Which of the following has a hinged shell: winkle, mussel or barnacle?

4 In what hemisphere are penguins found?

5 Frogs and toads make up almost nine-tenths of amphibians: true or false?

6 What is a kumquat?

7 Apart from some lizards, what other kinds of reptile can leap from trees and glide?

8 Which exotic spice is obtained from the stigmas of the crocus flower?

9 What do we call a group of chimpanzees?

10 Which nut tree did the Romans introduce to Britain: the hazel, the walnut or the sweet chestnut?

BACKGROUND BONUS

What is special about the whistling swan?

ANSWERS

1 In a tree **2** Flatfish **3** Mussel **4** Southern hemisphere **5** True **6** A fruit **7** Certain snakes **8** Saffron **9** A troop **10** The sweet chestnut

Background Bonus It has the most feathers of any bird

Scientifically Speaking

1 What is the only mammal that can fly?

2 What job does bile perform in the body?

3 Which type of insect makes huge mounds more than 2 m (6 ft) tall in Australia?

4 Which is the brightest planet, as seen from Earth?

5 How many sides has a parallelogram?

6 Barbary apes live in only one small part of Europe. Where is it?

7 Where in the human body is the trapezium?

8 What is the square root of 64?

9 If a doctor recommends taking insulin regularly, from what disorder is the patient suffering?

10 About 95 percent of the body's calcium is found in which two areas?

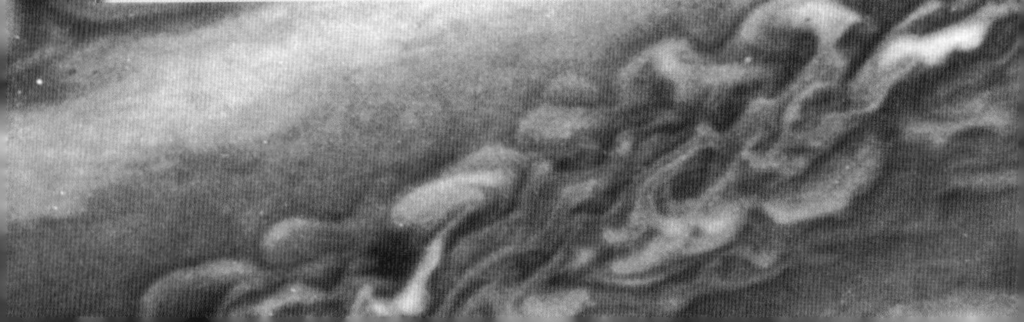

LEVEL 3 • QUIZ 140

Q 1

ANSWERS

1 A bat **2** It helps digest food **3** Termites **4** Venus **5** Four **6** Gibraltar
7 In the wrist (it's a bone) **8** 8 **9** Diabetes **10** Teeth and bones

Lights, Camera, Action!

Q 8

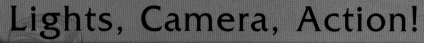

1 Who connects the movie epics *Lawrence of Arabia*, *Zorba the Greek* and *Barabbas*?

2 What character has been played on film by Bo Derek, Dorothy Dunbar and Maureen O'Sullivan?

3 Who played the president of the United States in the movie *Primary Colors?*

4 How are Curly, Larry and Mo collectively known on film?

5 Who played Oscar Madison in the movie *The Odd Couple?*

6 What board game is played by Steve McQueen and Faye Dunaway in *The Thomas Crown Affair?*

7 Who was the first British movie star to win a Best Actress Oscar?

8 Which actor starred as Mel Gibson's partner in the *Lethal Weapon* movies?

9 Which writer did Virginia McKenna portray in the 1966 movie *Born Free?*

10 In the movie *Peter's Friends*, which British comedy star played the title role?

ANSWERS

1 Anthony Quinn starred in them **2** Jane in the *Tarzan* movies **3** John Travolta **4** The Three Stooges **5** Walter Matthau **6** Chess **7** Vivien Leigh **8** Danny Glover **9** Joy Adamson **10** Stephen Fry

Total Trivia

1 Which Spanish percussion instrument is made from two wooden shells?

2 How many holes are there on a golf course?

3 Currants and raisins are dried what?

4 Which two German brothers wrote a famous collection of fairy tales?

5 What is the capital of Denmark?

6 Which musical features a lawyer called Billy Flynn, played by Richard Gere in the 2003 movie of the same name?

7 What is a private eye?

8 What is a newborn horse called?

9 What does a shark's skeleton comprise of?

10 If someone has a nest egg, what do they have?

Q 3

ANSWERS

1 Castanets **2** 18 **3** Grapes **4** The brothers Grimm **5** Copenhagen **6** *Chicago*
7 A private detective **8** A foal **9** Cartilage **10** Savings

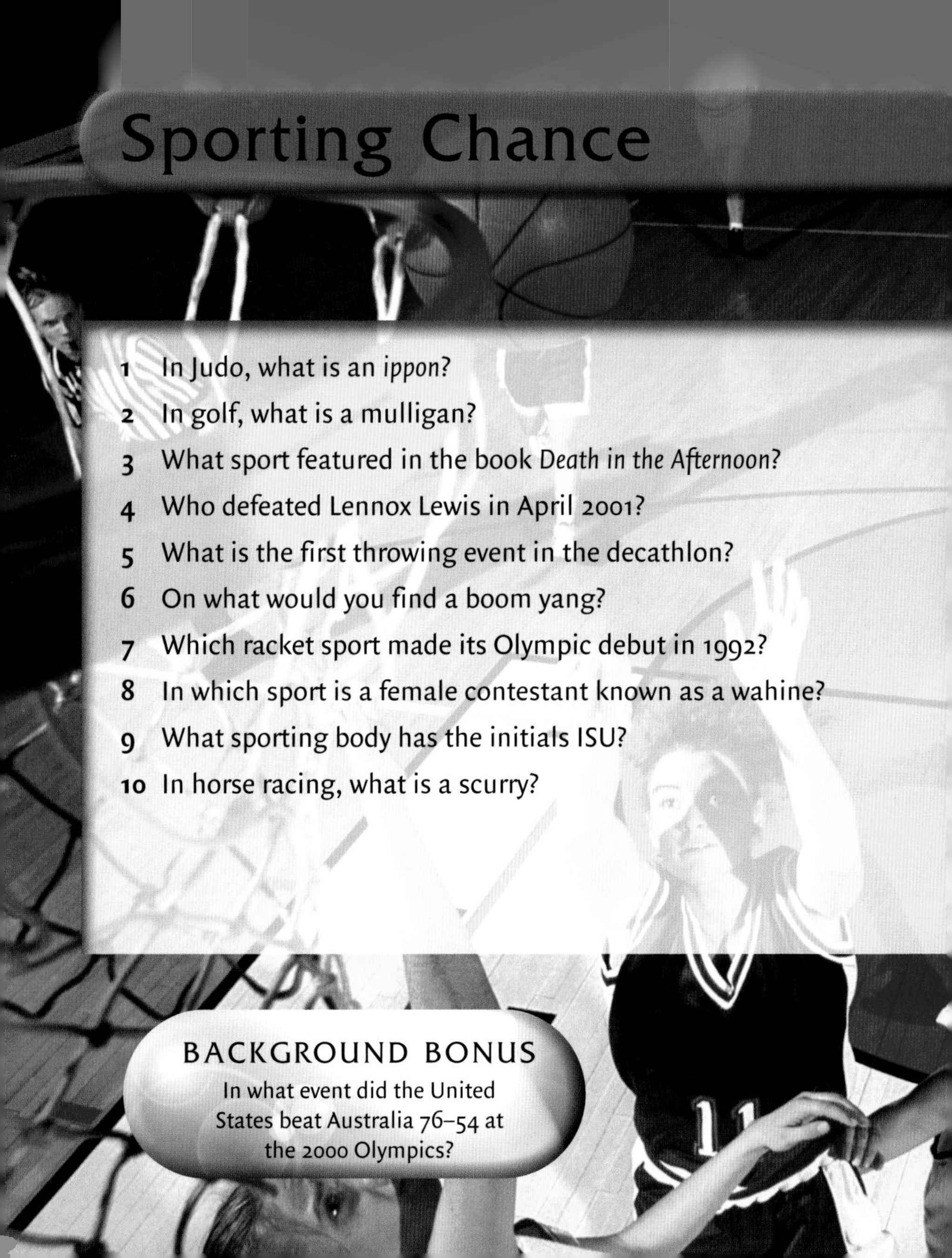

Sporting Chance

1 In Judo, what is an *ippon*?
2 In golf, what is a mulligan?
3 What sport featured in the book *Death in the Afternoon*?
4 Who defeated Lennox Lewis in April 2001?
5 What is the first throwing event in the decathlon?
6 On what would you find a boom yang?
7 Which racket sport made its Olympic debut in 1992?
8 In which sport is a female contestant known as a wahine?
9 What sporting body has the initials ISU?
10 In horse racing, what is a scurry?

BACKGROUND BONUS

In what event did the United States beat Australia 76–54 at the 2000 Olympics?

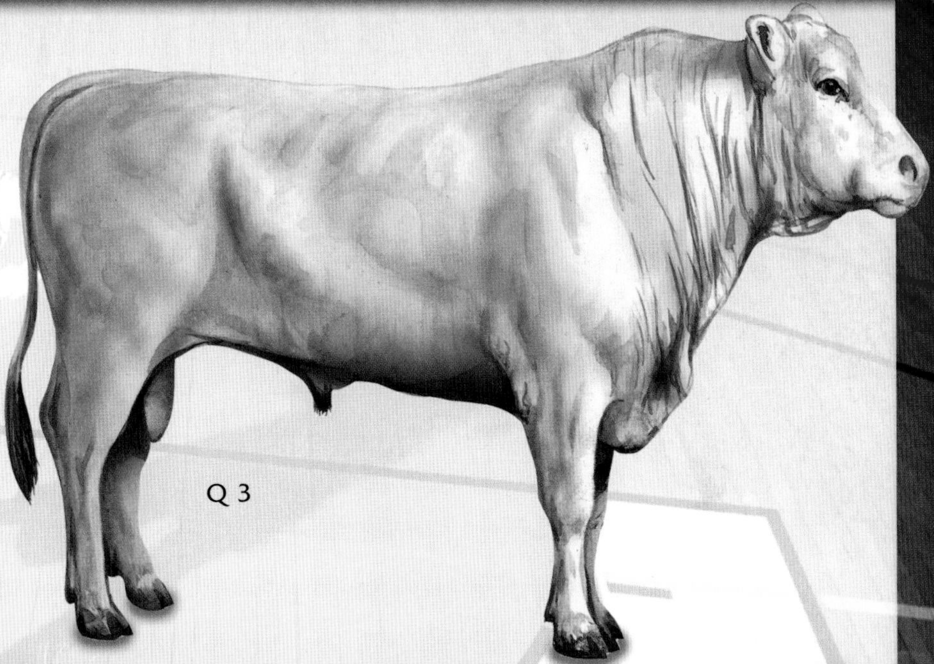

Q 3

ANSWERS

1 A winning point **2** A free shot **3** Bullfighting **4** Hasim Rahman **5** Javelin **6** A yacht **7** Badminton **8** Surfing **9** International Skating Union **10** A short sprint race

Background Bonus Women's basketball

Name the Object

Can you identify these objects?

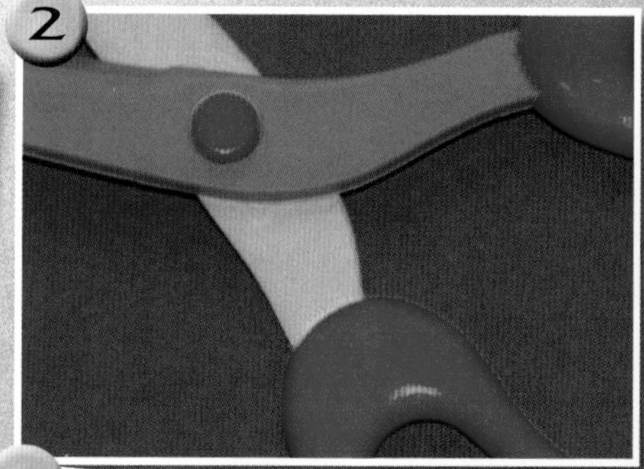

5

6

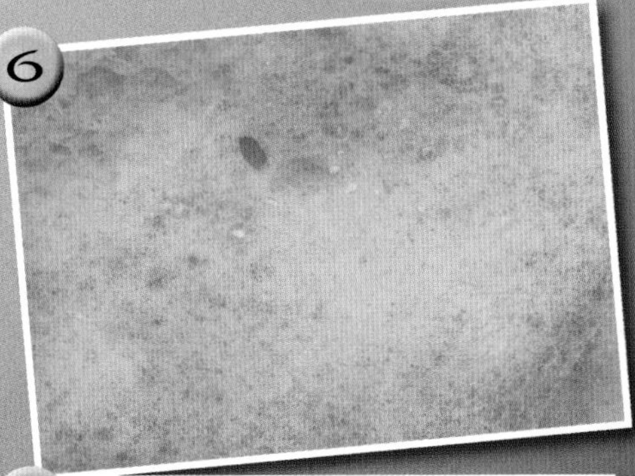

7

8

ANSWERS

1 Lipstick **2** Scissors **3** Paintbrush **4** Watering can **5** Drink cans **6** Sponge **7** Bucket and spade **8** Keys

Natural Selection

1 What is a thrush's anvil?
2 What does the Malaysian horned toad disguise itself as?
3 What happens to a honey bee after it uses its sting?
4 Which African mammal uses its head and very long neck as a club when fighting?
5 Why does the woodpecker have a liquid cushion inside its skull?
6 Which umbrella-like tree has no branches?
7 What does the antlion dig to catch its prey?
8 What is a caecilian?
9 Which rainforest mammal spends most of its life hanging upside down?
10 Where do tigers originate?

ANSWERS

1 A stone on which it smashes snails **2** It looks like a dead leaf **3** It dies **4** The giraffe **5** To protect its brain as it pecks trees **6** Palm tree **7** A pit in loose sand **8** A legless amphibian **9** The sloth **10** Siberia

Written Word: The Bible

Q 3

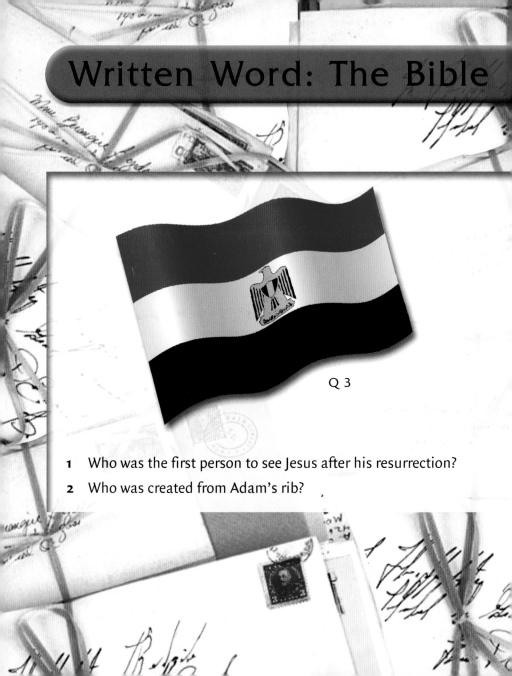

1 Who was the first person to see Jesus after his resurrection?

2 Who was created from Adam's rib?

LEVEL 3 · QUIZ 146

3 An angel appeared to Joseph telling him to take Mary and Jesus to what country?

4 What is the Seventh Commandment?

5 What was the name of Herod's stepdaughter?

6 How many books are there in the New Testament?

7 Who visited Mary to inform her that she was pregnant with the Son of God?

8 Which gospel writer was known as The Beloved Physician?

9 The Three Wise Men are believed to be buried in which German cathedral?

10 Who is the patron saint of tax collectors?

ANSWERS

1 Mary Magdalene 2 Eve 3 Egypt 4 Thou shalt not commit adultery 5 Salome 6 27 7 The Angel Gabriel 8 Luke 9 Cologne Cathedral 10 St. Matthew

Making History

1 In what year did India become independent of Britain?

2 What was built across the United States in 1869?

3 Which German composer wrote *The Messiah* and the *Water Music*?

4 How many thousands of years ago did the first modern humans appear?

5 Which English poet wrote *Kublai Khan*?

6 Who won the battle of Austerlitz in 1805?

7 Who became president of the United States in 1929?

8 Across which mountains did Lewis and Clarke lead an expedition?

9 Who were Ginger Rogers and Fred Astaire?

10 After which Greek god was the American manned Moon-landing spacecraft named?

ANSWERS

1 1947 **2** The first coast-to-coast railroad **3** Handel **4** 150,000 years ago **5** Samuel Taylor Coleridge **6** The French, led by Napoleon **7** President Hoover **8** The Rockies **9** A movie dance team **10** Apollo

Total Trivia

Q 4

LEVEL 3 · QUIZ 148

1 Where is singer Jim Morrison buried?

2 John, Ringo and George were three of the Beatles. Who was the fourth?

3 What kind of plant is marjoram?

4 What shape is *farfalla* pasta?

5 In which sea is the island of Crete?

6 Who wrote *Robinson Crusoe*?

7 Of which city were the Crusaders fighting for control?

8 What is the name for a small explosive charge that sets off a bomb?

9 Who was the only ruler of Britain who ruled instead of a king or a queen?

10 Which is the world's largest country?

ANSWERS

1 Paris **2** Paul McCartney **3** A herb **4** Bow-shaped **5** The Mediterranean **6** Daniel Defoe **7** Jerusalem **8** A detonator **9** Oliver Cromwell **10** The Russian Federation

Natural Selection

1 What goose migrates from Greenland to Mexico: the barnacle, Canada or snow goose?

2 How fast can tortoises move: 1 km/h (0.6 mph), 2 km/h (1.2 mph) or over 3 km/h (1.8 mph)?

Q 4

3 The 37 species of toucan all live on what continent?

4 Which popular small American squirrel crams food into its cheek pouches?

5 Which have bright, showy flowers: cone-bearing trees or broad-leaved trees?

6 Why do vultures have naked heads and necks?

7 Why do some South African geckoes have webbed feet?

8 What kind of animal is the sea mouse?

9 What is the odd one out: tuna, dolphin, dugong, sea otter?

10 Do the cones of the Australian bunya pine weigh: 1 kg (2.2 lb), 3 kg (6.6 lb) or 5 kg (11 lb) each?

ANSWERS

1 The snow goose **2** Up to 3.22 km/h (2 mph) over short distances **3** South America **4** The chipmunk **5** Broad-leaved trees **6** To keep clean when feeding **7** For moving through sand **8** Marine worm **9** Tuna is the only fish **10** 5 kg (11 lb)

Global Matters

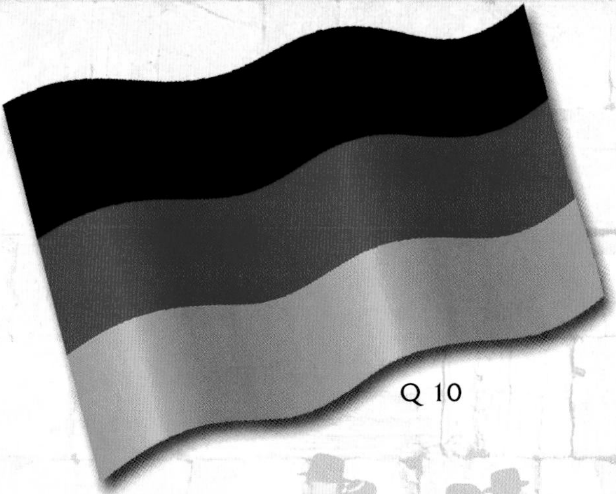

Q 10

1 In which country was the world's first public television service?

2 What country's flag features a blue globe in a yellow diamond on a green background?

BACKGROUND BONUS

What did the Western Wall in Jerusalem used to be known as?

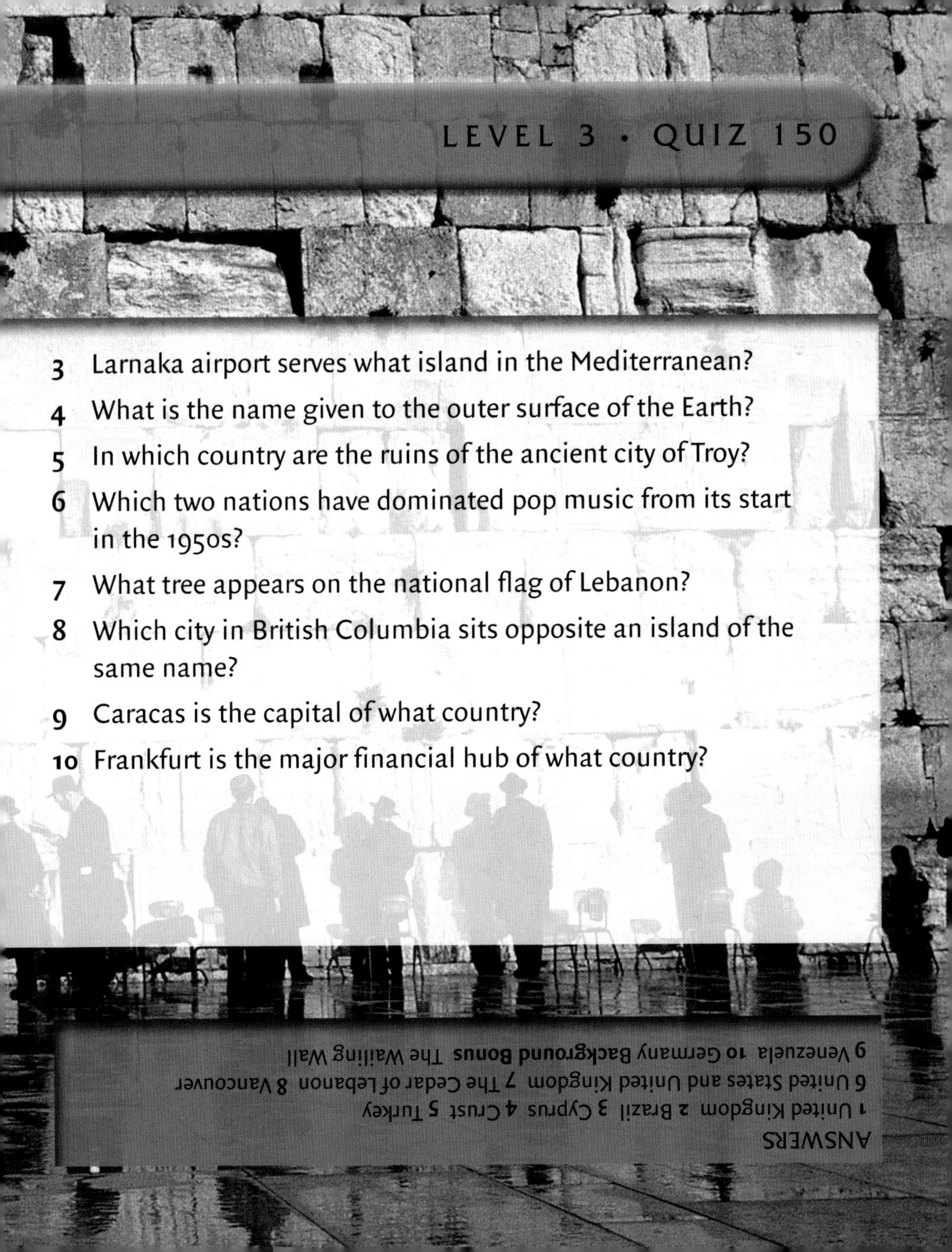

3 Larnaka airport serves what island in the Mediterranean?

4 What is the name given to the outer surface of the Earth?

5 In which country are the ruins of the ancient city of Troy?

6 Which two nations have dominated pop music from its start in the 1950s?

7 What tree appears on the national flag of Lebanon?

8 Which city in British Columbia sits opposite an island of the same name?

9 Caracas is the capital of what country?

10 Frankfurt is the major financial hub of what country?

ANSWERS

1 United Kingdom **2** Brazil **3** Cyprus **4** Crust **5** Turkey **6** United States and United Kingdom **7** The Cedar of Lebanon **8** Vancouver **9** Venezuela **10** Germany **Background Bonus** The Wailing Wall

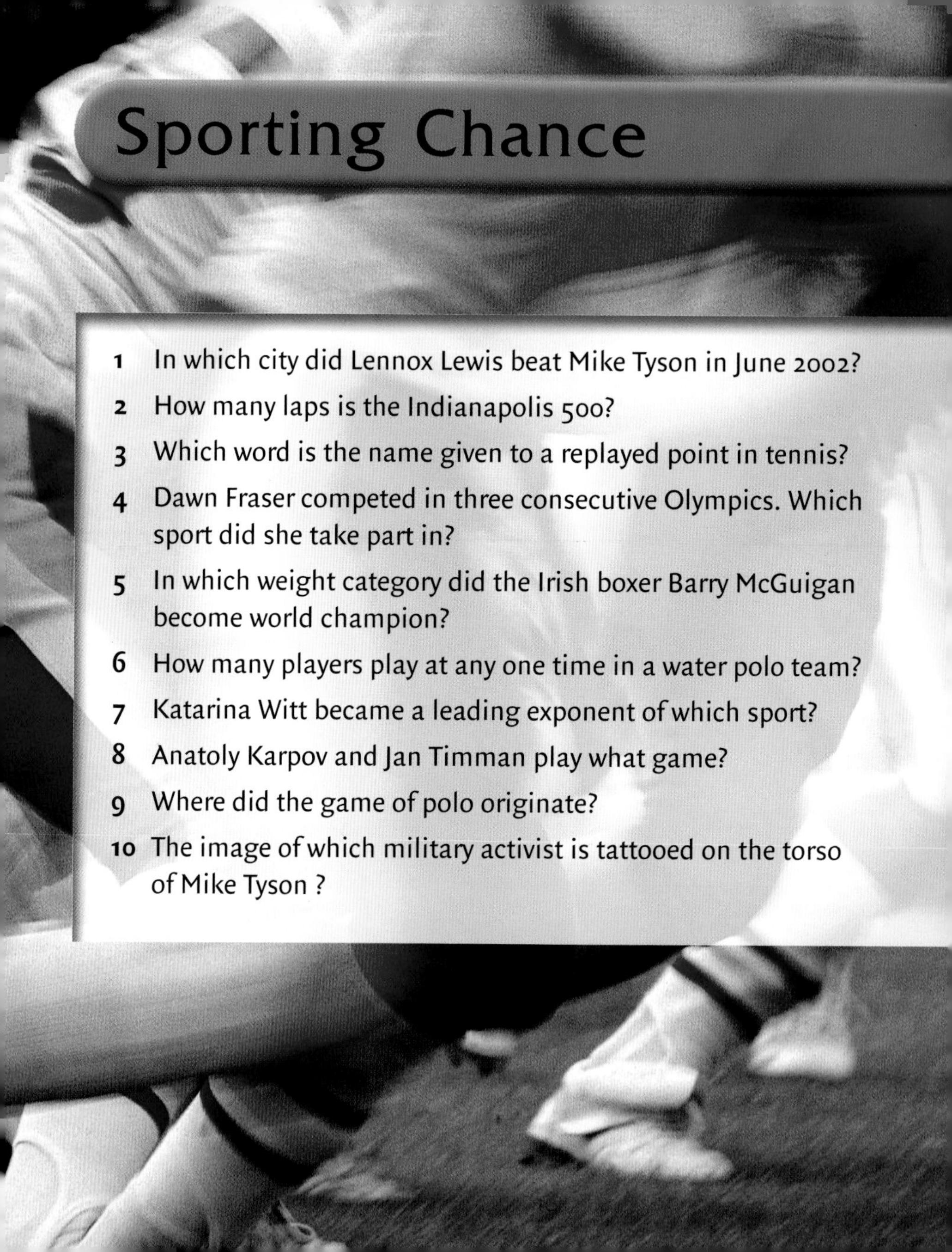

Sporting Chance

1 In which city did Lennox Lewis beat Mike Tyson in June 2002?

2 How many laps is the Indianapolis 500?

3 Which word is the name given to a replayed point in tennis?

4 Dawn Fraser competed in three consecutive Olympics. Which sport did she take part in?

5 In which weight category did the Irish boxer Barry McGuigan become world champion?

6 How many players play at any one time in a water polo team?

7 Katarina Witt became a leading exponent of which sport?

8 Anatoly Karpov and Jan Timman play what game?

9 Where did the game of polo originate?

10 The image of which military activist is tattooed on the torso of Mike Tyson ?

Q 7

ANSWERS

1 Memphis **2** 200 **3** Let **4** Athletics **5** Featherweight **6** Seven **7** Ice skating **8** Chess **9** Persia **10** Ché Guevara

Written Word

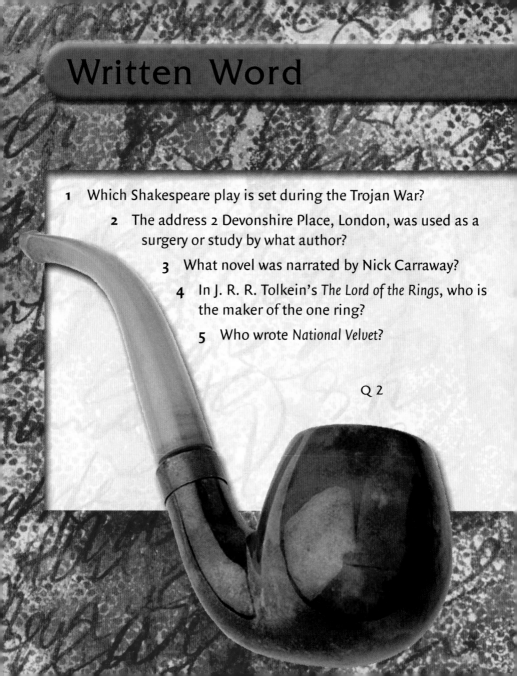

1 Which Shakespeare play is set during the Trojan War?

2 The address 2 Devonshire Place, London, was used as a surgery or study by what author?

3 What novel was narrated by Nick Carraway?

4 In J. R. R. Tolkein's *The Lord of the Rings*, who is the maker of the one ring?

5 Who wrote *National Velvet*?

Q 2

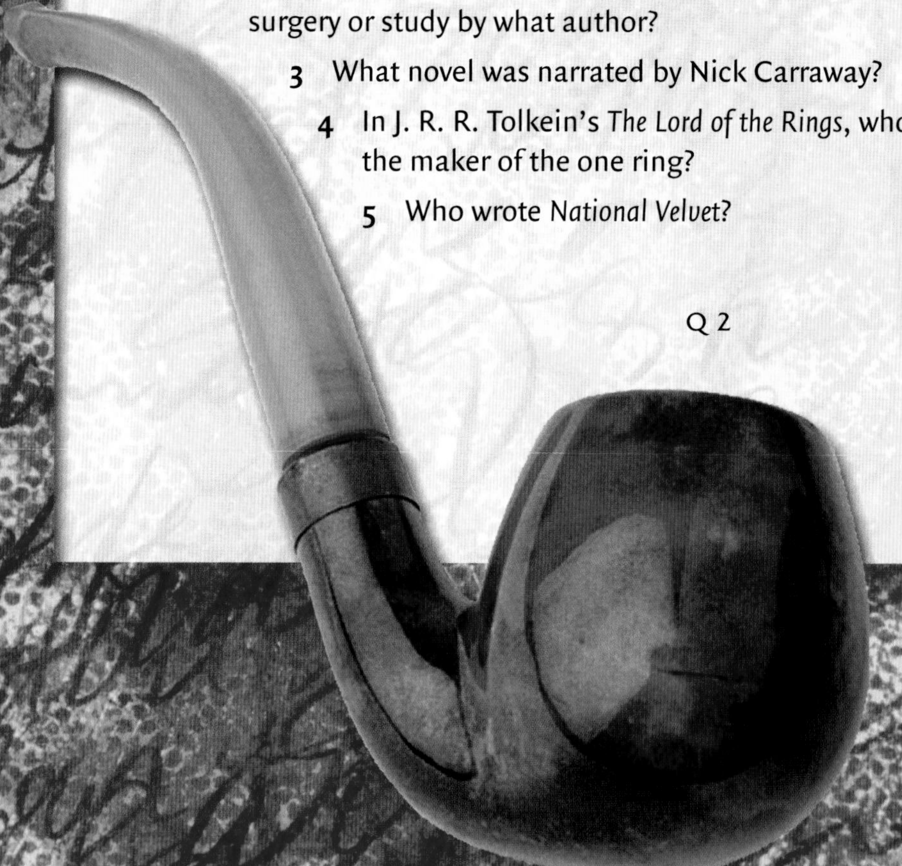

LEVEL 3 • QUIZ 152

6 What poet lived in a house called *Alloway*?

7 What is the surname of Anne of Green Gables?

8 Delores Haze is a central character of which controversial novel?

9 What do the initials H.E. stand for in the name of the author H.E. Bates?

10 What is the fictional village where Dr. Doolittle lives called?

ANSWERS

1 *Troilus and Cressida* 2 Arthur Conan Doyle 3 *The Great Gatsby* 4 Pangram 5 Enid Bagnold 6 Robert Burns 7 Shirley 8 *Lolita* 9 Herbert Ernest 10 Puddleby on Marsh

Scientifically Speaking

1 What type of instrument uses two or more lenses to make small objects appear much larger?

2 What in the body is the *deltoid* an example of?

3 What type of professional performs root canal treatments?

4 What name is given to the graphic recording of the electrical changes in the heart?

5 What metal does the chemical symbol Zn represent?

6 What is the closest natural satellite to Earth?

7 What did Ladislao Biro invent in 1933?

8 Which black-and-white mammal is of the genus *Equus*?

9 If an insect flaps its wings 30 times a second, how many times will it flap them in two minutes?

10 Pneumonia affects what part of the body?

BACKGROUND BONUS

What flower takes its name from the Turkish word for "turban"?

LEVEL 3 · QUIZ 153

ANSWERS
1 Microscope **2** Muscles **3** A dentist **4** ECG (electrocardiogram) **5** Zinc **6** The Moon **7** The ballpoint pen **8** Zebra **9** 3,600 **10** The lungs
Background Bonus Tulip

Making History

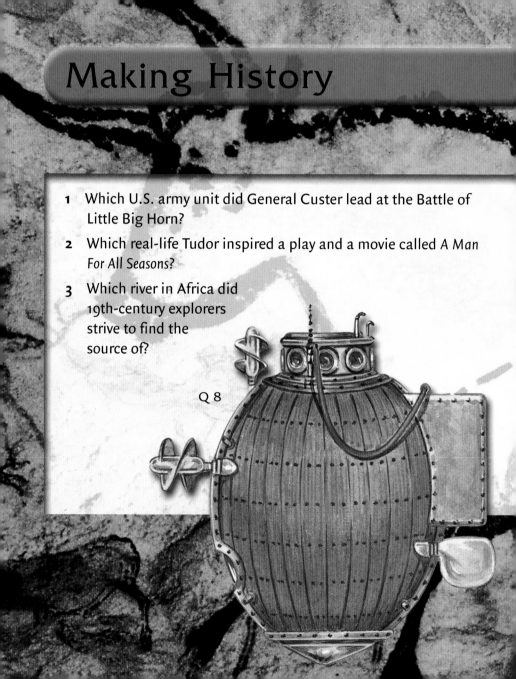

1 Which U.S. army unit did General Custer lead at the Battle of Little Big Horn?

2 Which real-life Tudor inspired a play and a movie called *A Man For All Seasons?*

3 Which river in Africa did 19th-century explorers strive to find the source of?

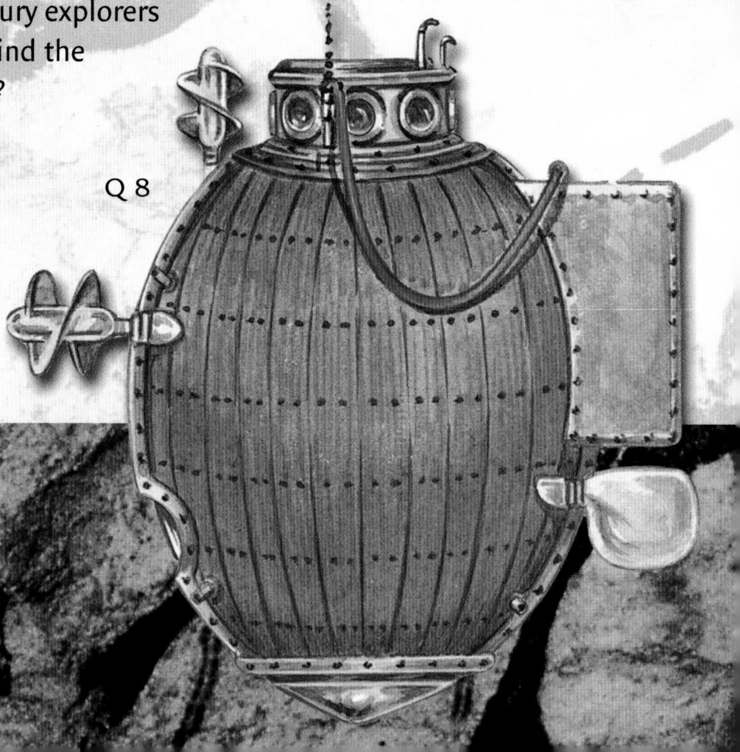

Q 8

4 Which bridge in London can open and close?

5 In 1971, East Pakistan became an independent country. What was it called?

6 What kind of prehistoric works of art were found in caves at Lascaux, France?

7 Balboa was the first European to see what, in 1513?

8 Was the *Turtle* of 1778 an early submarine, a tank or a rocket?

9 What country was the first to introduce the metric system of weights and measures, in 1795?

10 What islands was the Portuguese sea captain, Magellan, visiting when he was killed in a fight between rival tribes?

ANSWERS

1 The Seventh Cavalry 2 Sir Thomas More 3 The Nile 4 Tower Bridge 5 Bangladesh 6 Wall paintings 7 The Pacific Ocean 8 An early submarine 9 France 10 The Philippines

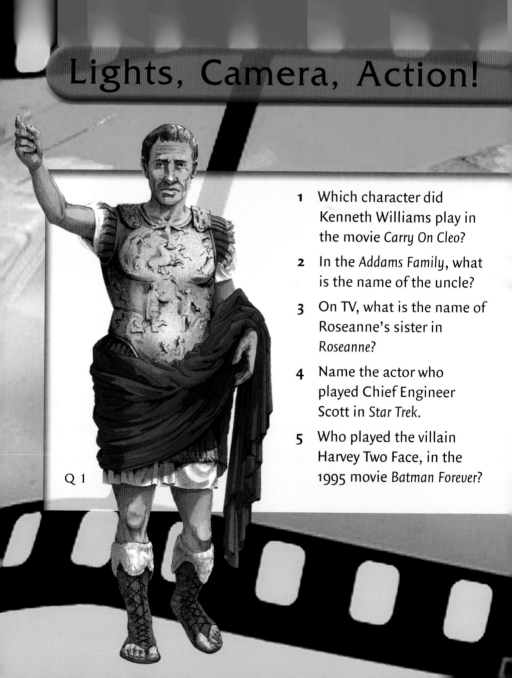

Lights, Camera, Action!

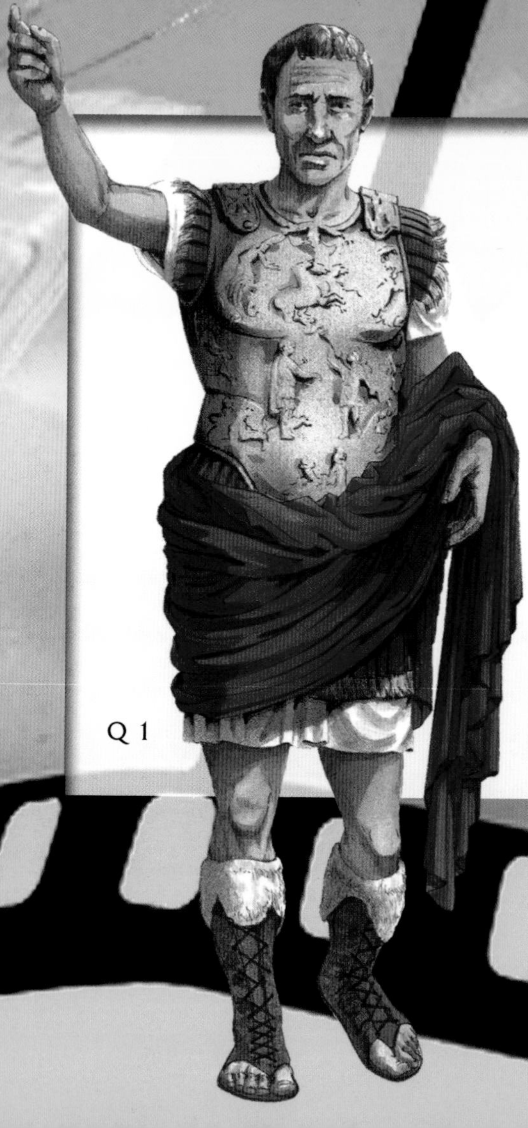

Q 1

1 Which character did Kenneth Williams play in the movie *Carry On Cleo?*

2 In the *Addams Family*, what is the name of the uncle?

3 On TV, what is the name of Roseanne's sister in *Roseanne?*

4 Name the actor who played Chief Engineer Scott in *Star Trek*.

5 Who played the villain Harvey Two Face, in the 1995 movie *Batman Forever?*

6 Which Belgian actor played a law enforcer in the movie *Timecop*?

7 What vehicle was Jock Ewing in when he was killed in the TV soap, *Dallas*?

8 Which female criminal was the subject of the movie *Dance With a Stranger*?

9 What author wrote the dramas *Pennies From Heaven* and *The Singing Detective*?

10 Which *Friends* star married Brad Pitt?

ANSWERS

1 Julius Caesar 2 Fester 3 Jackie 4 James Doohan 5 Tommy Lee Jones
6 Jean-Claude Van Damme 7 Helicopter 8 Ruth Ellis 9 Dennis Potter
10 Jennifer Aniston

Animal Antics

Can you guess the names of these animals from their fur, feathers and skin?

1

2

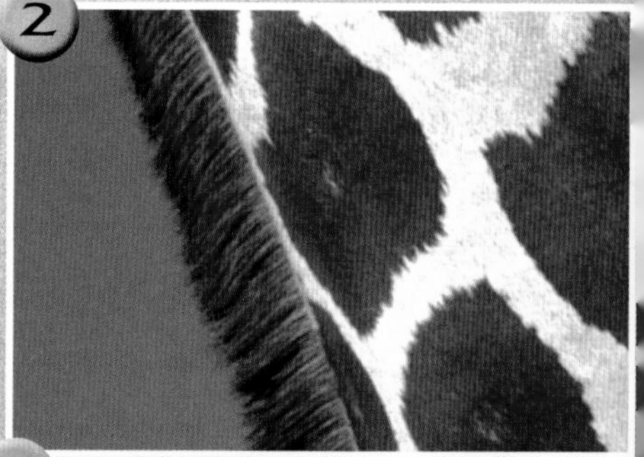

3

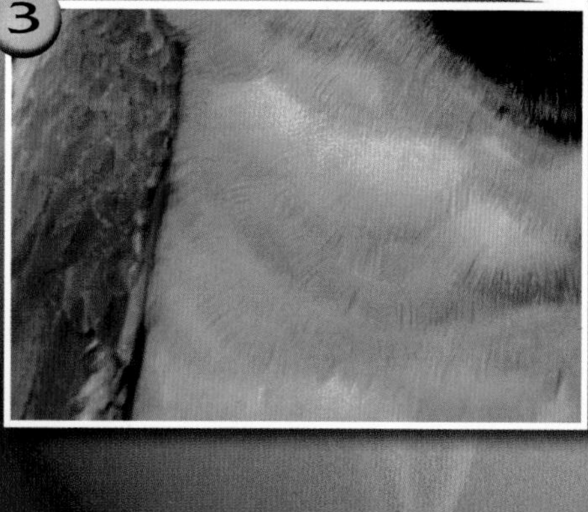

4

5

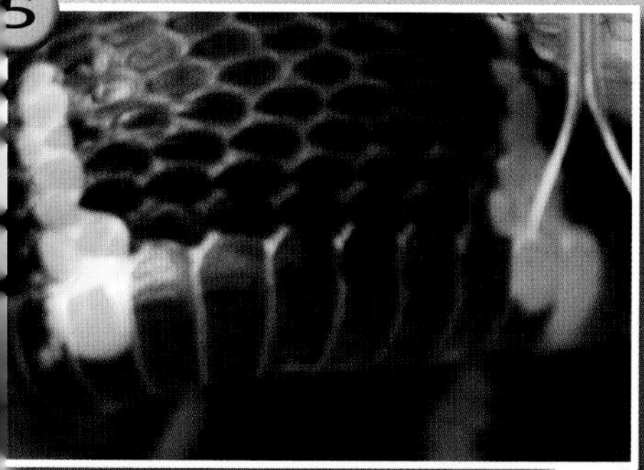

6

7

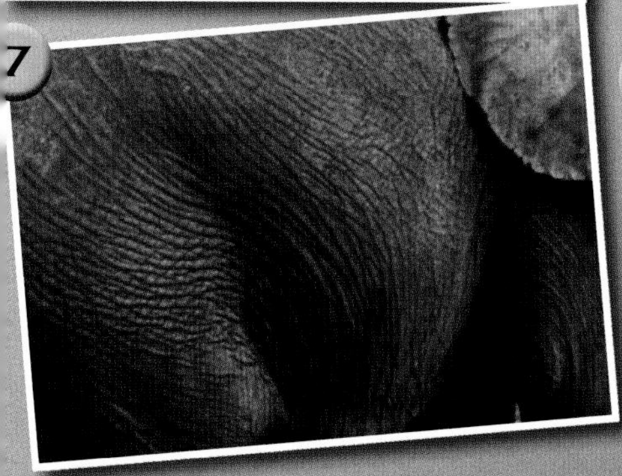

8

ANSWERS

1 Cheetah **2** Giraffe **3** Macaw **4** Butterfly **5** Snake **6** Lion **7** Elephant **8** Squirrel

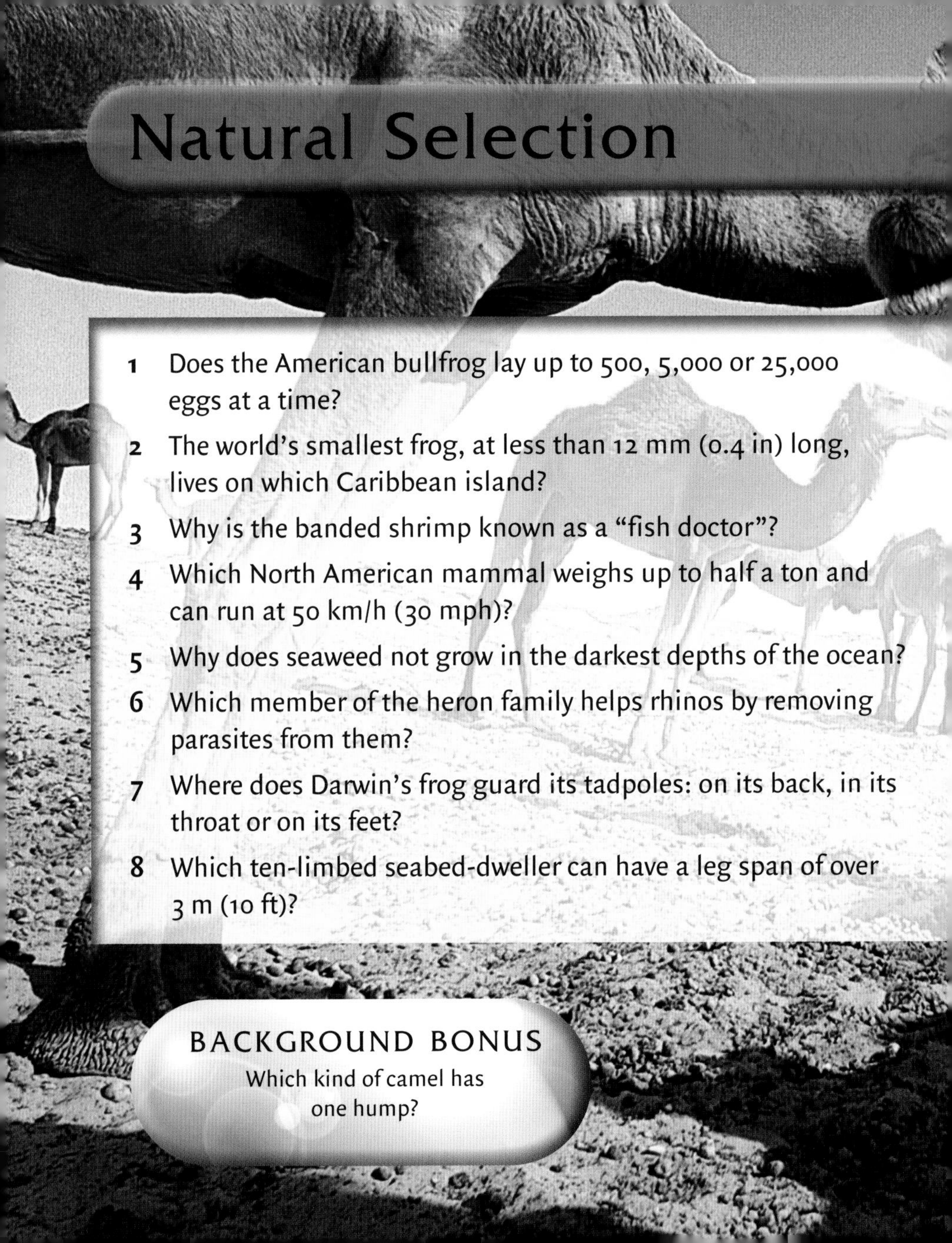

Natural Selection

1 Does the American bullfrog lay up to 500, 5,000 or 25,000 eggs at a time?

2 The world's smallest frog, at less than 12 mm (0.4 in) long, lives on which Caribbean island?

3 Why is the banded shrimp known as a "fish doctor"?

4 Which North American mammal weighs up to half a ton and can run at 50 km/h (30 mph)?

5 Why does seaweed not grow in the darkest depths of the ocean?

6 Which member of the heron family helps rhinos by removing parasites from them?

7 Where does Darwin's frog guard its tadpoles: on its back, in its throat or on its feet?

8 Which ten-limbed seabed-dweller can have a leg span of over 3 m (10 ft)?

BACKGROUND BONUS

Which kind of camel has one hump?

9 What member of the camel family was tamed 4,000 years ago in the Andes?

10 What bird of prey has New World and Old World varieties?

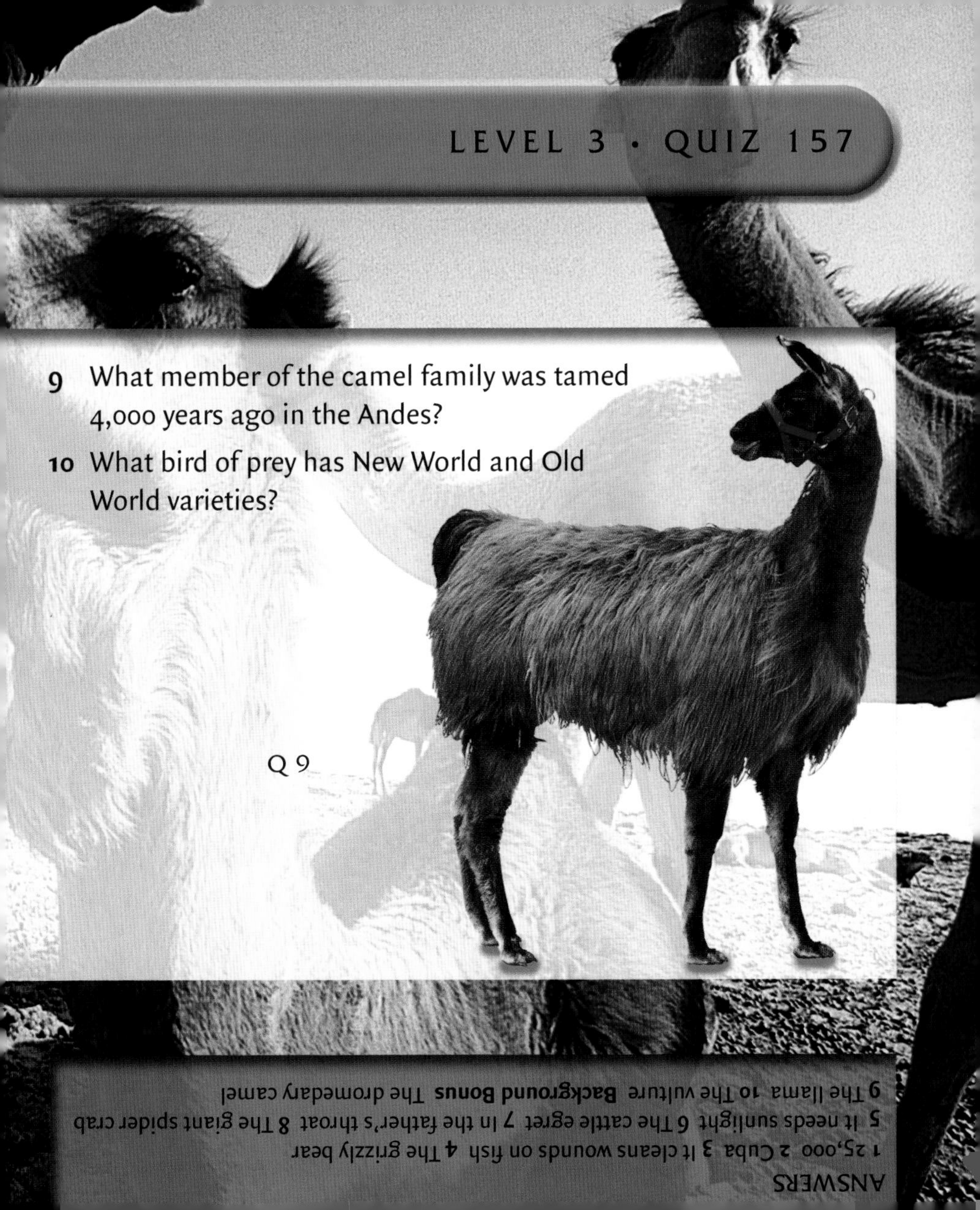

Q 9

ANSWERS

1 25,000 **2** Cuba **3** It cleans wounds on fish **4** The grizzly bear **5** It needs sunlight **6** The cattle egret **7** In the father's throat **8** The giant spider crab **9** The llama **10** The vulture **Background Bonus** The dromedary camel

Sporting Chance

Q 10

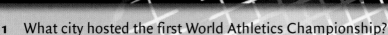

1 What city hosted the first World Athletics Championship?

2 In which U.S. city is the Pimlico horse racing track?

3 What sport employs the Stableford scoring system?

4 In which city is the Flinders Park tennis stadium?

5 Who was the first female tennis player to achieve the Grand Slam title?

6 In which U.S. city can the Kronk boxing stadium be found?

7 In the 1970s, what team won the World Series in three consecutive years?

8 Where is the world's highest golf course?

9 At what event was Al Oerter crowned Olympic champion in four successive games?

10 For which car company did Enzo Ferrari drive racing cars?

ANSWERS

1 Japan **2** A greyhound **3** 11 **4** Racketball **5** Silver **6** A bear **7** Virginia Wade **8** La Paz Golf Club, Bolivia **9** Discus **10** Alfa Romeo

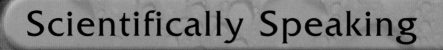

Scientifically Speaking

1 Which is larger: Mars or Saturn?

2 In 1782, which French brothers flew in a hot air balloon?

3 Combustion is the scientific term for what process?

4 In what disease do some of the body's cells go out of control and multiply?

5 Iron will only rust if exposed to air and what other substance?

6 What line of tropic runs through South America, Africa, and Australia?

7 If an engineer is measuring a moving object's RPMs, what is being checked?

8 Which two muscles are used to lift the forearm?

9 Which small weapon did Samuel Colt invent in 1835?

10 A block and tackle is a group of what?

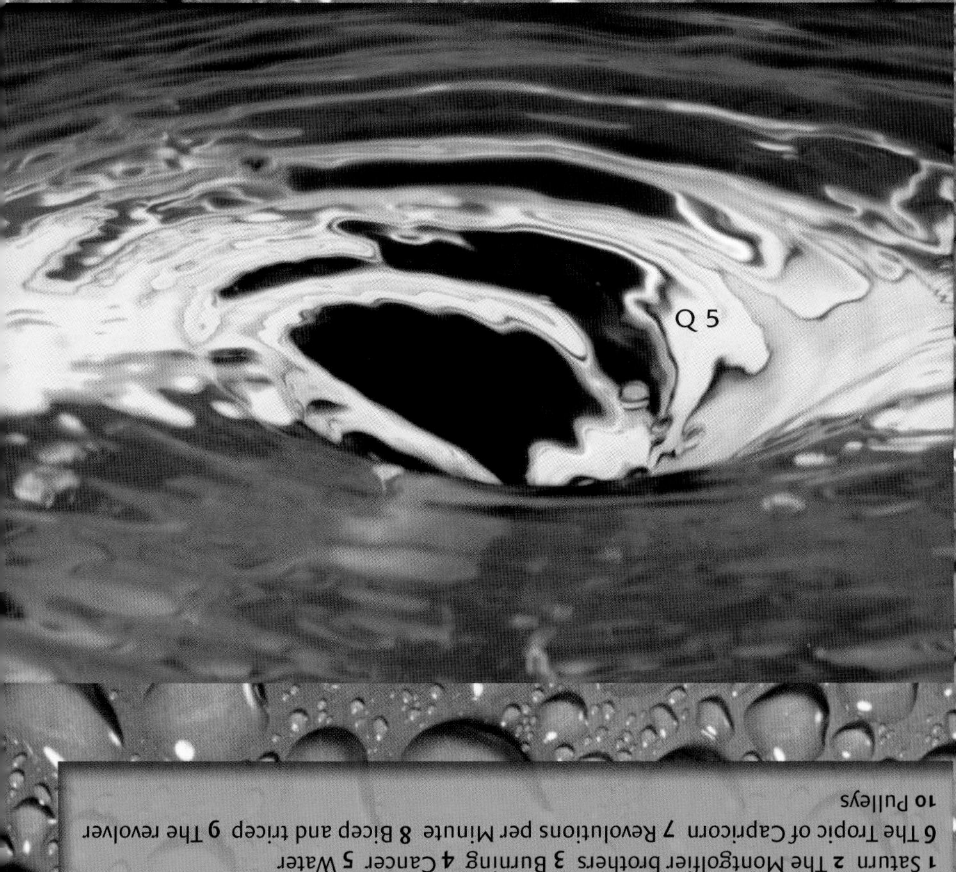

ANSWERS

1 Saturn **2** The Montgolfier brothers **3** Burning **4** Cancer **5** Water **6** The Tropic of Capricorn **7** Revolutions per Minute **8** Bicep and tricep **9** The revolver **10** Pulleys

Total Trivia

LEVEL 3 • QUIZ 160

1 What have larger ears: African or Indian elephants?

2 Could you jump higher on the Moon or on Earth?

3 Why do spiders build webs?

4 What countries make up Scandinavia?

5 What happens when an eclipse of the Sun occurs?

6 What does "to throw in the towel" mean?

7 Who wrote *The Twits*?

8 In which sport can you make a hole-in-one?

9 What was the code name for the day the Allied forces landed in Normandy during World War II?

10 What is the collective name for knives, forks and spoons?

Q 5

ANSWERS

1 African elephants 2 On the Moon 3 To catch their prey 4 Norway, Sweden and Denmark 5 The Moon hides the Sun from the Earth 6 To admit defeat 7 Roald Dahl 8 Golf 9 D-Day 10 Cutlery

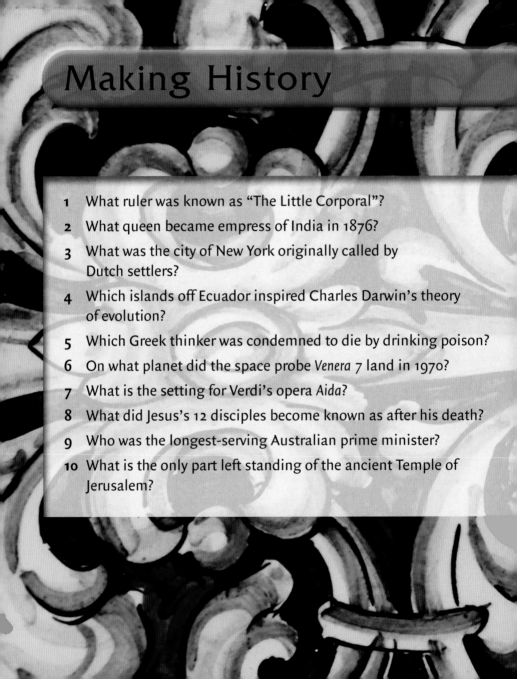

Making History

1. What ruler was known as "The Little Corporal"?
2. What queen became empress of India in 1876?
3. What was the city of New York originally called by Dutch settlers?
4. Which islands off Ecuador inspired Charles Darwin's theory of evolution?
5. Which Greek thinker was condemned to die by drinking poison?
6. On what planet did the space probe *Venera 7* land in 1970?
7. What is the setting for Verdi's opera *Aida*?
8. What did Jesus's 12 disciples become known as after his death?
9. Who was the longest-serving Australian prime minister?
10. What is the only part left standing of the ancient Temple of Jerusalem?

ANSWERS

1 Napoleon 2 Queen Victoria 3 New Amsterdam 4 Galapagos Islands 5 Socrates 6 On Venus 7 Ancient Egypt 8 The Apostles 9 Robert Menzies 10 The Western (Wailing) Wall

Written Word

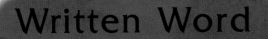

1 Who is the world's most successful horror writer, with books including *Misery*, *Rose Madder* and *The Shining*?

2 What was the name of Winnie the Pooh's small friend?

3 What word can mean to hobble and is also used to describe something that is floppy?

Q 4

LEVEL 3 • QUIZ 162

4 If canine equals dog what does vulpine equal?

5 Is a rotunda a round, domed building, a round musical instrument or a round brooch?

6 Which English word derives from the Italian meaning "little ball": balloon, ballot or ballet?

7 Who wrote *Sons and Lovers*?

8 Is a coracle: a prophet, a council meeting place, or a boat?

9 How does *Anno Domini* translate into English?

10 Dendrophobia is the morbid fear of what?

BACKGROUND BONUS

Which play by Alfred Uhry was made into an Oscar-winning movie?

ANSWERS

1 Stephen King **2** Piglet **3** Limp **4** Fox **5** A round domed building **6** Ballot **7** D.H. Lawrence **8** A boat **9** In the year of our Lord **10** Trees

Background Bonus *Driving Miss Daisy*

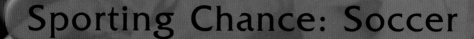

Sporting Chance: Soccer

1 In the 1940s, why was Maine Road host to Manchester United's home games?

2 Despite qualifying for the 1950 World Cup, why was India banned from competing?

3 Who was sacked as manager of Leeds United FC in June 2002?

4 Which paint company sponsored Liverpool when they won the double in 1986?

5 Which former Italian international soccer player was sacked as manager of Watford FC in 2002?

6 In 1931, what was the first London club to win the League title?

7 Who scored the winner when West Germany won the 1974 World Cup?

8 What team plays at the Nou Camp?

9 What nationality is former Arsenal player Christopher Wreh?

10 Which World Cup winner was sacked as manager of Portsmouth in 1999?

Q 9

ANSWERS
1 Old Trafford had been bombed **2** They refused to wear boots **3** David O'Leary **4** Crown Paints **5** Gianluca Vialli **6** Arsenal **7** Gerd Muller **8** Barcelona **9** Liberian **10** Alan Ball

Global Matters

1 What was the name of Austria's currency before the euro?

2 Valparaiso is a city in which South American country?

3 What is the capital of Australia's Northern Territory?

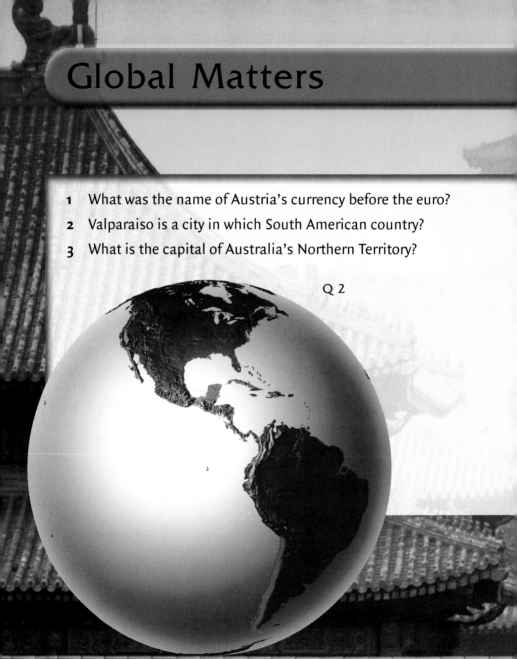

Q 2

LEVEL 3 • QUIZ 164

4 The Tagus river is found in which European country?

5 Which Asian country builds one in six of the world's ships: Japan, South Korea or Taiwan?

6 What nationality was the writer Mark Twain?

7 An artificial lake used to store water for drinking or to make electricity is known as what?

8 In which country would you find the city of Shanghai?

9 The Great Mosque at Djenne is in which African country?

10 If you were watching cricket at Galle or Kandy, what country would you be visiting?

ANSWERS

1 Schilling **2** Chile **3** Darwin **4** Portugal **5** South Korea **6** American **7** Reservoir **8** China **9** Mali **10** Sri Lanka

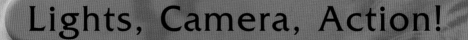

Lights, Camera, Action!

1 In which 2003 movie does Nick Nolte play the father of Dr. Bruce Banner?

2 What actor was America's most decorated soldier of World War II?

3 Who played the writer Joan Wilder in both *Romancing the Stone* and *Jewel of the Nile?*

4 In which movie did Jennifer Grey play the character of Baby Houseman?

Q 6

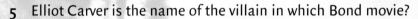

5 Elliot Carver is the name of the villain in which Bond movie?

6 Which 1990 movie features Leonardo, Donatello, Michelangelo and Raphael?

7 In which 1982 movie did Dustin Hoffman play the characters of Michael and Dorothy?

8 What was Cary Grant's real name?

9 In which movie did Elton John sing "Pinball Wizard"?

10 Who plays the role of Leo Getz in the *Lethal Weapon* movies?

BACKGROUND BONUS

Which Sinbad movie features a feline in its title?

ANSWERS

1 Hulk **2** Audie Murphy **3** Kathleen Turner **4** *Dirty Dancing* **5** *Tomorrow Never Dies* **6** *Teenage Mutant Ninja Turtles* **7** *Tootsie* **8** Archibald Leach **9** *Tommy* **10** Joe Pesci

Background Bonus *Sinbad and the Eye of the Tiger*

Making History

1 Which Native American people defeated General Custer at the Battle of Little Big Horn?

2 Who was the leader of the team that reached the South Pole in second place?

3 What was the last battle fought by Horatio Nelson?

4 Who did Britain fight in the 1839 Opium War ?

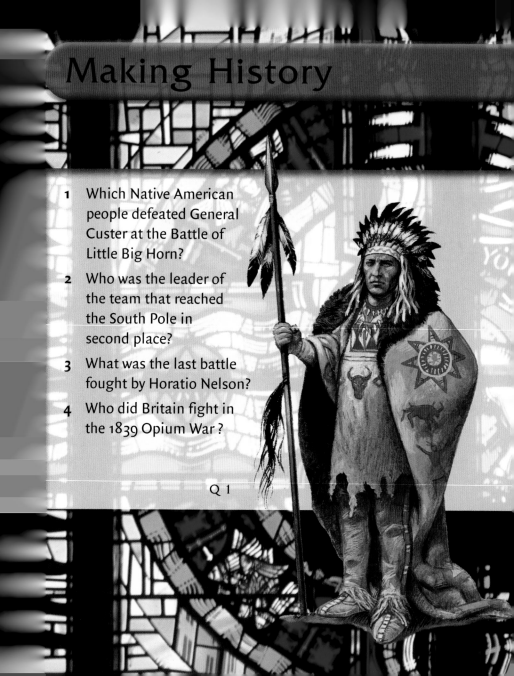

5 What emperor announced in 1946 that he was no longer a god?

6 Who wrote *The Lord of the Flies?*

7 At what siege did Davy Crockett die in 1836?

8 Which drink was invented by Dom Perignon?

9 Which waterfall in Africa was named after a British queen?

10 What pair of aviators first flew the Atlantic in 1919?

ANSWERS

1 Sioux **2** R.F. Scott **3** Trafalgar **4** The Chinese **5** Hirohito of Japan **6** William Golding **7** The Alamo **8** Champagne **9** Victoria Falls **10** John Alcock and Arthur Brown

Sporting Chance

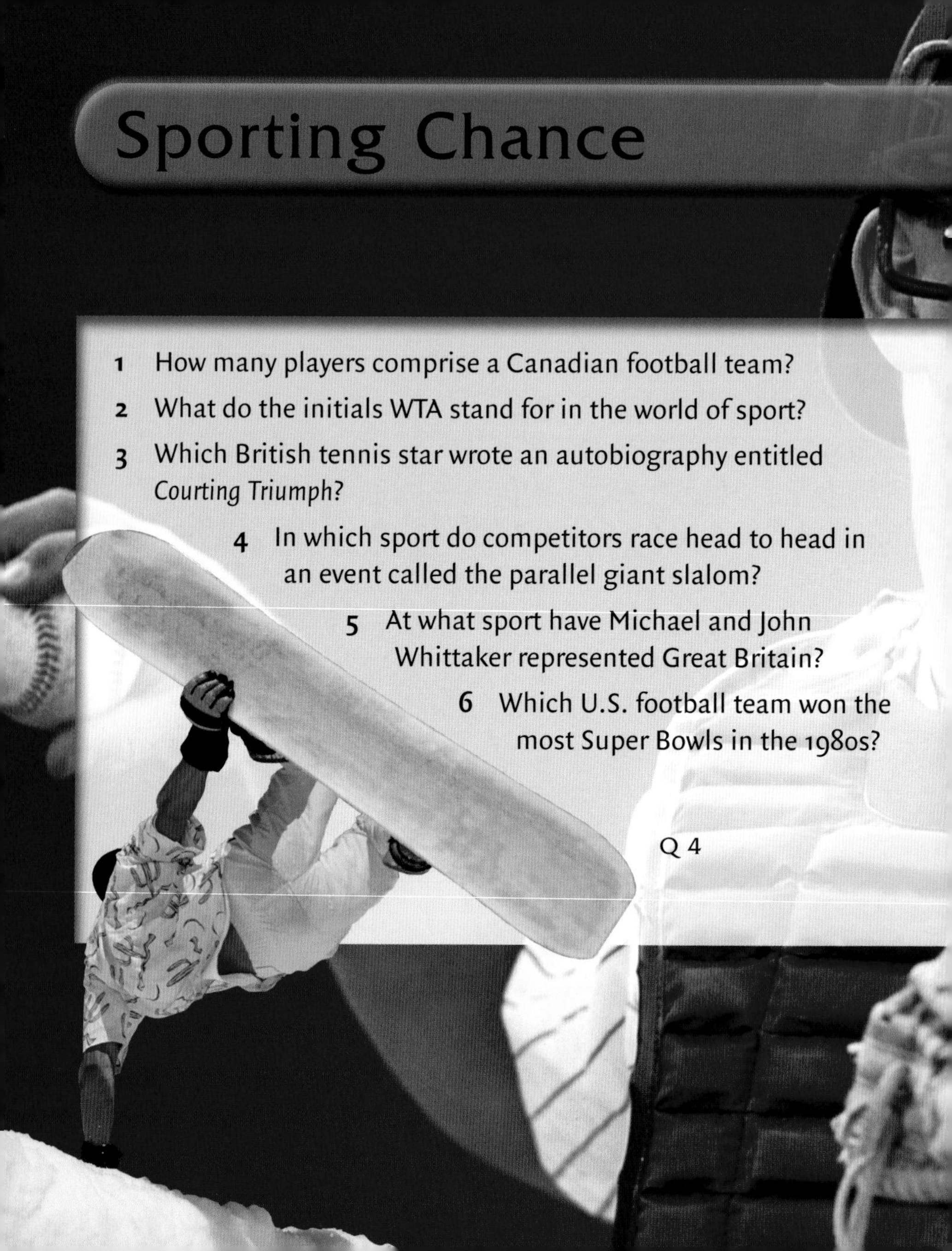

1 How many players comprise a Canadian football team?

2 What do the initials WTA stand for in the world of sport?

3 Which British tennis star wrote an autobiography entitled *Courting Triumph*?

4 In which sport do competitors race head to head in an event called the parallel giant slalom?

5 At what sport have Michael and John Whittaker represented Great Britain?

6 Which U.S. football team won the most Super Bowls in the 1980s?

Q 4

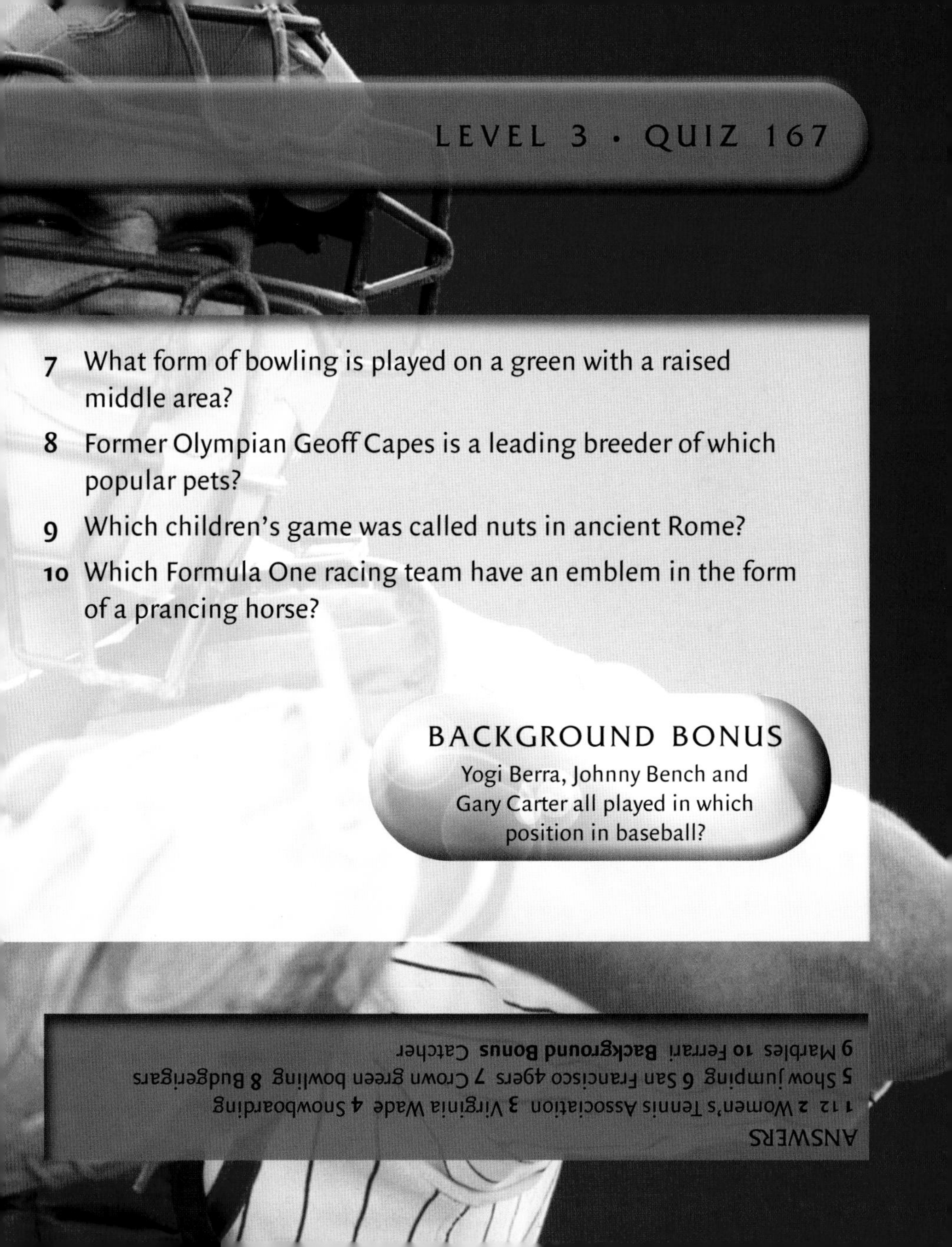

7 What form of bowling is played on a green with a raised middle area?

8 Former Olympian Geoff Capes is a leading breeder of which popular pets?

9 Which children's game was called nuts in ancient Rome?

10 Which Formula One racing team have an emblem in the form of a prancing horse?

BACKGROUND BONUS

Yogi Berra, Johnny Bench and Gary Carter all played in which position in baseball?

ANSWERS

1 12 **2** Women's Tennis Association **3** Virginia Wade **4** Snowboarding **5** Show jumping **6** San Francisco 49ers **7** Crown green bowling **8** Budgerigars **9** Marbles **10** Ferrari **Background Bonus** Catcher

Feeding Frenzy

Can you identify each of the foods in these pictures?

5

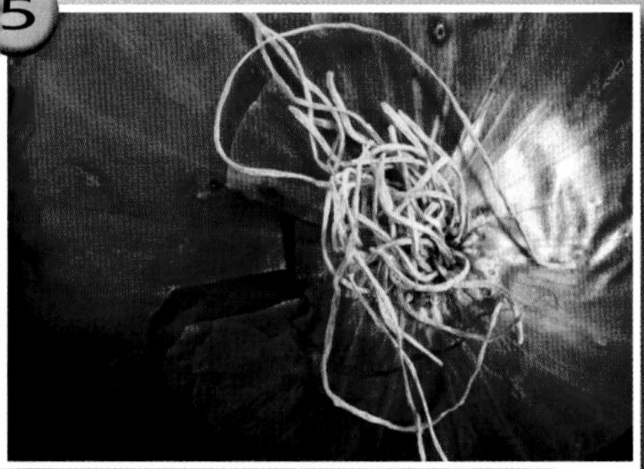

6

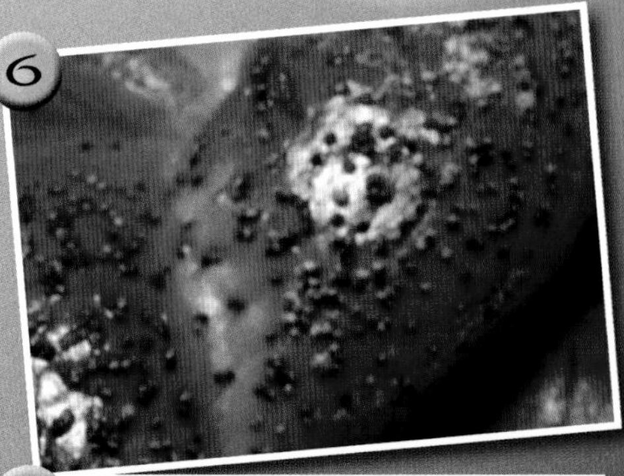

7

8

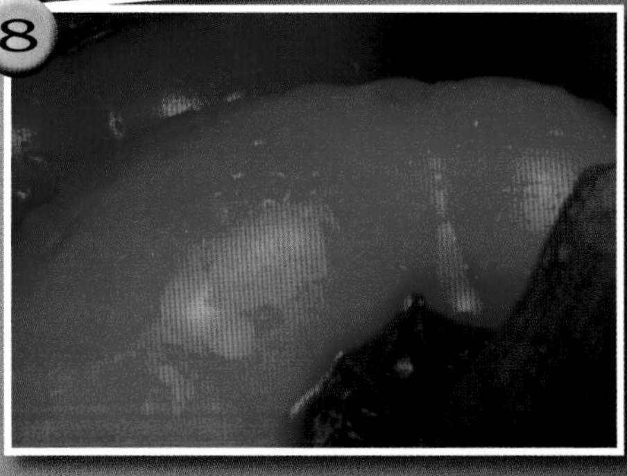

ANSWERS

1 Strawberry 2 Garlic 3 Pear 4 Tomato 5 Onion 6 Bread 7 Kiwi 8 Pepper

Written Word

1 Which book about a horse did Anna Sewell write?

2 Who wrote *My Family and Other Animals?*

3 Which Shakespeare play features the characters Viola, Malvolio and Sir Toby Belch?

4 What is the literal English translation of the Italian word *veto*?

5 In the novel 1984, what language do the authorities try to introduce?

6 Which S word is the name given to the highest order of angels in the celestial hierarchy?

7 *Captain Corelli's Mandolin* is set on which Greek island?

8 Bathsheba Everdene is the heroine of which novel by Thomas Hardy?

9 What is unusual about the word "facetious"?

10 What is a *croque monsieur*?

Q 10

ANSWERS

1 *Black Beauty* **2** Gerald Durrell **3** *Twelfth Night* **4** I forbid **5** Newspeak **6** Seraphim **7** Kephalonia **8** *Far From the Madding Crowd* **9** All the vowels appear in order **10** A toasted ham and cheese sandwich

Total Trivia

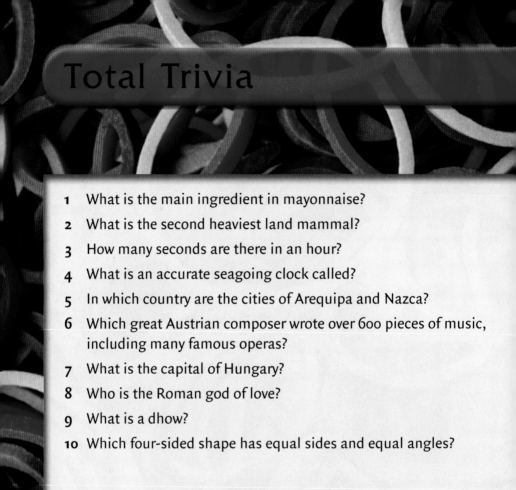

1 What is the main ingredient in mayonnaise?
2 What is the second heaviest land mammal?
3 How many seconds are there in an hour?
4 What is an accurate seagoing clock called?
5 In which country are the cities of Arequipa and Nazca?
6 Which great Austrian composer wrote over 600 pieces of music, including many famous operas?
7 What is the capital of Hungary?
8 Who is the Roman god of love?
9 What is a dhow?
10 Which four-sided shape has equal sides and equal angles?

LEVEL 3 • QUIZ 170

Q 1

ANSWERS

1 Egg yolk **2** The hippopotamus **3** 3,600 **4** A chronometer **5** Peru **6** Wolfgang Amadeus Mozart **7** Budapest **8** Aphrodite **9** An Arab sailing ship **10** A square

Written Word

Q 9

1 What part of the body is affected by glossitis?

2 What name is shared by a heavily spiked club and the spice made from nutmeg?

LEVEL 3 · QUIZ 171

3 Which A word describes a circular coral reef growing on top of a submerged mountain?

4 Which F word is the name given to the metal ribs on the fingerboard of a guitar?

5 What is the name of the sequel to *Bridget Jones's Diary?*

6 Which English king was portrayed by Shakespeare as a murderous hunchback?

7 Eugenics is the study of what?

8 If a meeting is held *sub rosa* what does this mean?

9 Which Italian poet wrote the *Divina Commedia?*

10 In which city is Shakespeare's *Romeo and Juliet* set?

ANSWERS

1 The tongue **2** Mace **3** Atoll **4** Frets **5** *The Edge of Reason* **6** Richard III **7** Selective breeding **8** In secret **9** Dante **10** Verona

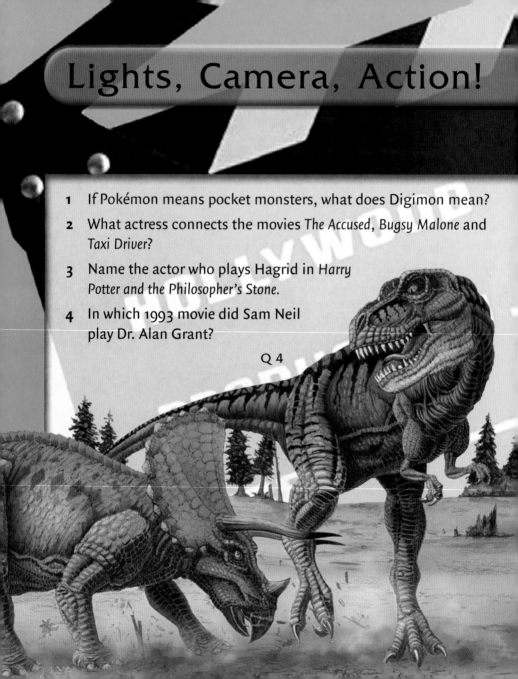

Lights, Camera, Action!

1 If Pokémon means pocket monsters, what does Digimon mean?

2 What actress connects the movies *The Accused*, *Bugsy Malone* and *Taxi Driver*?

3 Name the actor who plays Hagrid in *Harry Potter and the Philosopher's Stone.*

4 In which 1993 movie did Sam Neil play Dr. Alan Grant?

Q 4

5 Who played boat owner Charlie Allnut in the movie *The African Queen?*

6 In which country was *Dr. Zhivago* set?

7 In which country was Omar Sharif born?

8 In which 1987 movie did Michael Douglas play stockbroker Gordon Gecko?

9 Who provided the voice of Z-4195 in the 1998 movie *Antz?*

10 What bird inspired Walter Lantz to create his famous cartoon character, Woody?

ANSWERS
1 Digital monsters **2** Jodie Foster **3** Robbie Coltrane **4** *Jurassic Park*
5 Humphrey Bogart **6** Russia **7** Eygpt **8** *Wall Street* **9** Woody Allen **10** A woodpecker

Total Trivia

LEVEL 3 · QUIZ 173

1 What country has borders with France, Germany and Holland?

2 Which sea creature has species called European, Norway, spiny and American?

3 In which ocean is the island of Mauritius?

4 In which city are the main administrative offices of the European Union?

5 What type of animal is a grebe?

6 What country invaded Kuwait in 1990?

7 Which dish from New Orleans consists of rice, seafood, green peppers and spices?

8 What is an anemometer?

9 What is the capital of Mexico?

10 What do you call the coat of a sheep?

ANSWERS

1 Belgium **2** Lobster **3** The Indian Ocean **4** Brussels **5** A bird **6** Iraq **7** Jambalaya **8** A wind gauge **9** Mexico City **10** Fleece

Lights, Camera, Action!

1 Which famous composer was played by Tom Hulce in a 1984 Oscar-winning movie?

2 The movie *The Killing Fields* was set in what country?

3 Is Grandpa Simpson called Isaac, Abraham or Jacob?

4 What is the name of Bruce Wayne's butler in *Batman*?

5 What was the last movie that James Dean starred in?

6 In the movie *Romancing the Stone*, what kind of animal did the writer Joan Wilder own?

7 What is the title of the 1997 movie in which John Travolta plays an angel?

8 Which Hollywood actor, star of the movie *Some Like it Hot*, died in 2001 aged 76?

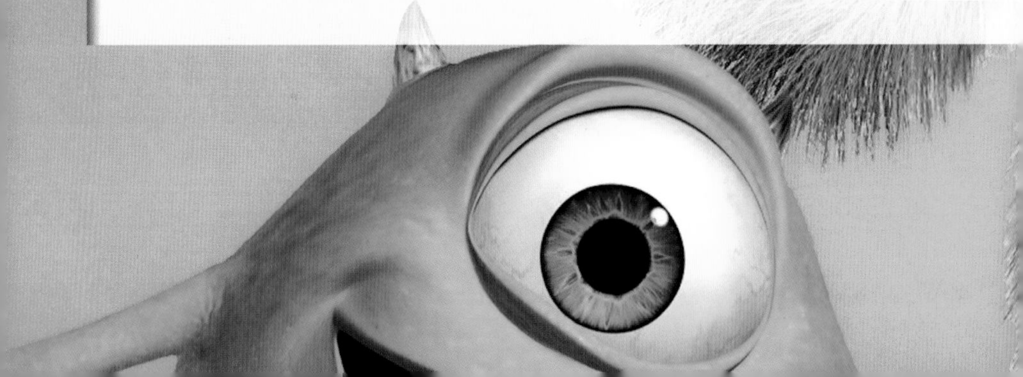

9 Who plays the character of Molly Brown in the 1997 disaster movie *Titanic?*

10 What instrument plays the theme music to the movie *O Brother, Where Art Thou?*

Q 8

ANSWERS
1 Wolfgang Amadeus Mozart 2 Cambodia 3 Abraham 4 Alfred 5 Giant 6 Iguana
7 Michael 8 Jack Lemmon 9 Kathy Bates 10 The banjo

Total Trivia

1 What is the hottest planet in our Solar System?

2 Where would you find a ligament?

3 Which western European nation has the largest population?

4 What river flows through Vienna?

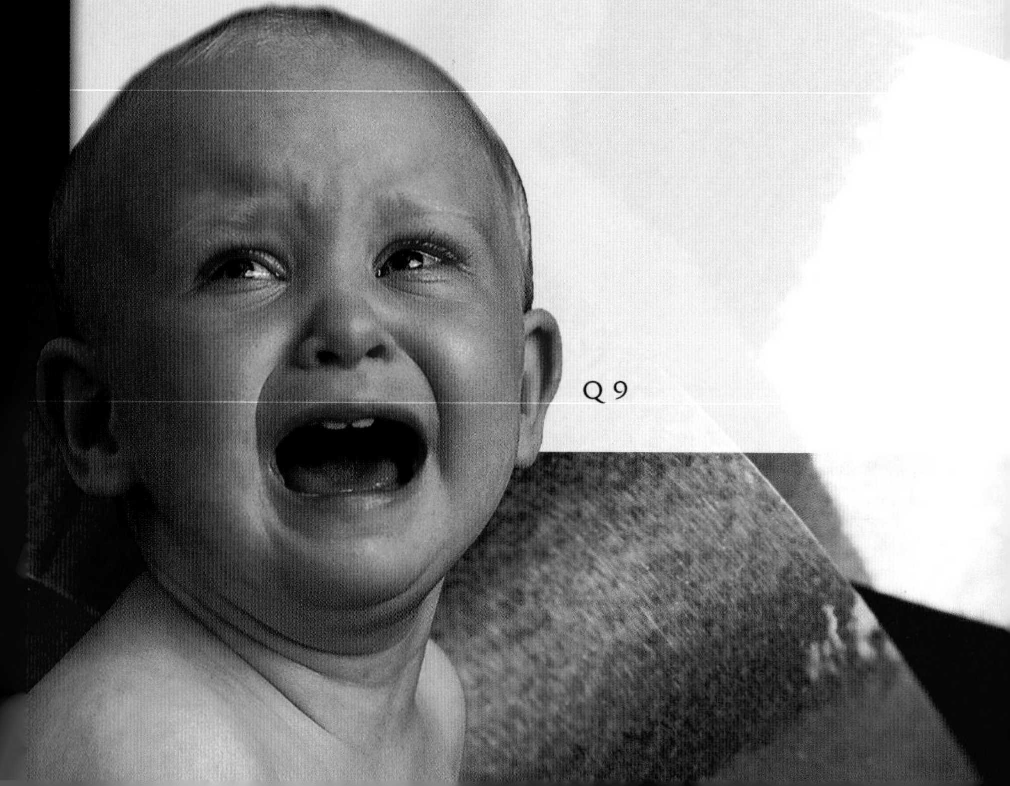

Q 9

5 Which emperor died in St. Helena?

6 One-third is approximately what as a decimal fraction?

7 What insect has larvae called daphnia?

8 Which African country takes its name from the Spanish for lion mountains?

9 What do the lachrymal glands produce?

10 What is the Irish name for Ireland?

ANSWERS

1 Mercury 2 In a joint 3 Germany (about 80 million people) 4 The Danube 5 Napoleon, in 1821 6 0.333 7 Dragonfly 8 Sierra Leone 9 Tears 10 Eire

Music Mania

Q 6

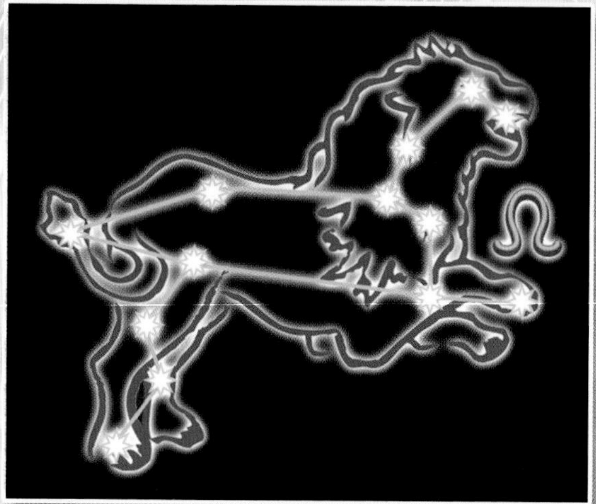

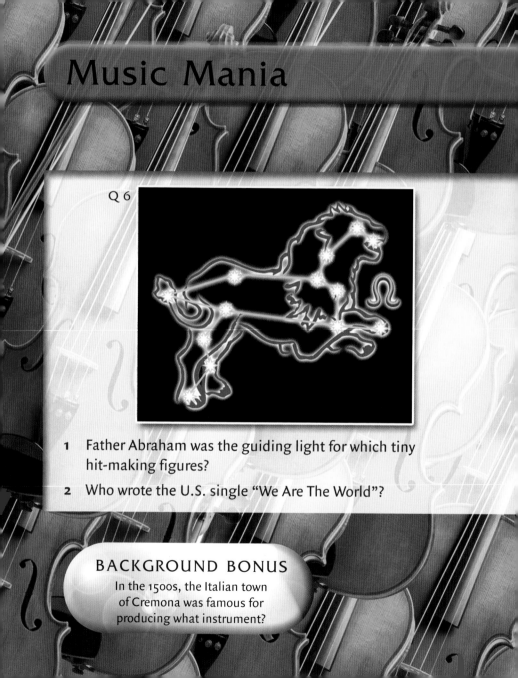

1 Father Abraham was the guiding light for which tiny hit-making figures?

2 Who wrote the U.S. single "We Are The World"?

BACKGROUND BONUS

In the 1500s, the Italian town of Cremona was famous for producing what instrument?

LEVEL 3 • QUIZ 176

3 Who wrote the Madonna hit song “Justify My Love”?

4 Who legally adopted a symbol to replace his name in 1993?

5 Who recorded “We All Stand Together” with The Frog Chorus?

6 “When I Need You” was a U.K. hit for what singer?

7 *The Rise and Fall* and *Keep Moving* were 1980s albums for which U.K. band?

8 Who joined Eurythmics on the song “Sisters Are Doin’ It For Themselves”?

9 What rapper performed at Bill Clinton’s inauguration?

10 “Hangin’ Tough” was a No.1 hit for which U.S. boy band?

ANSWERS

1 The Smurfs **2** Lionel Richie **3** Lenny Kravitz **4** Prince **5** Paul McCartney **6** Leo Sayer **7** Madness **8** Aretha Franklin **9** LL Cool J **10** New Kids on the Block

Background Bonus Violin

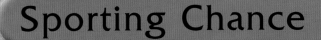

Sporting Chance

1 Petra Felke was the first woman to throw what over 80 m (260 ft)?

2 Which animal gives its name to an ice-skating move?

3 The name of what type of hall literally means naked exercise?

4 In chess, what moves with a rook in a move known as castling?

5 What is the highest grade awarded in judo?

6 Which former Wimbledon champion was knocked out of the 2002 tournament by an unseeded Swiss?

7 In tennis, does a ball travel faster on a grass or a clay court?

8 What sport is sometimes described as "bowls on ice"?

9 How many attempts is a pole-vaulter allowed at each height?

10 In 1980, what became the first communist country to win the Davis Cup in tennis?

Q8

ANSWERS

1 Javelin **2** Camel **3** Gymnasium **4** The king **5** 12th dan (white) **6** Pete Sampras **7** Grass court **8** Curling **9** Three **10** Czechoslovakia

Lights, Camera, Action!

1 In which country was *The Lord of the Rings* trilogy filmed?

2 Which star of the sitcom *Cheers* featured in the movie *Three Men and a Baby?*

3 Which famous model played the leading lady in *The Boy Friend?*

4 What is the name of the acting brother of Jeff Bridges?

5 Who links the movies *Seven* and *The Shawshank Redemption?*

6 Which singer played Breathless Mahoney in *Dick Tracy?*

7 What food do the Teenage Mutant Ninja Turtles like best?

8 Which James Bond comedy co-starred David Niven, Peter Sellers and Woody Allen?

9 Which pretty woman married Danny Moder in July 2002?

10 Who played the role of Gertie in ET?

BACKGROUND BONUS

What actress starred in the 1935 movie *Anna Karenina?*

ANSWERS

1 New Zealand **2** Ted Danson **3** Twiggy **4** Beau Bridges **5** Morgan Freeman **6** Madonna **7** Pizza **8** *Casino Royale* **9** Julia Roberts **10** Drew Barrymore

Background Bonus Greta Garbo

Total Trivia

1 What kind of heavenly body is made of very hot gas and gives out heat and light?

2 What name is given to a creature whose diet includes both plants and animals?

3 How many pairs of wings does a fly have?

4 In which country is McGill University?

5 Which Indian city produces more movies than Hollywood?

6 Where does the jaguar live?

7 In which country would you find a kibbutz?

8 What country is Beirut the capital of?

9 Which ancient civilization spilt a drop of blood every morning to please their gods?

10 What is the square of 11?

Q 1

ANSWERS

1 A star **2** An omnivore **3** Two **4** Canada **5** Bombay **6** In the forests of South America **7** Israel **8** Lebanon **9** The Aztecs **10** 121

Incredible Instruments

Can you guess the names of these eight musical instruments?

1

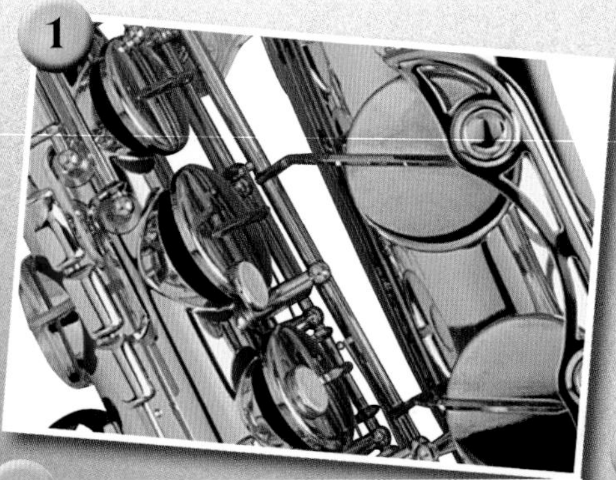

2

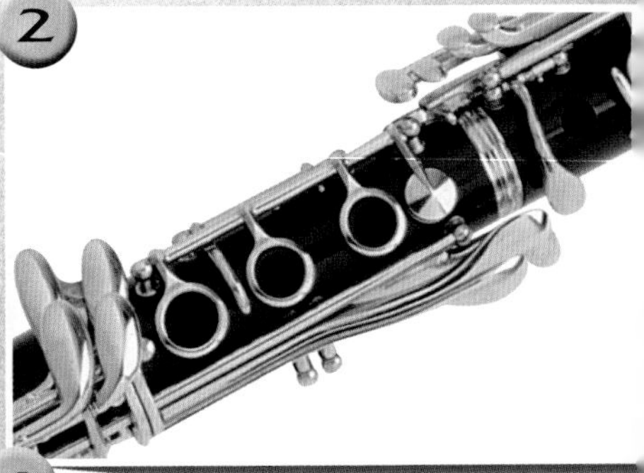

3

4

5

6

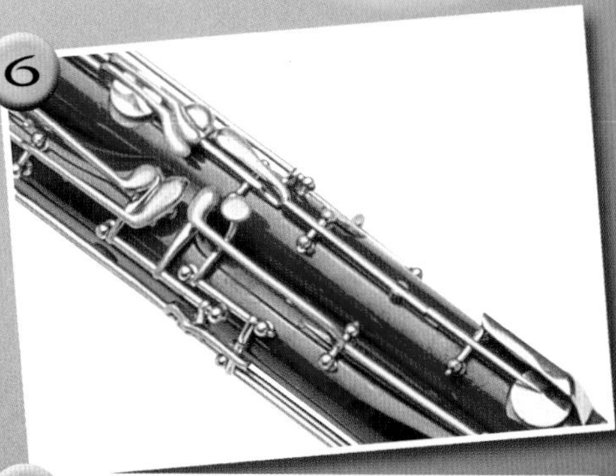

7

8

ANSWERS

1 Saxophone 2 Clarinet 3 Piano 4 Drum 5 Accordian 6 Bassoon 7 Harp 8 Guitar

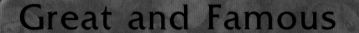

Great and Famous

1. Which U.S. actor of the 1940s and 1950s suffered a lip wound in World War I, giving him his distinctive appearance and voice?
2. In 1983, which English pop star was paid the highest sum ever to appear in a concert in California?
3. What was the name of the French inventor who devised a reading system for blind people?
4. Who wrote *Paradise Lost*?
5. Which fashion designer introduced the “New Look” in 1947?
6. *The Scream* and *The Dance of Life* were amongst which artist’s paintings?
7. The daughter of William Godwin and Mary Woolstencraft also became a famous writer. What was her name?

BACKGROUND BONUS

Which actress played the part of Sharon Stone in the 1994 movie *The Flintstones*?

8 Whose plays include *Uncle Vanya* and *The Three Sisters?*

9 Which writer created the character Jeeves?

10 Who was the second president of the United States?

Q 1

ANSWERS

1 Humphrey Bogart **2** David Bowie **3** Louis Braille **4** John Milton **5** Christian Dior **6** Edvard Munch **7** Mary Shelley **8** Anton Chekhov **9** P.G. Wodehouse **10** John Adams

Background Bonus Halle Berry

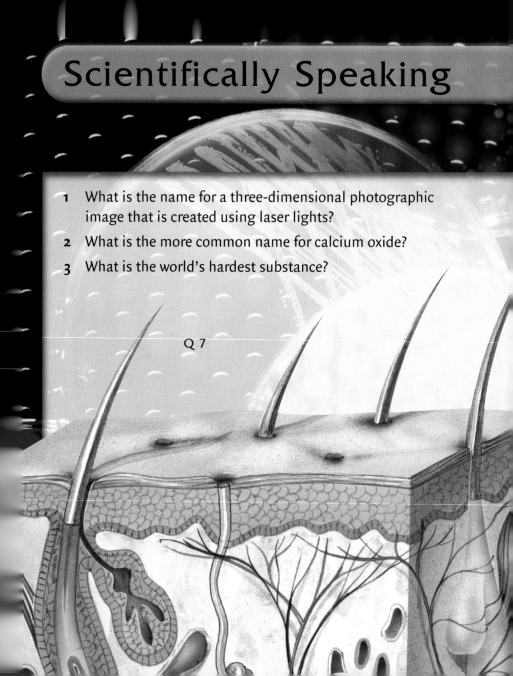

Scientifically Speaking

1. What is the name for a three-dimensional photographic image that is created using laser lights?
2. What is the more common name for calcium oxide?
3. What is the world's hardest substance?

Q 7

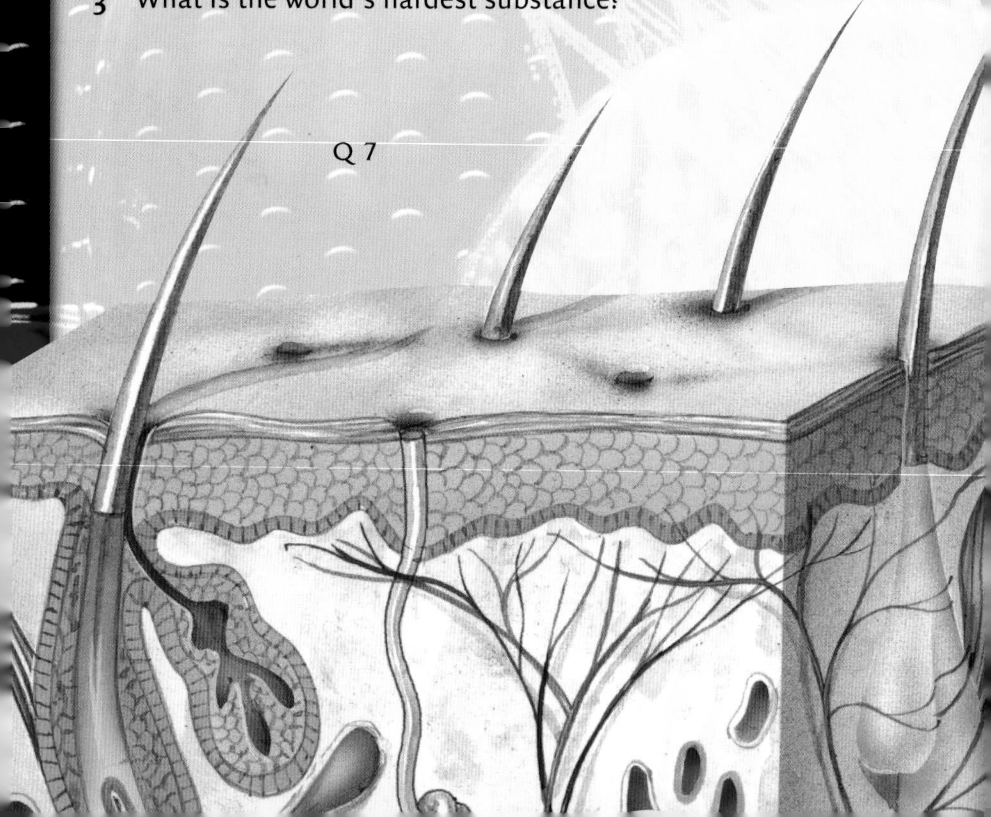

4 When water reaches its boiling point, what does it become?

5 What itchy condition, caused by a fungus, usually affects the area between the toes?

6 Which navigational device uses a magnet suspended or floated in a liquid?

7 What does a dermatologist study?

8 What gas makes up most of the air we breathe?

9 What is 20 percent of 20?

10 In which ocean does the Gulf Stream flow?

ANSWERS

1 Hologram **2** Quicklime **3** Diamond **4** Steam **5** Athlete's foot **6** A magnetic compass **7** The skin **8** Nitrogen (78.08%) **9** 4 **10** The Atlantic

Sporting Chance

1 How many players are in a handball team?

2 What is Frankie short for in the name of the jockey Frankie Dettori?

3 Which female athlete broke the world record at the 2003 London marathon?

4 What type of sporting contest includes calf roping and bull riding events?

5 Which athlete was stripped of the 100 m gold medal at the 1988 Olympics?

6 Which ice skater allegedly knew about the baton attack on her rival Nancy Kerrigan?

7 What city hosted the 1948 Summer Olympics?

8 In which sport do competitors make the Liffey Descent?

9 Which sports company are named after an African gazelle?

10 Mills Lane is a referee In which sport?

Q 9

ANSWERS

1 Seven 2 Lanfranco 3 Paula Radcliffe 4 Rodeo 5 Ben Johnson 6 Tonya Harding 7 London 8 Canoeing 9 Reebok 10 Boxing

Global Matters

Q 4

1 In which country are the headquarters of the International Olympic Committee?

2 What is the most common mineral found in rocks?

BACKGROUND BONUS

Which ancient Roman ruin once held crowds of 50,000 people?

3 What Polish city used to be known as Danzig?

4 In which country would you find Cape Guardafui?

5 A vehicle with the international registration ET comes from what country?

6 What sort of army is found in Xi'an, China?

7 Over what fish did Britain and Iceland battle in the 1970s?

8 What is the former name for Taiwan?

9 Which city is known as "the eternal city"?

10 Which four U.S. states begin and end with the same letter?

ANSWERS

1 Switzerland **2** Quartz **3** Gdansk **4** Somalia **5** Egypt **6** Terracotta army **7** The cod **8** Formosa **9** Rome **10** Alabama, Alaska, Arizona, Ohio

Background Bonus The Colosseum

Natural Selection

1 Why do South Africans call the brown hyena the beach wolf?

2 Does a polar bear's fur change from white to brown in summer?

3 What tree produces a substance that is essential to the automobile industry?

4 How does the basilisk lizard cross water?

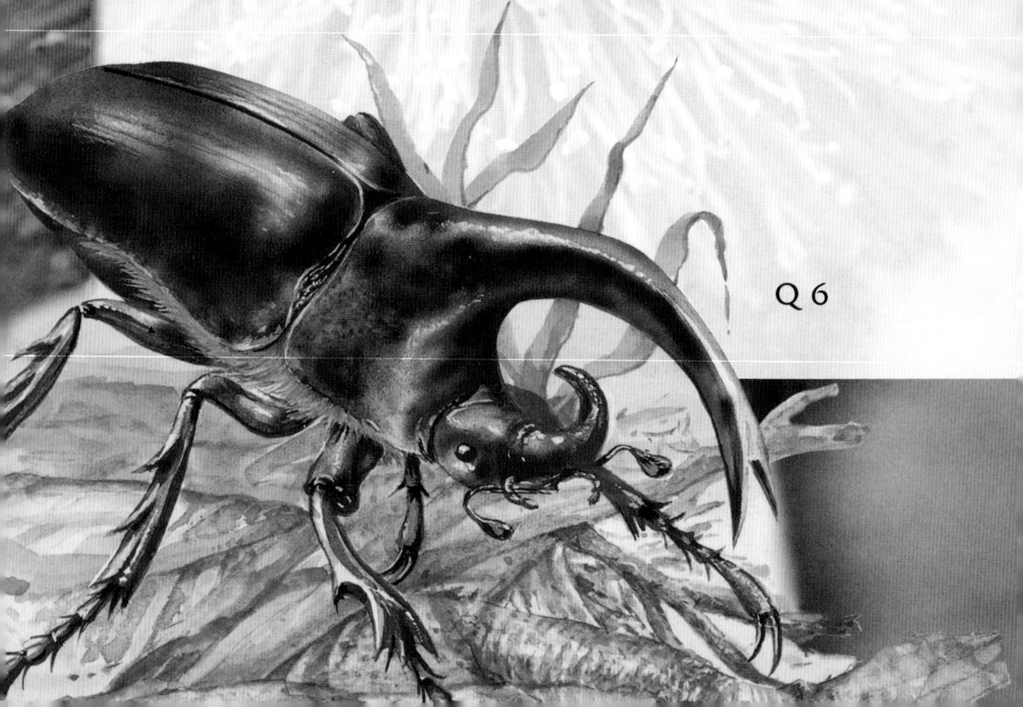

Q 6

5 Which flightless bird moves on rocks with a series of two-footed jumps?

6 What is the biggest beetle?

7 What does the spitting spider spit?

8 Do sloths live in forests or swamps?

9 What is another name for the manatee?

10 Which bird hardly ever lands, and can sleep while flying?

ANSWERS

1 It scavenges the tide line **2** No **3** The rubber tree **4** By running on its back legs **5** The rockhopper penguin **6** Rhinoceros or goliath beetle **7** A sort of glue or liquid silk **8** Forests **9** Sea cow **10** The swift

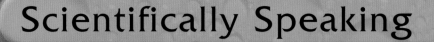

Scientifically Speaking

1 What do you call a scientist who studies volcanoes?

2 How many wisdom teeth can an adult grow?

3 How many cards are there in each suit of a deck of cards?

4 What do you do when you expectorate?

5 What part of a fraction is the dividend?

6 "Rheumatoid" is a type of which bone ailment?

7 Russian blue, Abyssinian and Maine coon are all examples of what?

8 Which term describes the amount of matter in an object?

9 What is the frequency of sound measured in?

10 What type of medical professional removes plaque?

Q 7

LEVEL 4 · QUIZ 186

ANSWERS

1 A vulcanologist **2** Four **3** 13 **4** Spit **5** The lower half **6** Arthritis **7** Domestic cat **8** Mass **9** Hertz (Hz) **10** A dentist or dental hygienist

Sporting Chance

BACKGROUND BONUS

What sport is Paradorn Srichaphan known for?

1 Which golfer won the Masters in 2001 and 2002?

2 Which country hosted the 2002 World Equestrian Games?

3 What is the name of the village in Berkshire where Queen Anne established a famous horseracing course?

4 Which gymnast won three gold medals at the 1972 Olympics?

5 In which city would you find teams called the Knicks, Giants and Yankees?

6 In which country did karate originate?

7 What does the word Olympiad mean?

8 What name is given to the skiing event where competitors have to swerve in and out to avoid flags?

9 Which athlete first broke the 4-minute mile in 1954?

10 What do the initials PU signify in the form guide of a racehorse?

ANSWERS

1 Tiger Woods **2** Spain **3** Ascot **4** Olga Korbut **5** New York **6** Japan **7** Every four years **8** Slalom **9** Roger Bannister **10** Pulled up

Background Bonus Tennis

Total Trivia

1 How many moons has Mars?

2 What lies under the ice at the North Pole?

3 Where is the Cape of Good Hope?

4 Who wrote *Pilgrim's Progress*?

5 What is laver bread made from?

6 Who starred as a singer who had changed her name from Sugar Kowalczyk to Sugar Kane in the 1958 movie *Some Like it Hot*?

7 According to Shakespeare, how many ages of man are there?

8 Doric, Ionic and Corinthian are all orders of what?

9 What Hollywood superstar narrated the movie *Armageddon*?

10 Who is king of the fairies?

Q 6

ANSWERS

1 Yes (Two, Deimos and Phobos) **2** Sea **3** At the southern tip of Africa **4** John Bunyan **5** Seaweed **6** Marilyn Monroe **7** Seven **8** Orders of architecture **9** Charleton Heston **10** Oberon

Lights, Camera, Action!

1 In which 1984 movie did Zach Galligan play a teenager who received a mogwai for Christmas?

2 In which TV show does a teenage witch live with her aunts and a talking cat?

3 In the movie *Great Balls of Fire!*, which rock and roller was played by Dennis Quaid?

4 Who won a Best Supporting Actress Oscar for her role in the movie *Ghost*?

5 Which movie, made in 2000, features Nicholas Cage as a car thief?

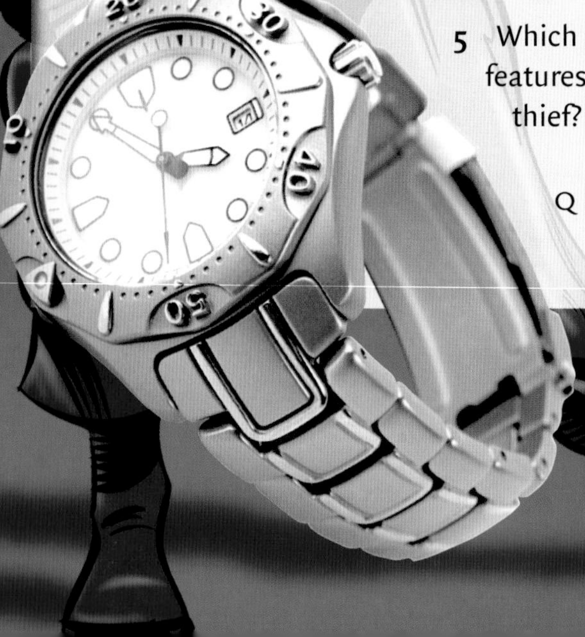

Q 5

6 Who won a Best Director Oscar for the movie *Titanic?*

7 In which classic Christmas movie did James Stewart attempt to commit suicide?

8 Who played the Bond girl, Pussy Galore and the Avenger, Cathy Gale?

9 Who played the role of Clark Griswold in the movie *National Lampoon's Christmas Vacation?*

10 In which movie did Anthony Hopkins say, "I'm having an old friend for dinner"?

ANSWERS

1 *Gremlins* **2** *Sabrina the Teenage Witch* **3** Jerry Lee Lewis **4** Whoopi Goldberg **5** *Gone in 60 Seconds* **6** James Cameron **7** *It's a Wonderful Life* **8** Honor Blackman **9** Chevy Chase **10** *Silence of the Lambs*

Natural Selection

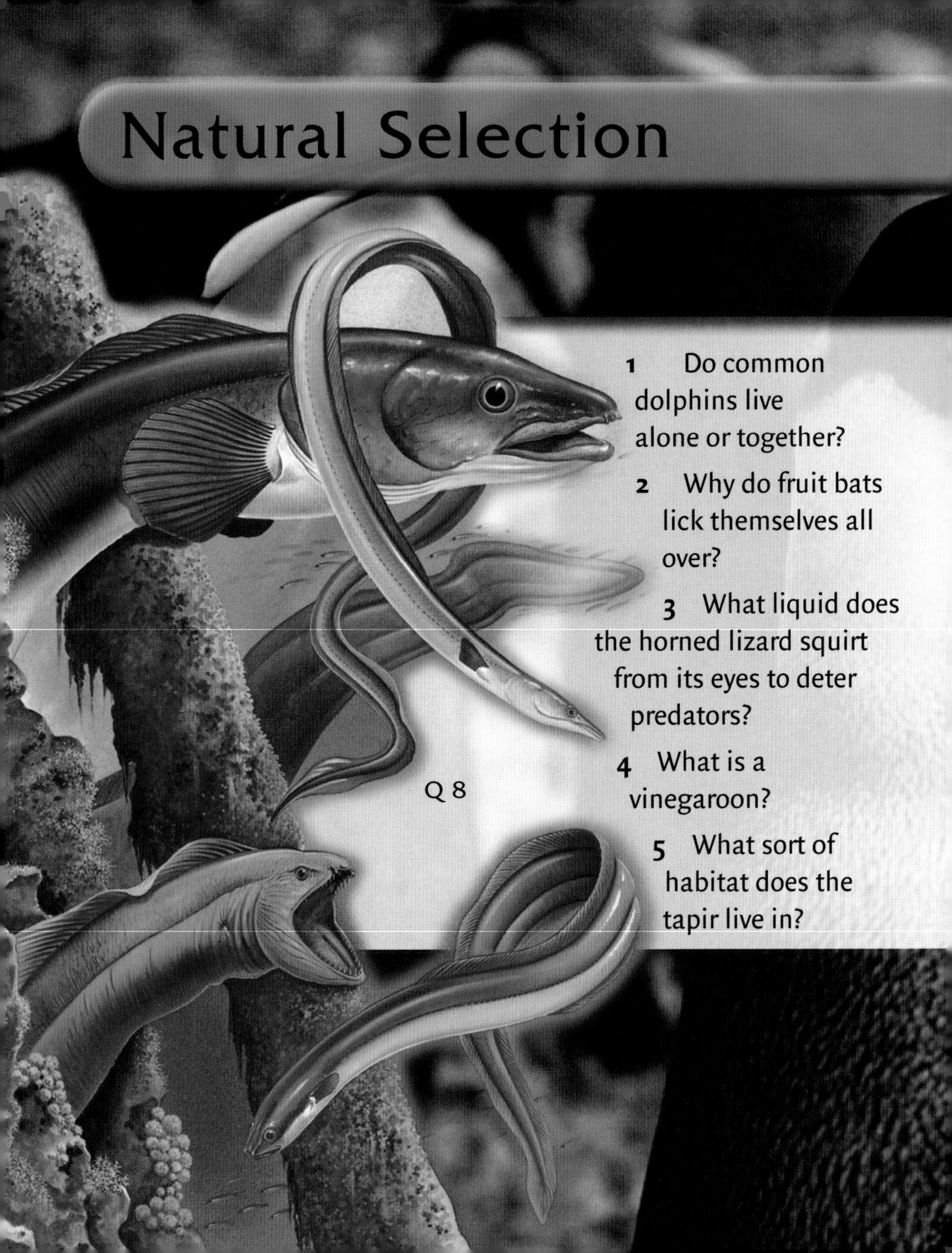

1 Do common dolphins live alone or together?

2 Why do fruit bats lick themselves all over?

3 What liquid does the horned lizard squirt from its eyes to deter predators?

4 What is a vinegaroon?

5 What sort of habitat does the tapir live in?

Q 8

6 What spider catches moths with a sticky ball on a long thread?

7 What crab has a shield-like body, covering five pairs of walking legs and a long tail spike?

8 Which snakelike fish did the ancient Romans keep as pets and decorate with jewels?

9 Which desert plant and moth share the same name?

10 Why do some owls bob their heads up and down?

ANSWERS

1 In a group 2 To keep cool 3 Blood 4 A false scorpion that squirts vinegar mixture 5 Dense forest (with streams) 6 The bolas spider 7 The horseshoe crab 8 The eel 9 The yucca bush and yucca moth 10 It helps judge distance

Total Trivia

1 Which sea creatures swim by squirting out water through a tube?

2 In which sport was the phrase "hat trick" first used?

3 Who wrote a book about Jemima Puddleduck?

4 What is the name for an area of space that sucks everything into itself, even light?

5 How many wings has a dragonfly?

6 Did the Egyptian god, Anubis, have the head of a cobra, jackal or falcon?

7 Who is the U.S. state of Virginia named after?

8 A sky with altocumulus clouds shares its name with what type of fish?

9 What was the name of the fairy in *Peter Pan?*

10 What is the only food which is consumed by vampire bats?

Q 3

ANSWERS
1 Squids and octopuses **2** Cricket **3** Beatrix Potter **4** Black hole **5** Four **6** Jackal **7** Queen Elizabeth I, the Virgin Queen **8** Mackerel **9** Tinkerbell **10** Blood

Beautiful Blooms

Can you guess the names of each of these plants?

1

2

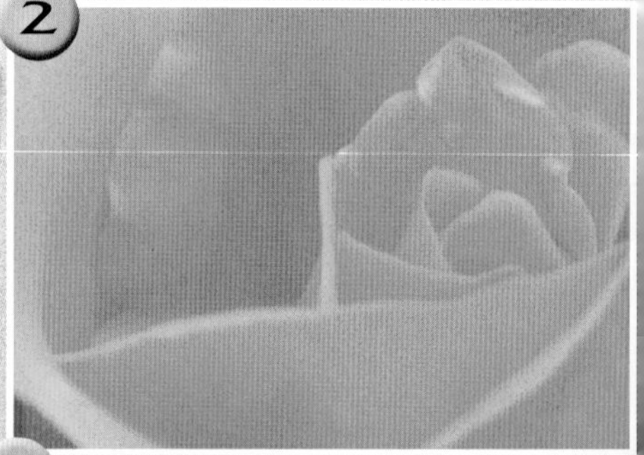

3

4

LEVEL 4 · QUIZ 192

5

6

7

8

ANSWERS

1 Lily **2** Rose **3** Sunflower **4** Columbine **5** Iris **6** Cactus **7** Orchid **8** Dandelion

Scientifically Speaking

1 Where would you find the rudder of an aircraft?

2 What material was used to produce LP records?

3 How many hours are there in five days?

4 What part of a fish aids buoyancy?

5 A fulcrum is an important part of what type of simple machine?

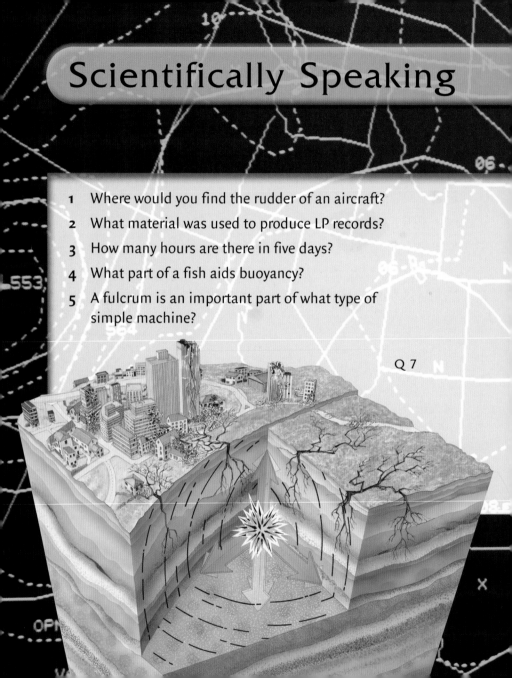

Q 7

LEVEL 4 • QUIZ 193

6 A fuel cell is a type of what?

7 What does a seismologist study?

8 What would a serial or parallel cable be used for?

9 What type of scientist would study quasars and asteroids?

10 You would find a cuticle at the base of what parts of the body?

BACKGROUND BONUS

What is another name for a synoptic chart?

ANSWERS

1 On the tail fin **2** Vinyl **3** 120 **4** Swim bladder **5** Lever **6** Battery **7** Earthquakes **8** Connecting devices to a computer **9** An astronomer **10** Fingernails and toenails

Background Bonus Weather map

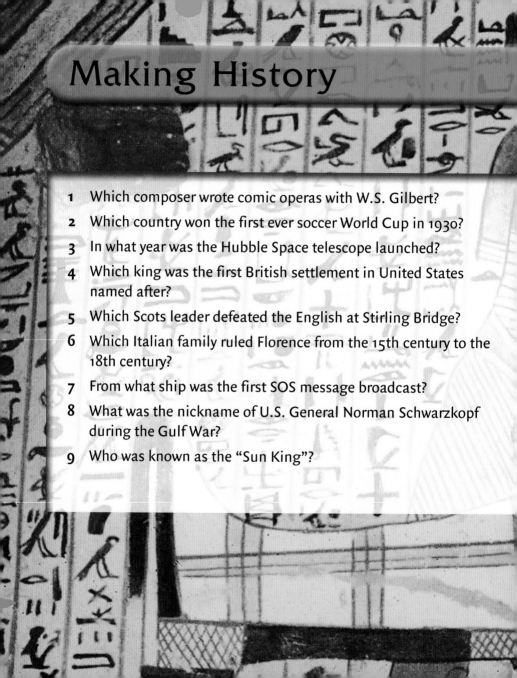

Making History

1 Which composer wrote comic operas with W.S. Gilbert?

2 Which country won the first ever soccer World Cup in 1930?

3 In what year was the Hubble Space telescope launched?

4 Which king was the first British settlement in United States named after?

5 Which Scots leader defeated the English at Stirling Bridge?

6 Which Italian family ruled Florence from the 15th century to the 18th century?

7 From what ship was the first SOS message broadcast?

8 What was the nickname of U.S. General Norman Schwarzkopf during the Gulf War?

9 Who was known as the "Sun King"?

10 In which World War I battle, lasting 141 days, did the British and French lose 600,000 men?

Q 7

ANSWERS

1 Arthur Sullivan **2** Uruguay **3** 1990 **4** James I (Jamestown) **5** William Wallace **6** The Medici family **7** The Titanic **8** Stormin' Norman **9** Louis XIV **10** The Somme

Great and Famous

Q 5

1 Who was known as "The Maid of Orleans"?

2 In the 2001 movie *Miss Congeniality*, which actress plays the undercover cop in a beauty contest?

3 Whose compositions include the operas *Tosca*, *Madame Butterfly* and *Turandot*?

4 What Marquis gave his name to the rules that govern the sport of boxing?

5 Which English explorer was imprisoned in the Tower of London and beheaded in 1618?

6 Which U.S. president introduced the New Deal?

7 Which British impresario was noted for his productions of Gilbert and Sullivan operettas?

8 Who became prime minister of India on its independence in 1947?

9 Who wrote *Don Quixote*?

10 Which astronomer first put forward the theory that the Earth and the planets revolve around the Sun?

ANSWERS

1 Joan of Arc **2** Sandra Bullock **3** Puccini **4** Queensberry **5** Sir Walter Raleigh **6** Franklin D. Roosevelt **7** Richard D'Oyly Carte **8** (Jawaharlal) Nehru **9** Miguel de Cervantes **10** Nicolas Copernicus

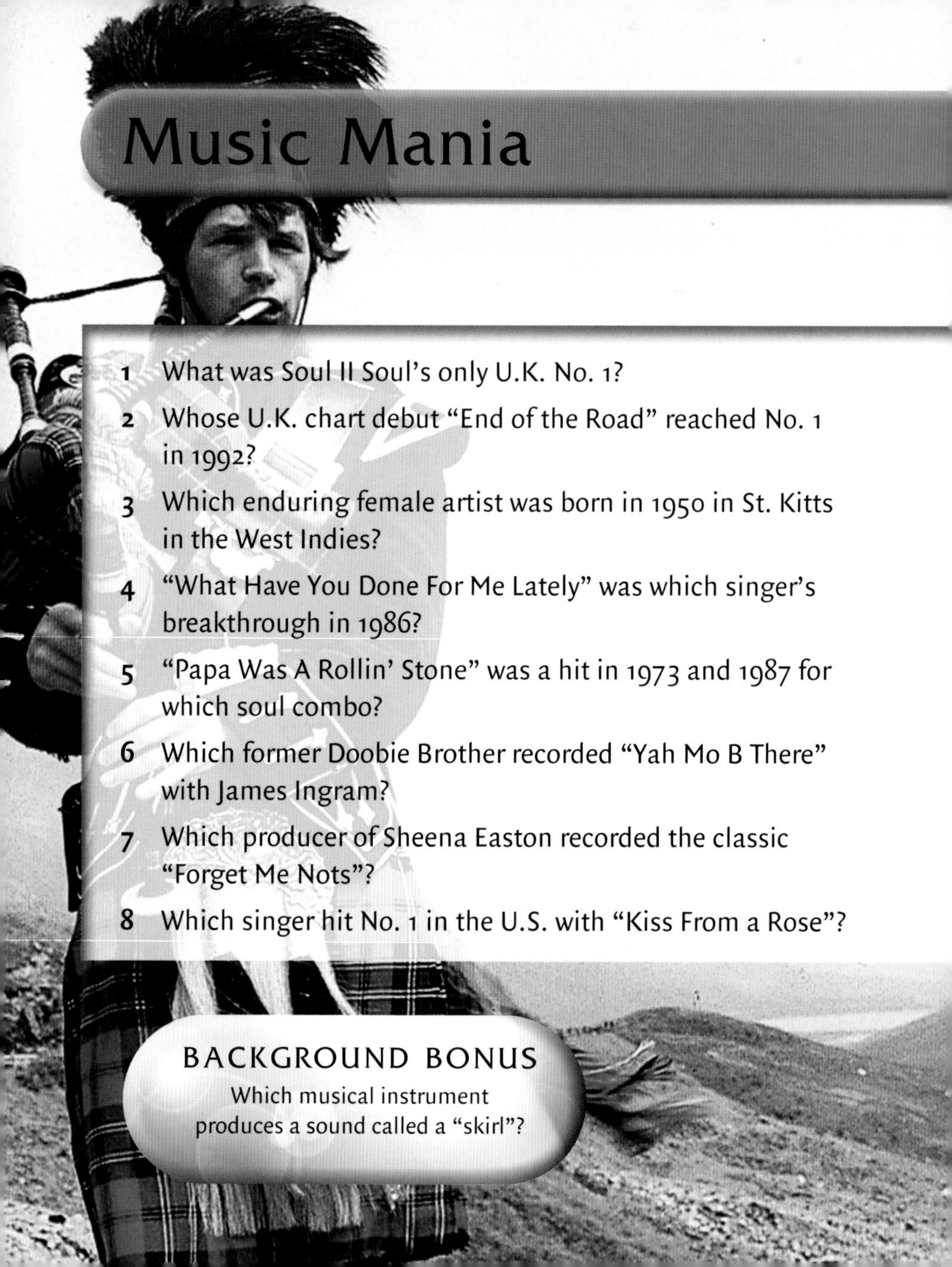

Music Mania

1 What was Soul II Soul's only U.K. No. 1?

2 Whose U.K. chart debut "End of the Road" reached No. 1 in 1992?

3 Which enduring female artist was born in 1950 in St. Kitts in the West Indies?

4 "What Have You Done For Me Lately" was which singer's breakthrough in 1986?

5 "Papa Was A Rollin' Stone" was a hit in 1973 and 1987 for which soul combo?

6 Which former Doobie Brother recorded "Yah Mo B There" with James Ingram?

7 Which producer of Sheena Easton recorded the classic "Forget Me Nots"?

8 Which singer hit No. 1 in the U.S. with "Kiss From a Rose"?

BACKGROUND BONUS

Which musical instrument produces a sound called a "skirl"?

9 Which diva scored a hit with "You Might Need Somebody" in 1997?

10 Who sang a duet with Marvin Gaye on "It Takes Two"?

Q 8

ANSWERS

1 "Back to Life" **2** Boyz II Men **3** Joan Armatrading **4** Janet Jackson **5** The Temptations **6** Michael McDonald **7** Patrice Rushen **8** Seal **9** Shola Ama **10** Kim Weston **Background Bonus** Bagpipes

Total Trivia

LEVEL 4 · QUIZ 197

1 In which type of object would you find a rampart above an escapement?

2 Who slept in the teapot at the Mad Hatter's tea party?

3 What is phlebitis the inflammation of?

4 In the 1950s, what war did the Treaty of Panmunjon end?

5 Which Alfred Hitchcock thriller was set mainly at Bodega Bay?

6 What was the infamous London address of the murderer John Christie?

7 What is the more common name for magnesium silicate?

8 What is a female fox called?

9 What type of passenger plane made its maiden flight in February 1969?

10 Who was Roman emperor when Jesus was crucified?

ANSWERS

1 A clock **2** The dormouse **3** A vein **4** The Korean War **5** The Birds
6 10 Rillington Place **7** Talcum powder **8** Vixen **9** Boeing 747 **10** Tiberius

Lights, Camera, Action!

1 In which movie does Tom Hanks play a prison guard called Paul Edgecomb?

2 Who has played the Prince of Wales, Charlie Chan and Hercule Poirot?

3 In which capital city was the actor Russell Crowe born?

4 Which heart-throb actor plays the father of the spy kids in the movie of the same name?

Q 1

5 Who played the title role in the epic movie *Spartacus?*

6 What was Billy Crystal's profession in the comedy movie *Analyze This?*

7 Who played Morpheus in the futuristic thriller *The Matrix?*

8 Name the third movie in the *Austin Powers* series.

9 What is the title of the 1964 movie which tells the story of an 1879 battle fought in Africa?

10 Which medieval author was portrayed by Paul Bettany in the movie *The Knight's Tale?*

ANSWERS

1 *The Green Mile* 2 Peter Ustinov 3 Wellington 4 Antonio Banderas 5 Kirk Douglas 6 Psychiatrist 7 Laurence Fishburne 8 Goldmember 9 Zulu 10 Geoffrey Chaucer

Making History

1 By what name is the religious group "The Society of Friends" better known?

2 What revolt did Wat Tyler lead in 1381?

3 Which famous pop star was shot dead in New York in 1980?

4 Which English king was defeated at Bosworth in 1485?

Q 3

5 What country offered Albert Einstein its presidency in 1948?

6 By what name is Mongol ruler Timur the Lame better known?

7 Where was Napoleon exiled after Waterloo?

8 Who won the Six Day War in 1967?

9 What instrument did Beethoven write his *Emperor Concerto* for?

10 What was Shakespeare's last play?

ANSWERS

1 The Quakers **2** The Peasants' Revolt **3** John Lennon **4** Richard III **5** Israel **6** Tamerlane **7** St. Helena **8** Israel **9** Piano (and orchestra) **10** Henry VIII

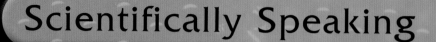

Scientifically Speaking

1 What word describes the horizontal and vertical lines on a graph?

2 What is classified by the letters A, B, AB and O?

3 What kind of plane was a Lancaster?

4 Does an electron have a positive, negative or neutral charge?

5 What is the process whereby yeast acts on sugar to produce alcohol and carbon dioxide?

6 Alfred Nobel, who founded the Nobel Prizes, invented what in 1866?

7 What system do submarines use to "hear" underwater?

8 What is the scientific name for rusting?

9 The Austrian monk Gregor Mendel is associated with what science?

10 What is the normal body temperature of a healthy person?

Q 3

ANSWERS
1 Axis 2 Blood types 3 A bomber 4 Negative 5 Fermentation 6 Dynamite 7 Sonar 8 Oxidation 9 Genetics 10 37°C (98.6°F)

Music Mania

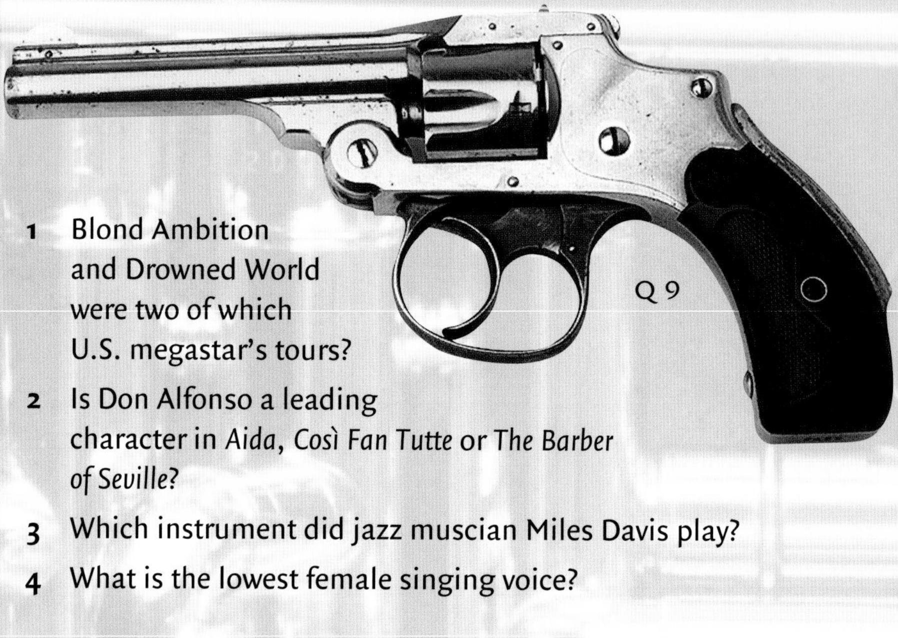

Q 9

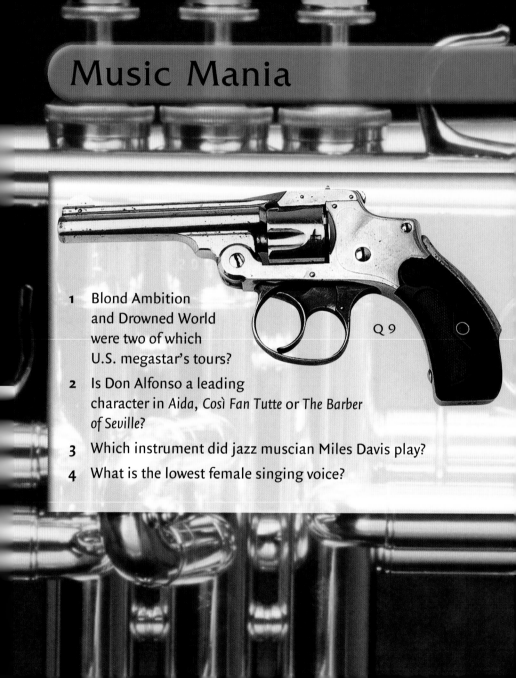

1 Blond Ambition and Drowned World were two of which U.S. megastar's tours?

2 Is Don Alfonso a leading character in *Aida*, *Così Fan Tutte* or *The Barber of Seville?*

3 Which instrument did jazz muscian Miles Davis play?

4 What is the lowest female singing voice?

5 Was classical composer Béla Bartók German, Hungarian or Polish?

6 Born in 1942, who acquired the nickname of The Queen of Soul Music?

7 By what name is U2 front man Paul Hewson better known?

8 Which reggae star sang with The Wailers and had a hit with "No Woman, No Cry"?

9 Sid Vicious replaced Glen Matlock in which controversial punk rock group?

10 Sky Masterson, Miss Adelaide and Nathan Detroit are characters In which musical?

ANSWERS

1 Madonna **2** Cosi Fan Tutte **3** Trumpet **4** Contralto **5** Hungarian **6** Aretha Franklin **7** Bono **8** Bob Marley **9** The Sex Pistols **10** Guys and Dolls

Global Matters

1 What is abrasion?

2 In which of the world's oceans would you find Kangaroo Island?

3 Which Australian town is further north: Cairns or Townsville?

4 In which continent would you find the Saltilla River?

5 The process of the continents moving apart over thousands of years is known by what name?

6 Which African country is now the only home of the oryx?

7 What is the state capital of Utah?

8 Cameroon was a colony of what country before becoming independent?

9 In which city can you find Michelangelo's famous sculpture called *David*?

10 What is the largest big cat in South America?

BACKGROUND BONUS

Which man-made structure, designed by Joseph B. Strauss, was completed in 1937?

ANSWERS

1 The process of wearing away **2** Indian Ocean **3** Cairns **4** North America **5** Continental drift **6** Chad **7** Salt Lake City **8** Germany **9** Florence, Italy **10** The jaguar **Background Bonus** Golden Gate bridge

Total Trivia

1 Which actress was married to Frank Sinatra, and Artie Shaw?

2 What flower was named after the Roman goddess of the rainbow?

3 If a dish is described as chantilly, what is it garnished with?

4 What sea creature is made up of 95% water and has no heart, brain, bones, eyes, gills or blood?

5 In which movie does Denzel Washington play the boxer Rubin Carter?

6 Is cynophobia the fear of cats, dogs or mice?

7 Who wrote the play *The Odd Couple*?

8 Where in the body is the tarsal joint?

9 In which city was John F. Kennedy assassinated?

10 Who invented the dynamo?

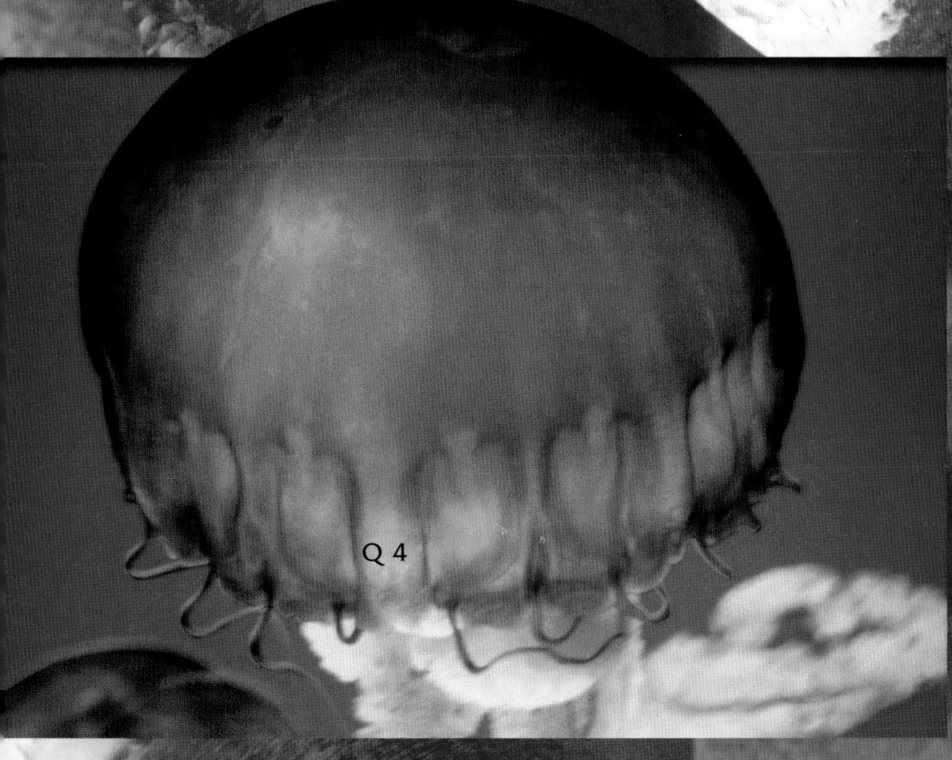

Q 4

ANSWERS

1 Ava Gardner **2** Iris **3** Whipped cream **4** Jellyfish **5** The *Hurricane* **6** Dogs **7** Neil Simon **8** The ankle **9** Dallas **10** Michael Faraday

Picture Perfect

Can you guess the names of the eight different artists who painted each of these famous paintings?

1

2

3

4
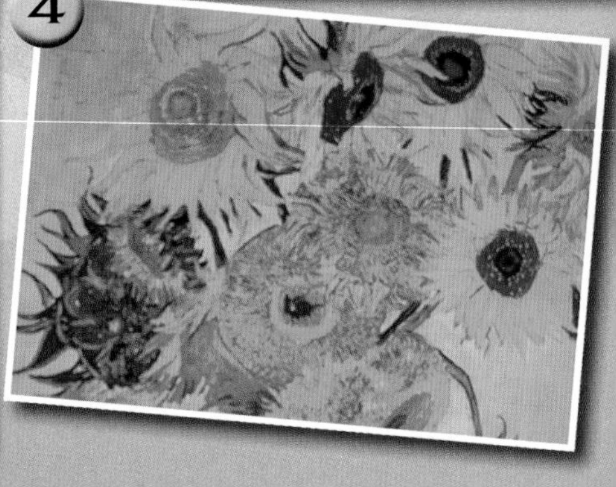

5

6

7

8

ANSWERS

1 Botticelli **2** Cezanne **3** Constable **4** Van Gogh **5** Renoir **6** Vemeer **7** Manet **8** Monet

Natural Selection

1 What is the smallest land mammal?

2 Which tree provided the main wood for English naval ships in the 18th century?

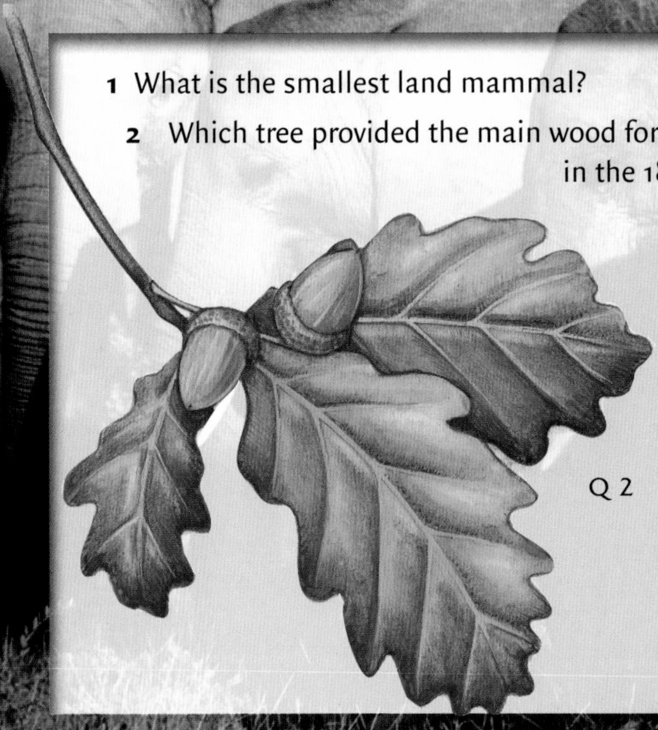

Q 2

BACKGROUND BONUS

Which type of elephant is biggest: the African or Asian?

LEVEL 4 • QUIZ 205

3 Which is the largest member of the dolphin family?

4 How does the chuckwalla lizard avoid predators?

5 How does the female Indian python help her eggs to hatch?

6 How does the frigate bird steal food?

7 Up to how many years can a lobster live: 50 years, 100 years or 150 years?

8 What does the perch fish eat?

9 What is a pond slider?

10 Which apes swing on long arms through the forests of Southeast Asia?

ANSWERS

1 Pygmy white-toothed shrew **2** Oak **3** The orca **4** It wedges its body in a rock crevice **5** By coiling around them **6** It harasses other birds **7** 100 years **8** Meat-eater **9** A turtle **10** Gibbons **Background Bonus** African Elephant

Lights, Camera, Action!

1 In which 1990 movie did Robert DeNiro play the patient of Robin Williams?

2 Which film blockbuster was promoted with the publicity blurb, "Protecting the Earth from the scum of the Universe"?

3 Who starred in *Breakfast at Tiffany's* and later played the leader of the *A-Team* on TV?

4 In which movie did James Bond come out of retirement to fight the evil SMERSH?

5 Who played the vigilante Paul Kersey in the *Death Wish* movies?

6 Which 1995 movies earned Susan Sarandon an Oscar for her role as a nun?

7 In which decade did Disney release the movie *Snow White and the Seven Dwarfs*?

8 Which TV police drama was adapted into a 1987 comedy movie co-starring Dan Aykroyd and Tom Hanks?

9 The movie *The Charge of the Light Brigade* was set during which war?

10 In which 1991 movie did Andrew Strong sing "Mustang Sally"?

Q 9

ANSWERS

1 Awakenings **2** Men in Black **3** George Peppard **4** Casino Royale **5** Charles Bronson **6** Dead Man Walking **7** 1930s (1937) **8** Dragnet **9** Crimean War **10** The Commitments

Making History

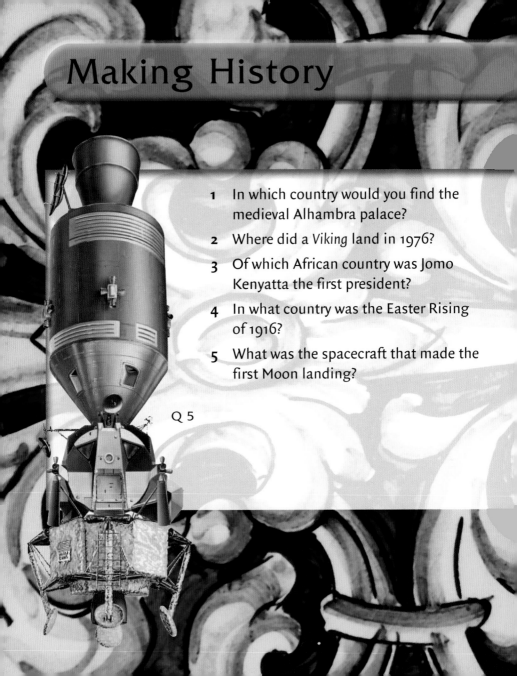

1 In which country would you find the medieval Alhambra palace?
2 Where did a *Viking* land in 1976?
3 Of which African country was Jomo Kenyatta the first president?
4 In what country was the Easter Rising of 1916?
5 What was the spacecraft that made the first Moon landing?

Q 5

6 Which U.S. president was known as "Ike"?

7 In which city was the first set of traffic lights set up in 1868?

8 What natural wonder is named after aviator James Angel?

9 A velocipede was an early name for what type of vehicle?

10 Who became president of France first in 1945 and later in 1968?

ANSWERS

1 Spain 2 Mars 3 Kenya 4 Ireland 5 Apollo 11 6 Dwight Eisenhower 7 London 8 The Angel Falls 9 Bicycle 10 Charles de Gaulle

Lights, Camera, Action!

1 Who played Garth in *Wayne's World?*

2 Which was the first movie set during the Vietnam War to win a Best Movie Oscar?

3 Which 1962 movie told the life story of T.E. Lawrence?

4 Susan Sarandon and Geena Davis play best friends in which 1991 movie?

5 What was the title of the movie in which Barbra Streisand was disguised as a man?

6 Who played Cornelius in the 1968 movie *Planet of the Apes?*

Q 8

7 In which movie did Julie Walters play a dancing teacher called Mrs. Wilkinson?

8 In which 1995 family movie did James Cromwell play Farmer Arthur Hoggett?

9 Who played the title role in the movie *Captain Corelli's Mandolin*?

10 In which 1976 horror movie did Piper Laurie play Sissy Spacek's mother?

BACKGROUND BONUS

Which 1996 movie starring Glenn Close has become a canine classic?

ANSWERS

1 Dana Carvey **2** *Platoon* **3** *Lawrence of Arabia* **4** Warren Beatty **5** *Yentl*
6 Roddy McDowall **7** *Billy Elliot* **8** *Babe* **9** Nicholas Cage **10** *Carrie*
Background Bonus *101 Dalmations*

Natural Selection

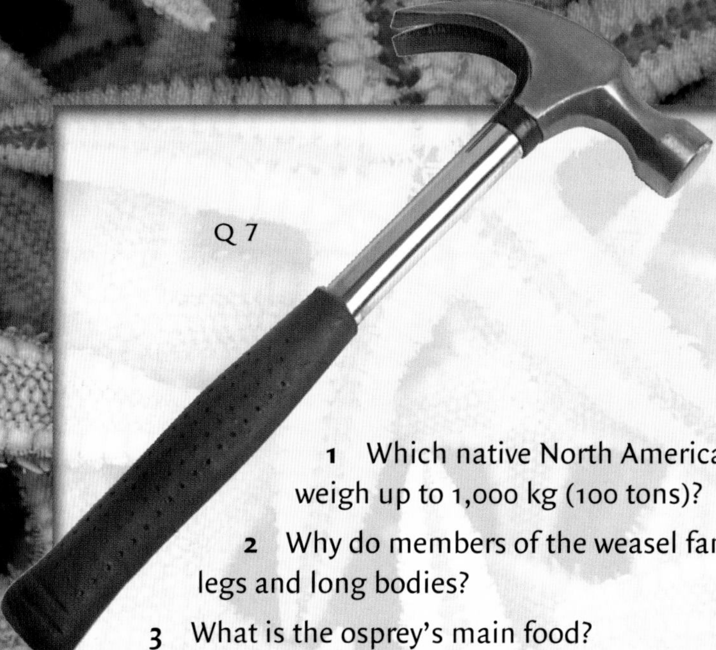

Q 7

1 Which native North American mammal can weigh up to 1,000 kg (100 tons)?

2 Why do members of the weasel family have short legs and long bodies?

3 What is the osprey's main food?

4 How does the Surinam toad carry its young?

5 Which forest spider lives in huge communities?

6 How does a snake swallow prey bigger than its own head?

7 Why are some birds known as anvil birds?

8 Which insect larva takes up to 15 years to become an adult with a noisy chirp?

9 Does the ostrich use its wings for courtship displays, shading its eggs or both?

10 Which two creatures have the most legs in the animal kingdom?

ANSWERS

1 The bison **2** So they can pursue prey underground **3** Fish **4** In pockets on their back **5** The dome-web spider **6** It unhinges its jaws **7** Their call is like a hammer on metal **8** The cicada **9** Both **10** Centipedes and millipedes

Music Mania

1 *A Northern Soul* was the precursor to which 90s album?

2 Dexy's Midnight Runners were searching for what in 1980?

3 How many studio albums did Kate Bush make in the period 1987 to 2000?

4 No. 1 in the U.K. and U.S., *Hysteria* was a huge seller for which British rock band?

5 Released the year before he died, what was the title of Otis Redding's *magnum opus*?

6 Whose debut album was entitled *Welcome to the Pleasuredome?*

7 Who had a 1983 No. 1 album called *Colour by Numbers?*

8 Which band was *Selling England by the Pound* in 1973?

9 Whose debut album was called *Tuesday Night Music Club?*

10 The 2000 album of which songstress was called *Rise?*

ANSWERS

1 *Urban Hymns* (The Verve) **2** *The Young Soul Rebels* **3** Two **4** Def Leppard **5** Otis Blue **6** Frankie Goes to Hollywood **7** Culture Club **8** Genesis **9** Sheryl Crow **10** Gabrielle

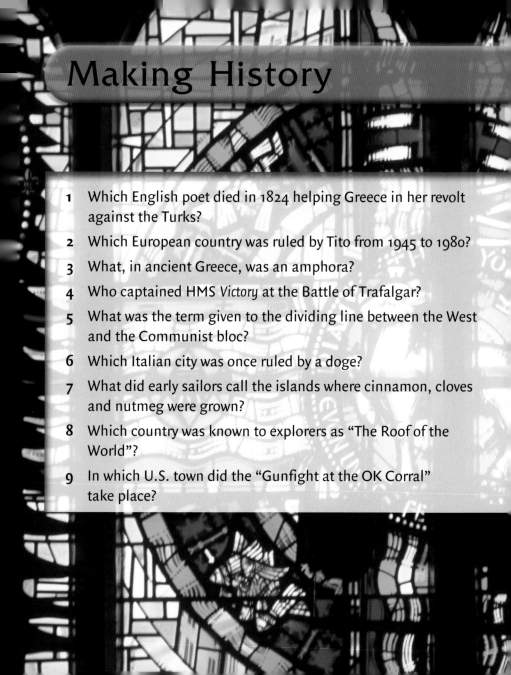

Making History

1 Which English poet died in 1824 helping Greece in her revolt against the Turks?

2 Which European country was ruled by Tito from 1945 to 1980?

3 What, in ancient Greece, was an amphora?

4 Who captained HMS *Victory* at the Battle of Trafalgar?

5 What was the term given to the dividing line between the West and the Communist bloc?

6 Which Italian city was once ruled by a doge?

7 What did early sailors call the islands where cinnamon, cloves and nutmeg were grown?

8 Which country was known to explorers as “The Roof of the World”?

9 In which U.S. town did the “Gunfight at the OK Corral” take place?

10 What shipboard disease did Captain Cook prevent by taking fresh fruit and fruit juice?

Q 1

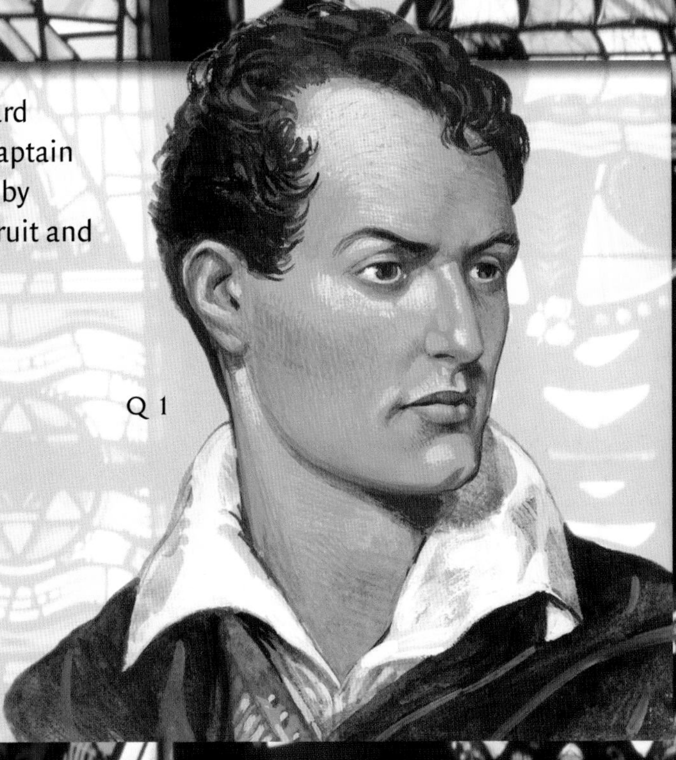

ANSWERS

1 Lord Byron **2** Yugoslavia **3** A big two-handled vase **4** Captain Hardy **5** The Iron Curtain **6** Venice **7** The Spice Islands **8** Tibet **9** Tombstone, Arizona **10** Scurvy

Global Matters

1 What fraction of the Earth's surface does the Pacific Ocean cover?

2 Is jute, cotton or silk Bangladesh's most important export?

3 Where do pilgrims circle the Kaaba Stone?

4 What is the abbreviation EU short for?

5 What is Mauna Loa?

6 What sea does the Orinoco River flow into?

7 Which large sea separates mainland Southeast Asia from the Philippine Islands?

8 A petrified forest is one that has been turned into what?

9 In which county is the English town of Preston?

10 Which large Japanese city was historically called Edo?

BACKGROUND BONUS

Which natural habitat covers just two percent of Earth's surface?

Q 10

ANSWERS

1 One-third **2** Jute **3** Mecca **4** European Union **5** Active volcano **6** Atlantic Ocean **7** South China Sea **8** Fossils **9** Lancashire **10** Tokyo

Background Bonus Rainforest

Total Trivia

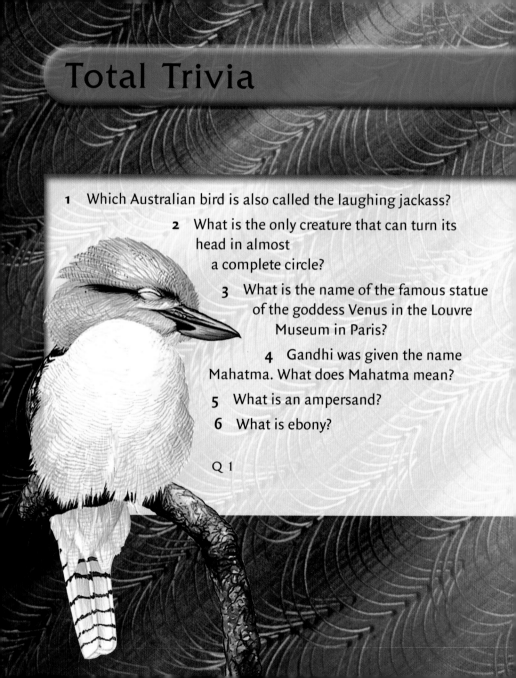

1 Which Australian bird is also called the laughing jackass?

2 What is the only creature that can turn its head in almost a complete circle?

3 What is the name of the famous statue of the goddess Venus in the Louvre Museum in Paris?

4 Gandhi was given the name Mahatma. What does Mahatma mean?

5 What is an ampersand?

6 What is ebony?

Q 1

7 What method of healing involves inserting needles into the body at certain points?

8 They jumped quickly through the hoop. Which is the adverb in that sentence?

9 What does the acronym NASA stand for?

10 What did William Wallace and Robert the Bruce fight for about 700 years ago?

ANSWERS

1 The kookaburra 2 The owl 3 Venus de Milo 4 Great soul 5 The character & 6 A hard jet-black wood 7 Acupuncture 8 Quickly 9 National Aeronautics and Space Administration 10 Scotland's independence

Sporting Chance

1 Which Belgian city hosted the 1920 Summer Olympics?

2 What city hosted the first Summer Olympics held outside Europe?

3 On a golf green, what is "the borrow"?

4 Hicham El Guerrouj won three successive world athletics titles at what event?

5 Lawrence Taylor was named MVP when the New York Giants won the Superbowl in which year?

6 On the Olympic flag, which of the five rings represents Europe?

7 Donovan Bailey won the Olympic 100 m gold medal in which year?

8 Which team defeated the Green Bay Packers to win Superbowl XXXII in 1998?

BACKGROUND BONUS

In which sport did Sir Steve Redgrave win five consecutive Olympic gold medals?

9 Which tennis star had a cameo appearance in the Jim Carrey movie *Me, Myself, and Irene?*

10 Which Australian won the men's Wimbledon Tennis Championships in 1987?

Q 10

ANSWERS

1 Antwerp **2** St. Louis (1904) **3** The slope of the green **4** 1,500 m **5** 1987 **6** The blue ring **7** 1996 **8** Denver Broncos **9** Anna Kournikova **10** Pat Cash

Background Bonus Rowing

Total Trivia

Q 10

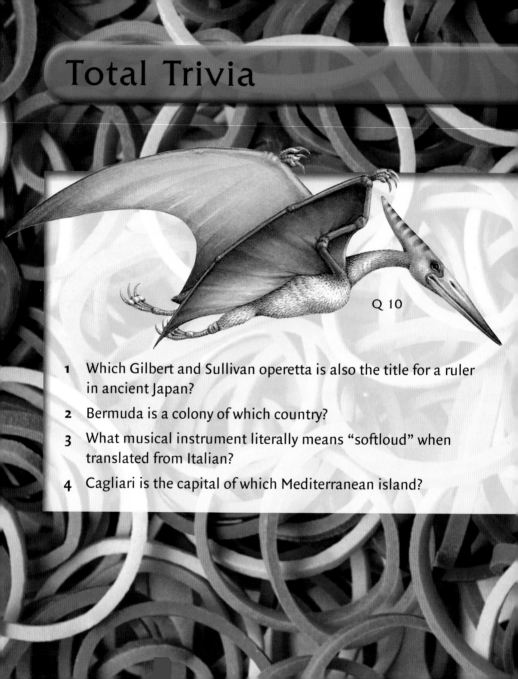

1 Which Gilbert and Sullivan operetta is also the title for a ruler in ancient Japan?

2 Bermuda is a colony of which country?

3 What musical instrument literally means “softloud” when translated from Italian?

4 Cagliari is the capital of which Mediterranean island?

5 What is the nearest capital city in the world to the Equator?

6 Pewter is an alloy of which two metals?

7 What is the name for the wearing away of land by running water, weather, ice and wind?

8 The musical *The Boys From Syracuse* was based on which Shakespeare play?

9 Red pinocchio and Floradora are varieties of what flower?

10 What is a pterodactyl?

ANSWERS

1 The Mikado 2 Britain 3 Pianoforte 4 Sardinia 5 Quinto, Ecuador 6 Tin and lead 7 Erosion 8 A *Comedy of Errors* 9 Rose 10 A prehistoric flying reptile

Feathered Friends

Do you know the names of these eight birds?

1

2

3

4

LEVEL 4 · QUIZ 216

5

6

7

8

ANSWERS
1 Kingfisher **2** Swan **3** Mallrd **4** Pelican **5** Canada goose **6** Ibis **7** Cardinal **8** Great horned owl

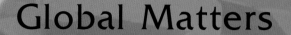

Global Matters

1 The Great St. Bernard's Pass links which two European countries?

2 Damask is a type of woven fabric that took its name from which city?

3 Accra is the capital city of which African country?

4 What is the most highly populated city in China?

5 What is the name given to the deepest part of the ocean floor?

6 In which Asian city would you shop in an area called the Ginza?

7 What is the capital of Libya?

8 The Khyber Pass links which two Asian countries?

9 In which European river would you find the Lorelei Rocks?

10 In which South American country is the city of Recife?

Q 4

ANSWERS
1 Italy and Switzerland **2** Damascus **3** Ghana **4** Shanghai **5** Abyssal plain **6** Tokyo **7** Tripoli **8** Afghanistan and Pakistan **9** The Rhine river **10** Brazil

Great and Famous

Q 3

1 In 1301, who led the Peasants' Revolt?

2 For what is Australian Nellie Melba famous?

3 What nationality was Nicolas Copernicus?

4 With what social reform is Elizabeth Fry associated?

5 Who composed the opera *Carmen*?

6 Which U.S. actor directed and starred in *Citizen Kane*?

7 John Macdonald became the first prime minister of which country in 1867?

8 Which admiral commanded the British fleet at the Battle of Jutland?

9 Who established the Presbyterian Church of Scotland in 1560?

10 Which French artist is renowned for his paintings of ballet dancers?

ANSWERS

1 Wat Tyler **2** Opera singing **3** Polish **4** Prison reform **5** Georges Bizet **6** Orson Welles **7** Canada **8** Admiral Jellicoe **9** John Knox **10** Edgar Degas

Total Trivia

Q 3

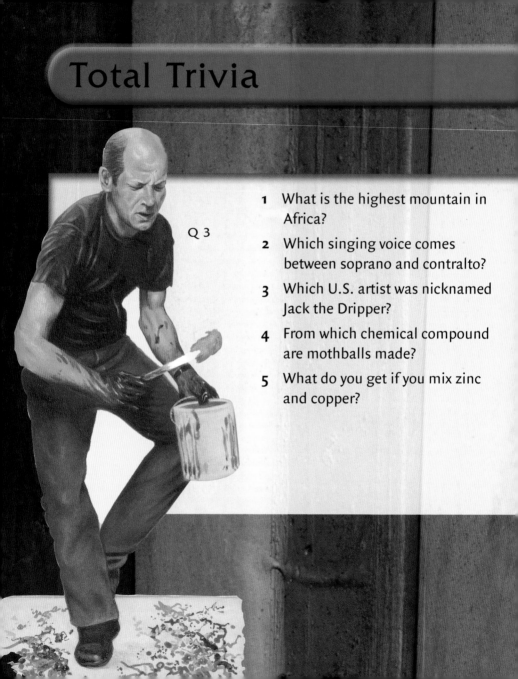

1. What is the highest mountain in Africa?
2. Which singing voice comes between soprano and contralto?
3. Which U.S. artist was nicknamed Jack the Dripper?
4. From which chemical compound are mothballs made?
5. What do you get if you mix zinc and copper?

6 What is the capital of Cambodia?

7 What do Frederick Ashton, Marie Rambert and Margot Fonteyn have in common?

8 Tom Selleck, Elliot Gould and Sarah Ferguson have all appeared in which TV show?

9 What kind of creature is a gila monster?

10 Where is the Rift Valley?

ANSWERS

1 Mount Kilimanjaro **2** Mezzo-soprano **3** Jackson Pollock **4** Naphthalene **5** Brass
6 Phnom Penh **7** Ballet **8** *Friends* **9** A lizard **10** Eastern Africa

Music Mania

1 "Complicated" and "Anything but Ordinary" featured on which singer's debut album?

2 Cat Stevens comes from which country?

3 Drummer Dave Grohl formed which band after the break-up of Nirvana?

4 *Play* and *18* are both album titles from which artist?

5 B-Real, Sen Dog, DJ Muggs are members of which band?

6 Who climbed a *White Ladder* to fame in 2000?

7 Which band's debut album was called *Pablo Honey*?

8 Whose only U.K. No.1 single was "My Ding-A-Ling" in 1972?

9 Who achieved the first ever million-selling single in the U.K.?

10 Monika Danneman found the dead body of which musical genius in 1970?

Q 8

ANSWERS

1 Avril Lavigne **2** England **3** The Foo Fighters **4** Moby **5** Cypress Hill **6** David Gray **7** Radiohead **8** Chuck Berry **9** Bill Haley & the Comets **10** Jimi Hendrix

Scientifically Speaking

1 Was the first electronic calculator manufactured in 1953, 1963 or 1973?

2 Brimstone is the old name for what element?

Q 10

3 How many minutes are there in three and a third hours?

4 What letter represents 1,000 in Roman numerals?

5 The Eustachian tube links the throat to which organ?

6 How are chlorofluorocarbon emissions more commonly known?

7 James Watson and Francis Crick discovered the structure of which substance?

8 Which branch of mathematics is concerned with sines and cosines?

9 Which planet has two moons called Deimos and Phobos?

10 What is removed from dehydrated food?

ANSWERS

1 1963 2 Sulphur 3 200 4 M 5 The ear 6 CFC gases 7 DNA 8 Trigonometry 9 Mars 10 Water

Making History

1 In which country was Emiliano Zapata a freedom fighter?

2 Of which country was Jan Smuts the prime minister in 1919?

3 Which language, spoken by white South Africans, is derived from Dutch?

4 What was the popular nickname for James Hickock?

5 Which African warriors fought in groups called *impis*?

Q 5

6 In which year was the modern state of Israel founded?

7 What instrument did Django Reinhardt play?

8 In which war was the Battle of Antietam (1862)?

9 Which European country conquered Brazil?

10 Who built the first nuclear reactor in a squash court in Chicago?

BACKGROUND BONUS

Which megalithic wonder was built in three stages over 1,000 years?

ANSWERS

1 Mexico **2** South Africa **3** Afrikaans **4** "Wild Bill" Hitchcock **5** Zulus **6** 1948
7 Guitar **8** The American Civil War **9** Portugal **10** Enrico Fermi
Background Bonus Stonehenge

Sporting Chance

1 Which Wimbledon tennis champion was conscripted in 2001?
2 Who ran the fastest 100 m of the 20th century?
3 Who was named Female Athlete of the Century by the International Athletic Federation?
4 Which U.S. tennis player won the women's singles gold medal at the 1996 Olympics?
5 In which country is the Flemington Park racecourse?
6 Which U.S. jockey was nicknamed "The Kentucky Kid"?
7 In the Olympic rings, which continent is represented by green?
8 Which female tennis star wrote a novel called *Total Zone*?
9 What nation's national anthem is played at the closing ceremony of the Olympic Games?
10 How many times did John McEnroe win the U.S. Open?

LEVEL 4 · QUIZ 223

Q 7

ANSWERS
1 Goran Ivanisevic **2** Maurice Greene **3** Fanny Blankers-Koen **4** Lindsay Davenport **5** Australia **6** Steve Cauthen **7** Oceania **8** Martina Navratilova **9** Greece **10** Four

Scientifically Speaking

1 Joules and calories are measurements of what?
2 What is the name for the tissue that connects bones?
3 A Maglev train travels by using what type of technology?
4 What does an audiologist study?
5 What are igneous rocks formed from?
6 The word "Mach", used for measuring speed, refers to what?
7 What is the body's largest gland?
8 Multiply 32 by the product of 2 and 4.
9 What does LCD stand for?
10 What is the main ingredient of paper?

Q 5

BACKGROUND BONUS

What is the name given to thin, transparent glass threads that transmit messages by light?

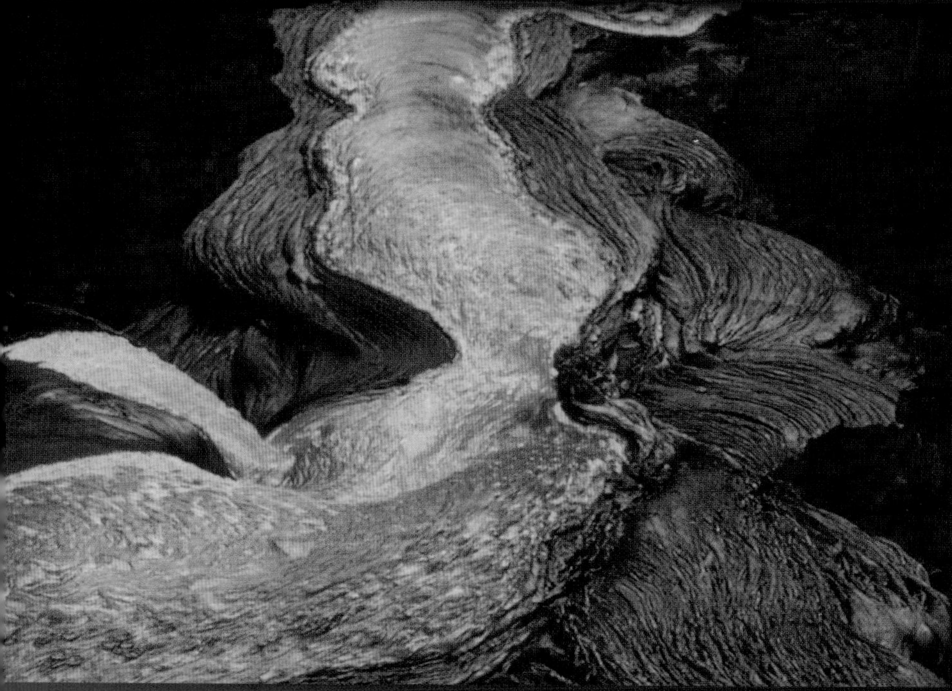

ANSWERS

1 Heat energy **2** Ligaments **3** Magnetic levitation **4** Human hearing **5** Lava **6** The speed of sound in the air **7** The liver **8** 256 **9** Liquid Crystal Display **10** Wood pulp **Background Bonus** Fibre optic cables

Great and Famous

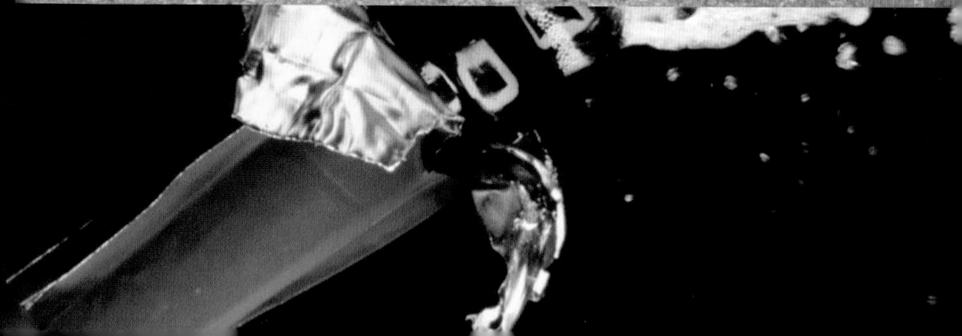

LEVEL 4 · QUIZ 225

1 In which country was Adolf Hitler born?
2 Which famous car was designed by Alec Issigonis in 1959?
3 Who wrote the original novel, *Les Misérables*?
4 Winston Churchill was half American: true or false?
5 What nationality was Abel Tasman, discoverer of New Zealand?
6 Who was Queen Elizabeth II's father?
7 Which of the Marx Brothers wore a painted false moustache?
8 What was David Livingstone's job?
9 In which country was the first national park set up in 1872?
10 How did African explorer H.M. Stanley earn his living?

ANSWERS

1 Austria **2** The Mini **3** Victor Hugo **4** True **5** Dutch **6** George VI **7** Groucho **8** Missionary **9** United States (Yellowstone) **10** He was a journalist

Total Trivia

1 What was the three-letter surname of the presiding judge in the O.J. Simpson murder trial?

2 In the United States, what was banned from 1917 to 1933 by the 18th Amendment?

3 Who was the first singer to have a U.K. No. 1 hit with the song "Unchained Melody"?

4 Which U.S. city is named after a British prime minister?

5 What does the medical condition DVT stand for?

6 What is the only marsupial native to North America?

7 Who was Robert Burns?

8 Would you weigh more or less on the Moon?

9 To what area of medicine does geriatrics refer?

10 What carries satellites into space?

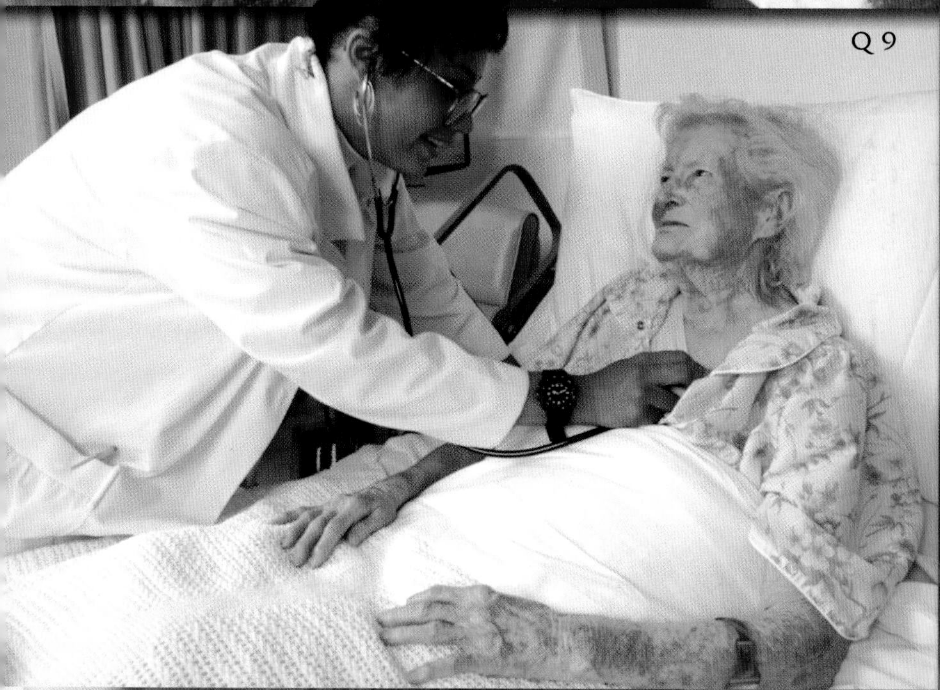

Q 9

ANSWERS
1 lto **2** Alcohol **3** Jimmy Young **4** Pittsburgh **5** Deep vein thrombosis **6** Opposum
7 A Scottish poet **8** Less **9** Old people **10** Rockets

Scientifically Speaking

1 The biggest spiders are members of which arachnid family?

2 What type of object can be either a red giant, a white dwarf or a black dwarf?

3 Smoking tobacco harms two major organs of the body; one is the lungs, what is the other?

4 What chemical element has the symbol Kr?

5 What is the boiling point of water on the Celsius scale?

6 What part of the body does arthritis affect?

7 What feature links penguins, rheas, ostriches and kiwis?

8 Which English scientist developed the first modern theory about how gravity works?

9 Where could you find a stigma, carpels and sepals?

10 What planets, apart from Saturn, have rings?

Q 1

ANSWERS

1 Tarantula **2** A star **3** The heart **4** Krypton **5** 100 degrees **6** The bones **7** They are all birds that cannot fly **8** Sir Isaac Newton **9** In a flower **10** Jupiter, Uranus and Neptune

Beneath the Waves

Can you guess the names of these underwater creatures?

1

2

3

4

5

6

7

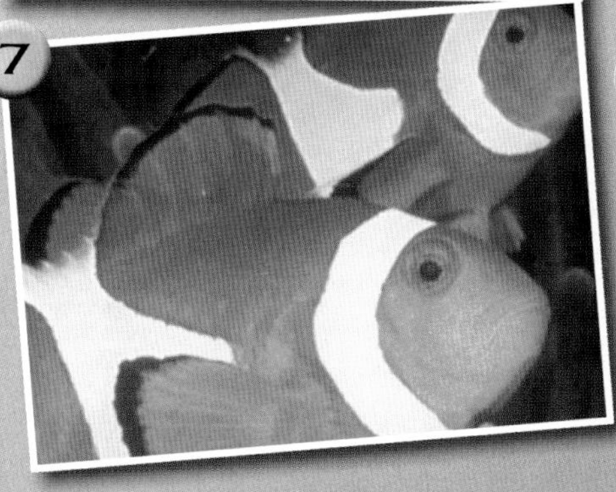

8

ANSWERS
1 Turtle **2** Butterfly fish **3** Great white shark **4** Angel fish **5** Unicorn fish **6** Crab **7** Clown fish **8** Whale shark

Natural Selection

1 How does the bee orchid attract bees to pollinate it?

2 How many compartments does a cow have in its stomach?

3 Which large Swiss dog was used for mountain rescue?

4 Which small, fierce freshwater fish hunts in shoals of thousands?

5 Why do eucalyptus trees have white bark and white leaves?

6 Which large sea bird can glide for a day without flapping its wings?

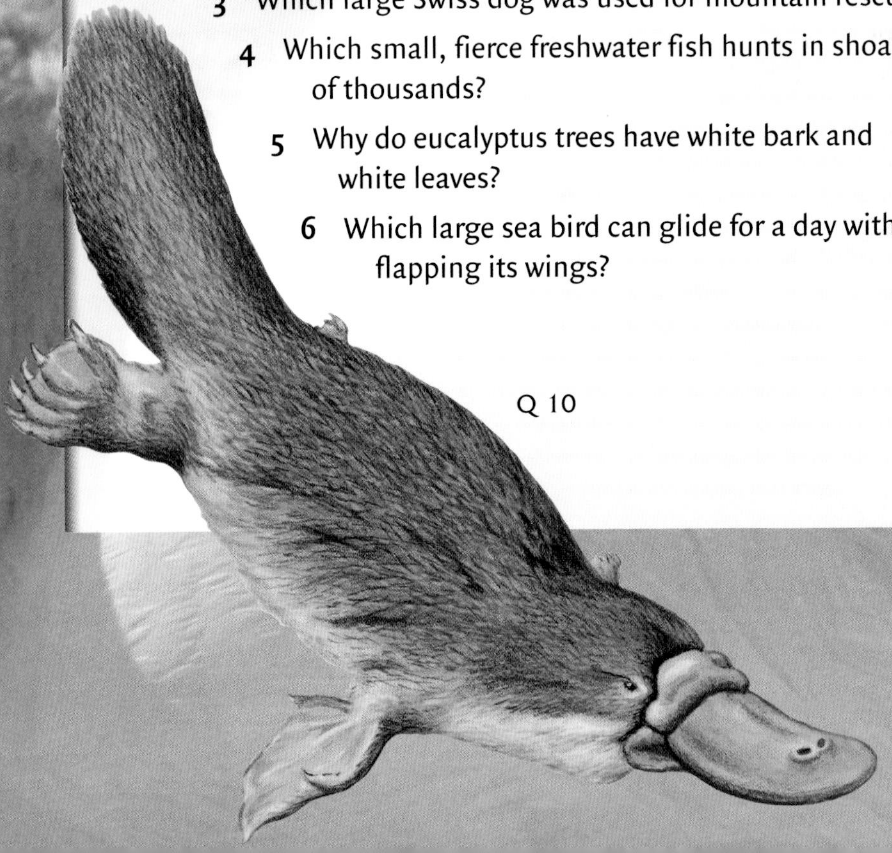

7 In which species of fish does the male incubate the young?

8 What is an ungulate?

9 What kind of animal is the whip-poor-will?

10 Which egg-laying mammal has venomous spurs on its hind legs?

BACKGROUND BONUS

What bird is the largest of North America's waterfowl?

ANSWERS

1 It resembles a bee **2** Four **3** The St. Bernard **4** The piranha **5** To reflect sunlight **6** The albatross **7** Seahorse **8** A hoofed mammal **9** Bird **10** The duck-billed platypus **Background Bonus** Trumpeter swan

Making History

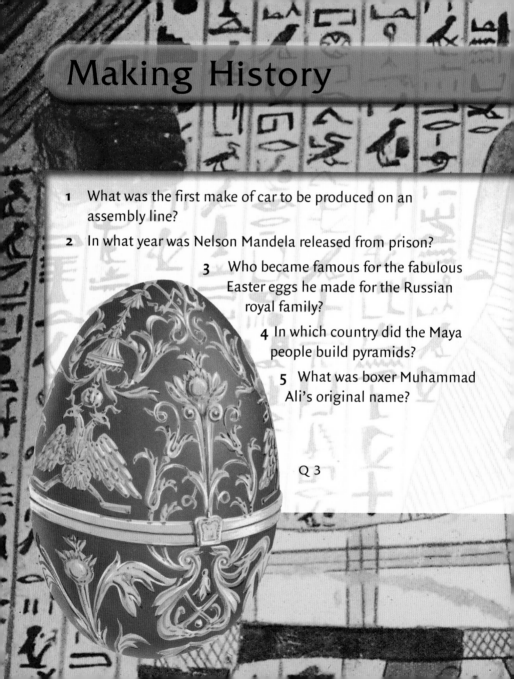

1 What was the first make of car to be produced on an assembly line?

2 In what year was Nelson Mandela released from prison?

3 Who became famous for the fabulous Easter eggs he made for the Russian royal family?

4 In which country did the Maya people build pyramids?

5 What was boxer Muhammad Ali's original name?

Q 3

6 Which Asian country was led by dictator Pol Pot?

7 In which year did the "Jack the Ripper" murders take place in London?

8 Which 18th-century Austrian composer had the Christian names Wolfgang Amadeus?

9 What weapon did Samson use to defeat the Philistines?

10 What kind of bomber was a World War II *Stuka*?

ANSWERS

1 The Ford Model-T **2** 1990 **3** Carl Fabergé **4** Mexico **5** Cassius Clay **6** Cambodia **7** 1888 **8** Mozart **9** An ass's jawbone **10** Dive-bomber

Lights, Camera, Action!

1 Who did Kurt Russell play in the movie *Tombstone?*

2 The phrase "Book 'em, Danno" was associated with which TV show?

3 The actress Holly Hunter won an Oscar for her role in which 1993 movie?

4 In which 2000 movie did Russell Crowe play Maximus Decimus Meridus?

5 In which 1997 movie did Harrison Ford play President James Marshall?

6 Who directed the 2001 movie *Gosford Park?*

7 Marion Morrison was the real name of which U.S. film star?

8 Which cult TV show was created by Gene Roddenberry?

9 What is the name of Roseanne's sister in the TV series *Roseanne?*

BACKGROUND BONUS

Which 1999 movie starred Leonardo DiCaprio and Virginie Ledoyen?

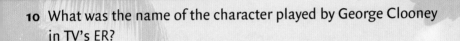

10 What was the name of the character played by George Clooney in TV's ER?

Q 5

ANSWERS
1 Wyatt Earp **2** Hawaii 5 O **3** The Piano **4** Gladiator **5** Airforce One **6** Robert Altman **7** John Wayne **8** Star Trek **9** Jackie **10** Dr. Doug Ross
Background Bonus The Beach

Total Trivia

1. Who was shipwrecked in a land of tiny people?
2. What type of jellyfish has a name relating to a country?
3. Why does the Moon shine?
4. Who was the Italian Fascist leader during World War II?
5. What does a barometer measure?
6. In which war were tanks first used?
7. What is fog?
8. In which sport did teams compete for the Jules Rimet trophy?
9. What is the past tense of "strike"?
10. What planet is nearest to the Sun?

Q 2

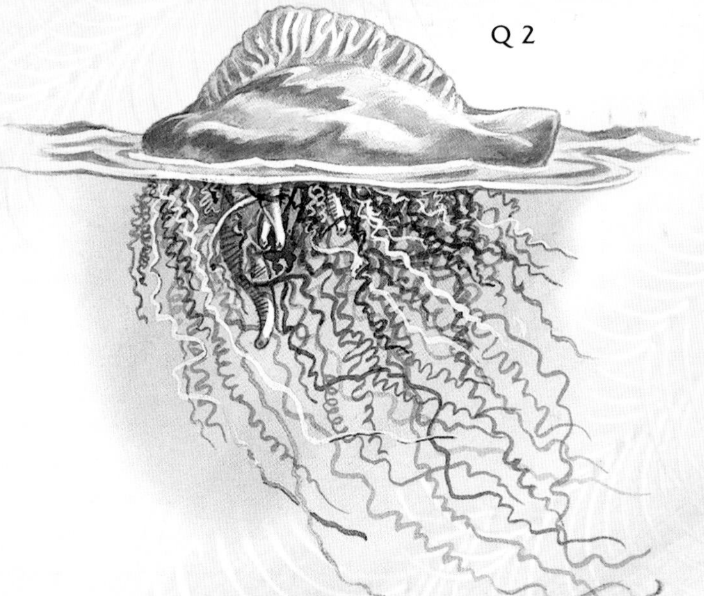

ANSWERS

1 Gulliver **2** Portuguese man o' war **3** Because it reflects light from the Sun **4** Benito Mussolini **5** Air pressure **6** World War I **7** A cloud that forms close to the ground **8** Soccer **9** Struck **10** Mercury

Natural Selection

Q 3

1 What animal makes a shallow, grassy nest called a form?

2 What insect has a wingspan of up to 14 cm (5.5 in) and lays its eggs on or near water?

3 What is a mudpuppy?

4 What is a mandrake?

5 What mammal needs to drink 70–90 l (18–24 gal) of water a day?

6 Which type of grass grows the tallest and thickest?

7 Why is the tokay gecko lizard so named?

8 What does the bulldog bat do with its long foot claws as it swoops over water?

9 What does a mussel use its "beard" for?

10 What common weed spreads its seeds by feathery-looking parachutes?

ANSWERS

1 The hare **2** The dragonfly **3** A salamander **4** A poisonous plant **5** The elephant **6** Bamboo **7** After its call **8** Drags fish from the surface of the water **9** It anchors it to rocks **10** The dandelion

Lights, Camera, Action!

1 In which movie did Tom Hanks play a boy trapped in a 32-year-old man's body?

2 In the title of a 1999 movie, what animal is crouching when a dragon is hidden?

3 When Olivia de Havilland played Maid Marian, who played Robin Hood?

4 What was Frank Sinatra's nickname?

5 Which Oscar-winning movie star is the daughter of the film director John Huston?

6 In which 1990 movie did Julia Roberts and Keifer Sutherland play medical students?

7 In which 1968 movie did Sally Anne Howes play Truly Scrumptious?

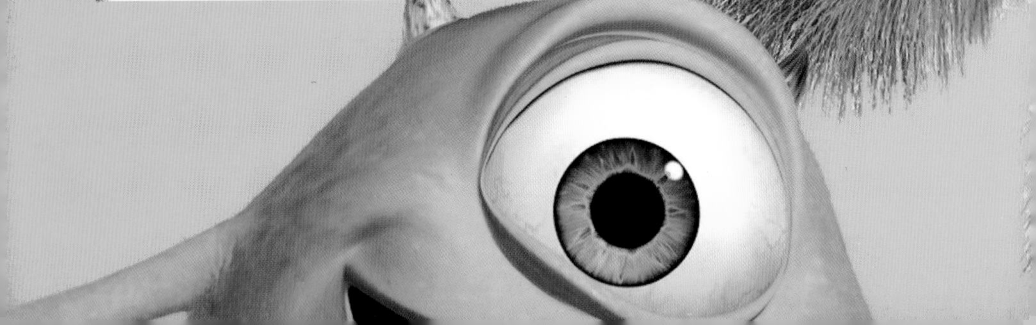

LEVEL 4 • QUIZ 234

8 In which 1997 movie did Gaz, Gerald, Guy and Dave shed their clothes?

9 Which Scottish comedian played an auctioneer in the movie *Indecent Proposal*?

10 In a 1993 version of *The Three Musketeers*, who played the character D'Artagnan?

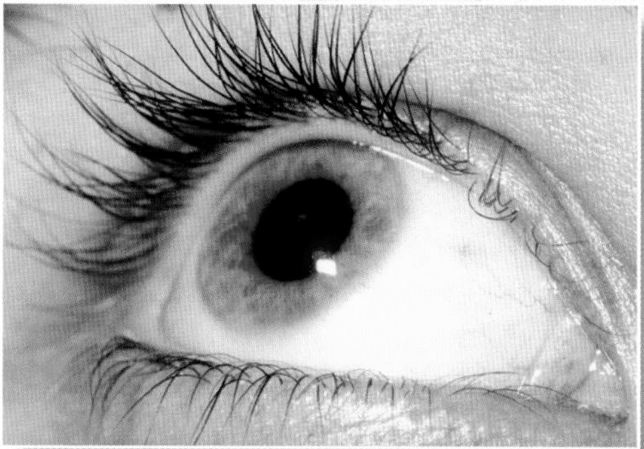

Q 4

ANSWERS

1 Big **2** *Tiger* **3** Errol Flynn **4** "Ol' Blue Eyes" **5** Angelica Huston **6** *Flatliners* **7** *Chitty Chitty Bang Bang* **8** *The Full Monty* **9** Billy Connolly **10** Chris O'Donnell

Total Trivia

Q 5

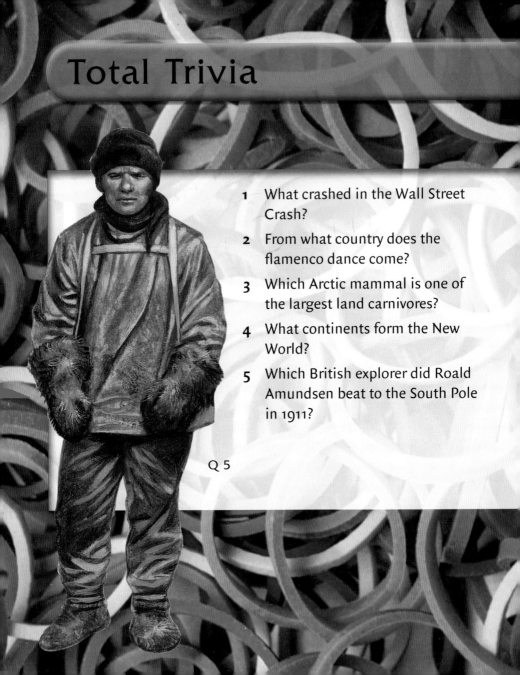

1 What crashed in the Wall Street Crash?

2 From what country does the flamenco dance come?

3 Which Arctic mammal is one of the largest land carnivores?

4 What continents form the New World?

5 Which British explorer did Roald Amundsen beat to the South Pole in 1911?

LEVEL 4 · QUIZ 235

6 What does a forensic scientist do?

7 What does the Bayeux Tapestry show?

8 Where is Tierra del Fuego?

9 How does a radio telescope see objects that are too dim for an ordinary telescope?

10 What layer of special oxygen in the atmosphere blocks out dangerous radiation from the Sun?

ANSWERS

1 U.S. Stock Market 2 Spain 3 Polar bear 4 North and South America 5 Robert Scott 6 Gives technical details about a crime 7 The 1066 invasion of England 8 Southern tip of South America 9 Collects radio waves from space 10 Ozone layer

Sporting Chance

1 How many gold medals did Jesse Owens win at the 1936 Olympics?

2 At what Olympic Games did Carl Lewis win four gold medals?

3 In tennis, what is the term for a very high lob?

4 What does "judo" mean in Japanese?

5 What racehorse won the 2003 Dubai World Cup?

6 Which baseball star married Marilyn Monroe?

7 In what month is the Kentucky Derby run?

8 The Fastnet Race is contested In which sport?

9 A telltale, a service box and a tin can be found on the court in which racket sport?

10 How is Edson Arantes do Nascimento better known as?

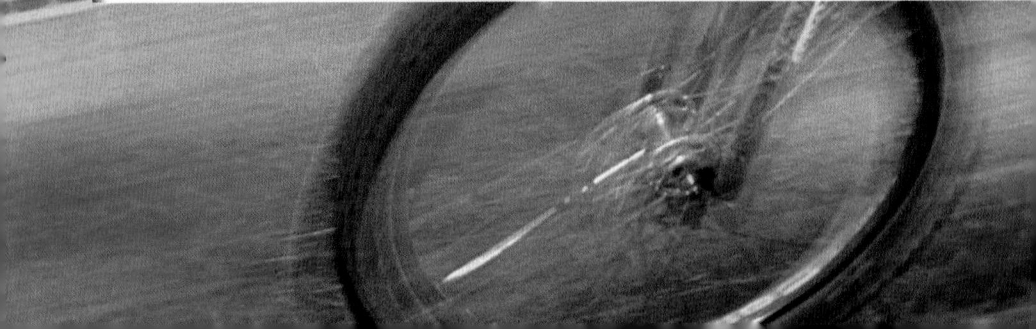

Q 3

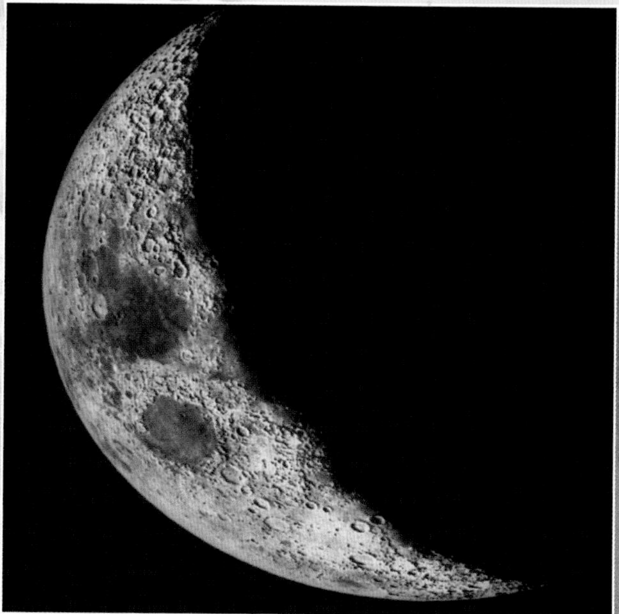

ANSWERS

1 Four **2** 1984, Los Angeles **3** Moon ball **4** "The Gentle Way" **5** Moon Ballad **6** Joe DiMaggio **7** May **8** Yachting **9** Squash **10** Pelé

Global Matters

Q 8

1 The Maracana Stadium is found in which South American city?

2 What do Arica in Chile and Death Valley in the U.S. have in common?

3 Into which body of water does the River Niagara flow?

4 What is the currency of Cuba?

5 What is the capital of Jamaica?

6 What is jet a hard, solid form of?

7 What is the abbreviation GNP short for?

8 What country is Kampala the capital of?

9 In which country is the Camargue horse?

10 The Nurburgring Racing Circuit is found in which European country?

BACKGROUND BONUS

Mount Kilimanjaro can be found in which African country?

ANSWERS

1 Rio de Janiero 2 They are two of the world's driest places 3 Lake Ontario 4 The Cuban Peso 5 Kingston 6 Coal 7 Gross National Product 8 Uganda 9 France 10 Germany **Background Bonus** Kenya

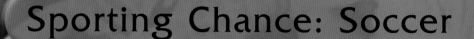

Sporting Chance: Soccer

1 Which country did goalkeeper Peter Schmeichel represent at international level?

2 In what year was the first World Cup organized?

3 Eusebio played for what country?

4 Which European club plays at the Stadio Delle Alpi?

5 Which French club won their seventh league title in 2000?

6 Which Italian club did Asprilla and Zola play for?

7 Who won the 1970 FA Cup final?

8 From which Scottish club did Leeds United buy striker Mark Viduka?

9 Who was the first person to have managed both England's and Australia's national teams?

10 What club is generally accepted as being the oldest in England?

LEVEL 4 · QUIZ 238

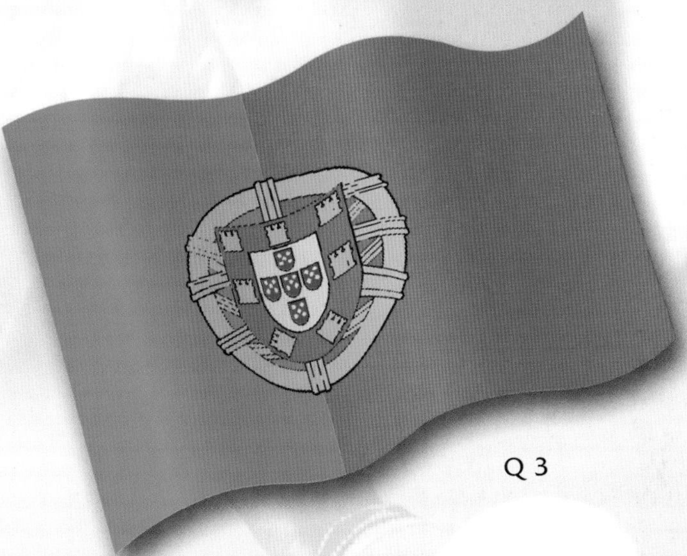

Q 3

ANSWERS
1 Denmark **2** 1930 **3** Portugal **4** Juventus **5** Monaco **6** Parma **7** Chelsea **8** Celtic
9 Terry Venables **10** Notts County

Written Word

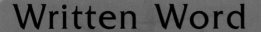

1 Who wrote *For Whom the Bell Tolls?*

2 What name is given to a line on a map that connects points of the same height?

3 *West Side Story* is based on what play by Shakespeare?

4 What is the name of Dorothy's dog in *The Wizard of Oz?*

5 What is the only letter that is worth five points in Scrabble: J, K or V?

6 Who wrote the novel *Bridget Jones's Diary?*

7 What is studied by an ichthyologist?

8 Where is Armistead Maupin's *Tales of the City* series set?

9 In the James Bond novels, who is his boss?

10 What was the name of the captain in pursuit of Moby Dick?

ANSWERS
1 Ernest Hemmingway **2** Contour **3** Romeo and Juliet **4** Toto **5** K **6** Helen Fielding
7 Fish **8** San Francisco **9** M **10** Captain Ahab

Country Clues

Each of the pictures below is a clue to a different country. Can you guess each one?

1

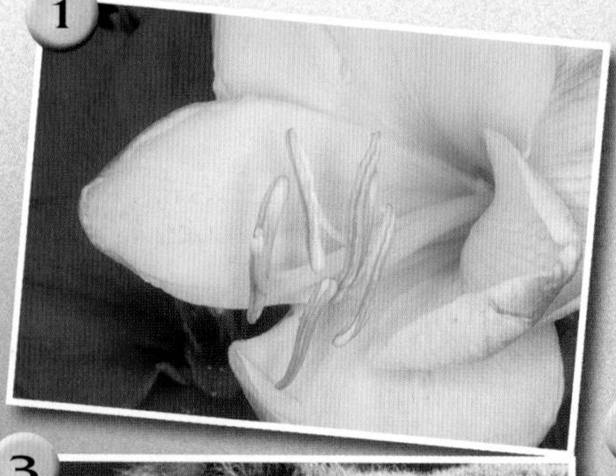

2

3

4

5

6

7

8

ANSWERS

1 France **2** USA **3** Australia **4** Wales **5** Japan **6** Holland **7** India **8** Italy

Sporting Chance

1 Which British horse racing course is the largest in the world?

2 In golf, an eagle is how many holes under par?

3 What city hosted the 1972 Olympic Games?

4 What is the perfect score in tenpin bowling?

5 Which is the only British city to have hosted the Summer Olympics in the 20th century?

6 In which sport would you do a *Harai goshi*?

7 What was the first country beginning with the letter M to host the Summer Olympics?

8 In chess, when can a pawn move diagonally?

9 In which sport would you use a shot called a "boast"?

10 *Petanque* originated in which country?

LEVEL 4 • QUIZ 241

Q 7

ANSWERS

1 Newmarket **2** Two **3** Munich **4** 300 **5** London **6** Judo **7** Mexico **8** When it's taking another piece **9** Squash **10** France

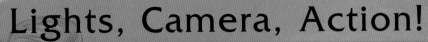

Lights, Camera, Action!

1 Who played the role of Harry Lime in the movie *The Third Man*?

2 How many musical items were included in the movie *Fantasia*?

3 Reckless was the name of which TV family's pet dog?

4 What sport featured in the 1985 movie *American Flyers*?

5 What profession is represented by the TV series *NYPD Blue*?

6 Which multi-Oscar winning actor played Captain John Miller in the movie *Saving Private Ryan*?

7 In which 1967 movie did Paul Newman eat 50 eggs in one hour?

8 Who starred in the movie *Chinatown*?

9 Which 1953 movie opens with Doris Day singing "The Deadwood Stage"?

10 In which city is *Cagney and Lacey* set?

LEVEL 4 • QUIZ 242

Q 10

ANSWERS

1 Orson Wells **2** Eight **3** The Waltons **4** Cycling **5** U.S. police force **6** Tom Hanks **7** Cool Hand Luke **8** Jack Nicholson **9** Calamity Jane **10** New York

Music Mania

BACKGROUND BONUS

In 1984, "Caribbean Queen" was a worldwide hit for which soul sensation?

1 Carl, Dennis, Brian, Mike and Al are collectively known as what group?

2 In which movie did Elvis Presley sing "Wooden Heart"?

3 Which jazz legend recorded the album *Giant Steps*?

4 Who won eight Grammy Awards for the album *Supernatural*?

5 What movie directed by Mike Leigh chronicled the life story of the composers Gilbert and Sullivan?

6 What is the world's largest opera house?

7 Which Puccini opera heroine leaps to her death from a castle in Rome?

8 What is the nationality of the composer Bela Bartok?

9 The rebec was an early form of what instrument?

10 Catfish Row provides the setting for what opera?

ANSWERS

1 The Beach Boys **2** G.I. Blues **3** John Coltrane **4** Carlos Santos **5** Topsy Turvy **6** The Metropolitan Opera House in New York **7** Tosca **8** Hungarian **9** Violin **10** *Porgy and Bess* **Background Bonus** Billy Ocean

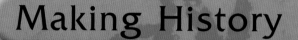

Making History

1 What is the name of the official body that elects popes?

2 What was discovered by Robert Ballard in 1985?

3 Which historical figure said, "Put your trust in God and keep your powder dry"?

4 What was founded in 1831 by King Louis Philippe to assist in the control of French colonies?

5 Which capital city was formerly called Krung Threp?

6 What conflict was ended by the Treaty of Panmunjon?

7 Sarnia was the Roman name for what island?

8 What artefact was discovered on the island of Melos in 1822?

9 What state did the United States purchase from France in 1603?

10 What was the first organization to win the Nobel Peace Prize twice?

Q 5

ANSWERS
1 The Council of Cardinals **2** The wreck of the Titanic **3** Oliver Cromwell **4** The Foreign Legion **5** Bangkok **6** The Korean War **7** Guernsey **8** Venus de Milo **9** Louisiana **10** The International Red Cross

Global Matters

Q 1

1 What city is overlooked by the Blue Mountains and is served by Kingsford Smith International Airport?

2 Which European capital city stands on Faxey Bay?

LEVEL 5 • QUIZ 245

3 What country is separated from Spain by the Straits of Gibraltar?

4 According to an old saying, which Italian city should you visit before you die?

5 What kind of geographical feature can be rain-shadow, continental or tropical?

6 Which European capital city stands on the River Aare?

7 To what country do the Galapagos Islands belong?

8 What river flows into the world's largest delta?

9 Which capital city was formerly called Christiana?

10 What country is the smallest island of the Greater Antilles?

ANSWERS

1 Sydney 2 Reykjavik 3 Morocco 4 Naples 5 Deserts 6 Berne 7 Ecuador 8 The Ganges 9 Oslo 10 Puerto Rica

Total Trivia

Q 2

1 What does a phillumenist collect?

2 Which country has the world's oldest national flag?

3 On what river does the Angel Falls stand?

4 To what religion do Sangha monks belong?

5 What is the name given to the Turkish dish that comprises honey and nuts in filo pastry?

6 Who is the Greek god counterpart of the goddess Amphitrite?

7 In 1936, who was voted *Time Magazine* Woman of the Year?

8 What was the surname of the famous painter Rembrandt?

9 What is potamophobia a fear of?

10 In which country was Leon Trotsky assassinated in 1940?

ANSWERS
1 Matchbox labels **2** Denmark **3** Carrao River **4** Buddhist **5** Baklava **6** Poseidon **7** Wallis Simpson **8** Van Rijn **9** Rivers, or running water **10** Mexico

Scientifically Speaking

1 Where on the body is your occiput?

2 What is the more common name for magnesium sulphate?

3 What is the only chemical element named after an American state?

4 What is studied by an oneirologist?

Q 4

LEVEL 5 • QUIZ 247

5 Copper was named after what island?

6 What planet was discovered in 1846?

7 What is coprolite?

8 What is the final stage in the life cycle of a star called?

9 What kind of gas is produced by the Haber-Bosch process?

10 Which class of rocks are formed from the wastage of earlier rocks?

ANSWERS

1 The back of the head 2 Epsom salts 3 Californium 4 Dreams 5 Cyprus 6 Neptune 7 Fossilized dinosaur dung 8 White dwarf 9 Ammonia 10 Sedimentary

Natural Selection

1 If an animal is described as succivorous, what does it feed on?

2 In which country did pheasants originate?

3 If an animal is described as oviporous, what does it mean?

4 *Orcinus orca* is the scientific name for what creature?

5 If an object is described as testudinal, what animal is it shaped like?

6 Which bird family does the mynah bird belong to?

7 From what type of creature is the incense onycha obtained?

8 *Galapago* is the Spanish name for what animal?

9 What bird has varieties called Australian brown, American white and spot-billed?

10 The kowhai is the national flower of what country?

ANSWERS

1 Sap **2** China **3** It lays eggs **4** Killer whale **5** Tortoise **6** Starling **7** Marine snails **8** Tortoise **9** Pelican **10** New Zealand

Great and Famous

1 Which two U.S. presidents received the Nobel Peace Prize in the 20th century?

2 Who won an Oscar playing a character called Loretta Castorini?

3 In which country was the explorer Ferdinand Magellan born?

4 Which U.S. president married Mary Todd?

5 Which artist once said, "My curiosity crosses over every frontier of curiosity"?

6 At what battle did Horatio Nelson lose his arm?

7 In 1989, who invented the World Wide Web?

8 Harry Houdini was born In which city?

9 *The Small Woman* is the biography of which missionary?

10 What is the nationality of the man who designed the Sydney Opera House?

Q 8

ANSWERS

1 Theodore Roosevelt and Woodrow Wilson **2** Cher in the movie *Moonstruck* **3** Portugal **4** Abraham Lincoln **5** Pablo Picasso **6** The Battle Of Santa Cruz **7** Tim Berners-Lee **8** Budapest **9** Gladys Aylward **10** Danish, Jorn Utzon

Acknowledgements

The publishers would like to thank the following sources for the use of their photographs:

Quiz 44 (C) Twentieth Century Fox/Pictorial Press; 67 (L) Universal/DreamWorks/Scott Free/Pictorial Press; 72 Pictorial Press; 78 (L) TCF/Icon/Ladd/Pictorial Press; 100 (R) Rank/Parkfield/Pictorial Press; 165 (L) Twentieth Century Fox/Pictorial Press; 198 (L) Warner/Castle Rock/Pictorial Press

Cover photographs:

David Beckham/Daniel Garcia/AFP; Mike Powell/Eric Fererberg/AFP; Charlton Heston/MGM/AFP; Stephen Hendry/Pornchai Kittiwongsakul/AFP; New York Yankees/Henny Ray Abrams/AFP

All other pictures from:

CASE, Castrol, Corel, Digital Vision, digitalSTOCK, FlatEarth; Hemera, ILN, PhotoAlto, PhotoDisc, Stockbyte

The publishers would like to thank the following artists for contributing to this book:

Syd Brak, John Butler, Steve Caldwell, Martin Camm, Vanessa Card, Jim Channell, Peter Dennis, Richard Draper, Wayne Ford, Nicholas Forder, Chris Forsey, Mike Foster/Maltings Partnership, Terry Gabbey, Luigi Galante, Terry Grose, Alan Harris, Sally Holmes, Richard Hook, Ian Jackson, Rob Jakeway, John James, Mick Loates, Janos Marffy, Andrea Morandi, Helen Parsley, Roger Payne, Gill Platt, Terry Riley, Steve Roberts, Martin Sanders, Peter Sarson, Mike Saunders, Susan Scott, Rob Sheffield, Ted Smart, Guy Smith, Sarah Smith, Gwen Touret, Rudi Vizi, Mike White